NONPROFIT LAW MADE EASY

Bruce R. Hopkins

WILEY

John Wiley & Sons, Inc.

NONPROFIT LAW
MADE EASY

Bruce R. Hopkins

WILEY

John Wiley & Sons, Inc.

For general information on our other products and services, or technical support, please contact our Customer Care Department within the United States at 800-762-2974, outside the United States at 317-572-3993 or fax 317-572-4002.

Wiley also publishes its books in a variety of electronic formats. Some content that appears in print may not be available in electronic books.

For more information about Wiley products, visit our Web site at *www.wiley.com*.

Library of Congress Cataloging-in-Publication Data:

Hopkins, Bruce R.
  Nonprofit law made easy / Bruce R. Hopkins.
     p. cm.
  Includes index.
  ISBN 0-471-70973-5 (cloth : alk. paper)
  1. Nonprofit organizations—Law and legislation—United States.   I. Title.
  KF1388.Z9H673 2005
  346.73′064—dc22

                             2004029117

Printed in the United States of America
10 9 8 7 6 5 4 3 2 1

About the Author

Bruce R. Hopkins is a lawyer in Kansas City, Missouri, with the firm of Polsinelli Shalton Welte Suelthaus PC, having practiced law in Washington, D.C., for 26 years. He specializes in the representation of tax-exempt organizations. His practice ranges over the entirety of tax matters involving exempt organizations, with emphasis on the formation of nonprofit organizations, acquisition of recognition of tax-exempt status for them, the private inurement and private benefit doctrines, the intermediate sanctions rules, legislative and political campaign activities issues, public charity and private foundation rules, unrelated business planning, use of exempt and for-profit subsidiaries, joint venture planning, review of annual information returns, Internet communications developments, the law of charitable giving (including planned giving), and fundraising law issues.

Mr. Hopkins served as chair of the Committee on Exempt Organizations, Tax Section, American Bar Association; chair, Section of Taxation, National Association of College and University Attorneys; and president, Planned Giving Study Group of Greater Washington, D.C. He was accorded the Assistant Commissioner's (IRS) Award in 1984.

Mr. Hopkins is the series editor of Wiley's Nonprofit Law, Finance, and Management Series. In addition to *Nonprofit Law Made Easy*, he is the author of *The Law of Tax-Exempt Organizations, Eighth Edition*; *The Tax Law of Charitable Giving, Third Edition*; *The Law of Fundraising, Third Edition*; *650 Essential Nonprofit Law Questions Answered*; *The Nonprofits' Guide to Internet Communications Law*; *The Law of Intermediate Sanctions: A Guide for Nonprofits*; *The First Legal Answer Book for Fund-Raisers*; *The Second Legal Answer Book for Fund-Raisers*; *The Legal Answer Book for Nonprofit Organizations*; *The Second Legal Answer Book for Nonprofit Organizations*; *The Nonprofit Law Dictionary*; and *Starting and Managing a Nonprofit Organization: A Legal Guide, Fourth Edition*.

In addition, Mr. Hopkins is the co-author, with Jody Blazek, of *Private Foundations: Tax Law and Compliance, Second Edition*; also with Ms. Blazek, *The Legal Answer Book for Private Foundations*; and with Thomas K. Hyatt, *The Law of Tax-Exempt Healthcare Organizations, Second Edition*. He also writes *Bruce R. Hopkins' Nonprofit Counsel*, a monthly newsletter, published by John Wiley & Sons, Inc.

Mr. Hopkins earned his J.D. and L.L.M. degrees at the George Washington University and his B.A. at the University of Michigan. He is a member of the bars of the District of Columbia and the state of Missouri.

Table of Contents

Preface

My editor, Susan McDermott, asked me to write this book. That fact is not entirely unique; that also happened recently (*650 Essential Nonprofit Law Questions Answered* (2005)). Indeed, previous editors at Wiley have requested—or at least suggested—books. (My response to each of these requests has been consistent and swift: yes.)

This book, however, *is* unique in another respect: it blatantly mimics another Wiley book, titled *Not-for-Profit Accounting Made Easy*. Lawyers and accountants in the nonprofit realm populate overlapping universes, so this companion volume is a natural. Susan wanted a law book to accompany this accounting book; here it is.

I have never discussed this accounting book with its author, Warren Ruppel. I cannot imagine, however, that he extracted as much enjoyment from the process as I did. After years of writing technical and long books about various aspects of nonprofit law, writing this one was pure fun. The biggest challenge, not surprisingly, was what to include and (the painful part) what to leave out. This book thus reflects my take on what constitutes the fundamentals of the law of nonprofit organizations. (The title of my book also reflects my ongoing disagreement with the accounting profession and others over the use of *not-for-profit* rather than *nonprofit*.)

In any event, I had an easier time of it than Mr. Ruppel did. He had to *create* his book: I had merely to *imitate* it. The substance obviously is different but the format is unabashedly copied. Consequently, the book is about the same length, there also are a dozen chapters, each chapter opens with an inventory of what is coming and ends with a chapter summary, and there are no footnotes. Both books share a similar jacket design. So, Mr. Ruppel and Wiley designed the vessel; I poured my descriptions of the law into it.

Back to this matter of what to include and what to exclude. I included the absolute basics (such as the private inurement doctrine, the lobbying rules, the unrelated business rules, and planned giving) but I wanted to include more, so I toyed with some emerging concepts.

Nonprofit law is as dynamic as law can get; capturing what appears to be the "basics" at a point in time can be elusive. For example, as this book goes to press, nonprofit corporate governance principles are rapidly developing. Congress (the 109th, meeting 2005-2006) seems poised to enact major tax-exempt organizations legislation, the IRS has ambitious regulations and rulings projects, and the courts are certain to contribute their share of new law. I have tried to inject references to the prospects of this and other coming law among the summaries of the basics.

As a non-accountant in the nonprofit field, I am glad to have *Not-for-Profit Accounting Made Easy* as a guide to the basics of the accounting principles and rules. I have tried to emulate Mr. Ruppel's work, to provide an equally valuable volume for the non-lawyer who wants a grounding in nonprofit law.

BRUCE R. HOPKINS

2005

CHAPTER 1

Forming a Nonprofit Organization

The purpose of this chapter is to provide basic information about the law concerning the formation of nonprofit organizations. This will serve as a basis for understanding much of the law summarized in the subsequent chapters. Specifically, this chapter will:

- Provide a nonprofit organizations philosophical framework
- Define the term *nonprofit organization*
- Address the matter of the organization's *purposes*
- Explain the selection of the *form* of the organization
- Explain where to *locate* the organization
- Focus on the composition of the organization's *governing body*
- Address the matter of the organization's *officers* and *key employees*

A PHILOSOPHICAL FRAMEWORK

Before delving into the law of nonprofit organizations, one may ask: Why are there nonprofit organizations in the United States?

The answer is that the United States was founded on several principles, with one of the chief ones being distrust of the state—that is, government. Consequently, there has been heavy reliance on nonprofit organizations in our society since the birth of the nation. From the beginning, the U.S nonprofit sector has served as an alternative to the governmental sector as a means for addressing society's problems.

1

This, then, is a matter of political philosophy. The emergence and role of nonprofit organizations was not stimulated by the tax law. The key concept underlying this philosophy is *pluralism;* more specifically, the pluralism of institutions, which features competition among various institutions in the three sectors of U.S. society (nonprofit entities, governmental agencies, and for-profit businesses). In this context, the competition is between the nonprofit and governmental sectors. This philosophy is embodied in the writings of philosophers such as John Stuart Mill and Alexis de Tocqueville. The latter wrote that Americans were constantly forming associations and societies, rather than turning to government for solutions to problems.

Much literature exists on this subject. This philosophy is well articulated in, for example, the Report of the Commission on Private Philanthropy and Public Needs (1975). The Secretary of the Treasury told the House Committee on Ways and Means that charities are an "important influence for diversity and a bulwark against overreliance on big government" (1973). John Gardner wrote that the "private pursuit of public purpose is an honored tradition in American life" (1979). Max Lerner wrote that the "associative impulse is strong in American life." Richard C. Cornuelle wrote that "[w]e have been unique because another sector, clearly distinct from the other two, has, in the past, borne a heavy load of public responsibility." John D. Rockefeller III wrote that the "third sector is . . . the seedbed for organized efforts to deal with social problems."

This conflict and tension among the sectors—a sorting out of the appropriate role of government and nonprofit organizations—is, in a healthy society, a never-ending process, ebbing and flowing with the sentiments and politics of the day. Indeed, it is because of this tension that there is a healthy society to begin with—which is to say, a free society.

The federal income tax exemption for nonprofit organizations thus is a reflection of and is in furtherance of the American way of life. The exemption is a manifestation of a free society. It is based on the previously expressed view that many of society's problems can be solved by means other than the intervention of governmental agencies. Individuals can rarely act alone in this regard; they must function collectively, which means either through nonprofit organizations or governmental bodies. The American bias, based on distrust of government, is to favor the former.

The policy rationale for tax exemption is thus rested on this political philosophy, rather than tax policy. When a constitutional income tax came into existence in 1913, Congress created tax exemption for charitable organizations but did not leave any legislative history on the subject. It is generally assumed that Congress, back then, viewed tax exemption for charitable organizations as the only way to consistently correlate tax policy to political theory on the point, and saw the exemption of charities as an extension of comparable practice throughout the whole of history. One observer stated that the "history of mankind reflects that our early legislators were not setting precedent by exempting religious or charitable organizations" from income tax.

The charitable contribution deductions (in the income, gift, and estate tax law) are likewise part of the federal tax law because of the belief of Congress that the services provided by charitable organizations are valuable to U.S. society and that the existence of these organizations is inherently a significant part of the American social order. These deductions are in the law to stimulate contributions to charitable organizations. The charitable deduction is based on the same philosophical premise as the tax exemption. The Supreme Court wrote, in 1983, that, in enacting both the exemption and deduction provisions, "Congress sought to provide tax benefits to charitable organizations, to encourage the development of private institutions that serve a useful public purpose or supplement or take the place of public institutions of the same kind."

One of the issues of the day is whether tax exemption and the charitable deductions amount to government subsidies. Those who argue that they are assert that tax exemption is merely a subsidy provided by government to the nonprofit sector. Likewise, this view has it that the charitable deduction is a subsidy of a donor that is provided either by the government or by all other taxpayers. This view is based on the fact that, absent the workings of the deduction, more funds would flow to the U.S. treasury. The contrary view is that the subsidy rationale is misguided because it is based on the assumption (almost always unstated) that the subsidy is of funds to which the government is initially entitled. Yet, the rationale for the exemption and deduction make it clear that tax exemptions are beneficial to the social order, to promote pluralism.

The government generally leaves the nonprofit sector alone

when it comes to taxation. The money flowing to the sector does not belong to the government to begin with; thus, there cannot be a subsidy. The practical problem, obviously, is that, like any tax preference, tax exemptions and deductions shrink the tax base involved, so that one can (superficially) argue that they constitute subsidies. But, in the realm of charity, this approach takes the exemptions and deductions out of context, and—in an example of an analytical approach that the Supreme Court on occasion has labeled *wooden, unthinking,* and *crabbed*—ignores the philosophical construct. To paraphrase the Supreme Court, to treat exemptions and deductions as government subsidies is to "tear them from their roots."

In one of its first pronouncements on the point, the U.S. Supreme Court (albeit somewhat hesitantly) concluded, soon after enactment of the constitutional income tax in 1913, that the foregoing rationalization was the basis for the federal tax exemption for charitable entities. The Court wrote in 1924 that "[e]vidently the exemption is made in recognition of the benefit which the public derives from corporate activities of the class named, and is intended to aid them when not conducted for private gain." In 1970, the Court wrote that the state "has an affirmative policy that considers these groups [that is, tax-exempt charities] as beneficial and stabilizing influences in community life and finds this classification useful, desirable, and in the public interest."

In 1983, the Court wrote (this time without hesitancy) that "[c]haritable exemptions are justified on the basis that the exempt entity confers a public benefit—a benefit which the society or the community may not itself choose or be able to provide, or which supplements and advances the work of public institutions already supported by tax revenues." In this opinion, the Court added that tax exemptions "for certain institutions thought beneficial to the social order of the country as a whole, or to a particular community, are deeply rooted in our history, as in that of England. The origins of such exemptions lie in the special privileges that have long been extended to charitable trusts." The Court reviewed case law and concluded that "[t]hese statements clearly reveal the legal background against which Congress enacted the first charitable exemption statute in 1894: charities were to be given preferential treatment because they provide a benefit to society."

The Court has viewed tax exemption and the charitable contribution deductions as subsidies provided by government. It first indicated its view in this regard in 1983, when it observed: "When the Government grants exemptions or allows deductions all taxpayers are affected; the very fact of the exemption or deduction for the donor means that other taxpayers can be said to be indirect and vicarious 'donors.'"

Oddly, this was not the original view of the Court. In 1970, it conceded that granting tax exemption "necessarily operates to afford an indirect economic benefit." But it also observed that the "grant of a tax exemption is not sponsorship [that is, not a subsidy] since the government does not transfer part of its revenue" to exempt organizations.

The current federal and state governments' crackdown on charitable and other nonprofit organizations shows that the governmental sector can become intolerant of the nonprofit sector. Tax exemption and the charitable contribution deductions are not protected by constitutional law principles. Thus, the nonprofit sector is always open to government regulation. The sector is dependent on restraint by government as to regulation of it, so as to preserve pluralism. It is always a perilous position for the sector to be in.

Note Most of the law discussed in this book is federal tax law as administered and enforced by the Internal Revenue Service (IRS), a component of the Department of the Treasury. Appropriate state law should also be consulted, such as a state's nonprofit corporation act and the states' charitable solicitation act. Other federal, state, and local law may be applicable, however (see Chapter 12).

DEFINING NONPROFIT ORGANIZATION

The term *nonprofit organization* consistently generates confusion. For one thing, the term does not refer to an organization that is prohibited by law from earning a *profit* (that is, an excess of revenue over expenses). In fact, is it quite common for nonprofit organizations to generate profits. Rather, the definition of nonprofit organization essentially relates to requirements as to what must be done with the profits earned.

A nonprofit organization may be contrasted with a *for-profit organization*. The for-profit organization has owners that hold equity in the enterprise, such as stockholders of a corporation. For-profit entities are operated for the benefit of their owners: the profits of the business undertaking are passed through to them, such as by the payment of dividends on shares of stock. That is what is meant by the term for-profit organization: It is one designed and operated to generate a profit for its owners. The transfer of profits through the organization to its owners is known as *private inurement*.

By contrast, nonprofit organizations are not supposed to engage in private inurement. They are expected to devote their profits to their nonprofit purposes and activities. Consequently, the doctrine of private inurement is the substantive defining characteristic that distinguishes nonprofit organizations from for-profit entities.

Another source of confusion is use of the term *tax-exempt organization*. The two terms do not mean the same, although there is considerable overlap. An organization can be a nonprofit one without being tax-exempt. Nearly all tax-exempt organizations, however, are nonprofit entities. State law usually determines whether an organization is a nonprofit entity. The federal tax law generally is the basis for an organization's tax-exempt status (if any).

A third source of confusion is the term *charitable organization*. Just as all nonprofit organizations are not tax-exempt, not all tax-exempt organizations are charitable in nature. The term charitable, while it certainly has its technical elements, generally embraces organizations that are educational, scientific, religious, and the like. The Supreme Court held that all of these organizations must meet "certain common law standards of charity—namely, that an institution seeking tax-exempt status [as a charitable entity] must serve a public purpose and not be contrary to established public policy." Further, contributions to these entities are generally eligible for the *charitable contribution deduction*.

PURPOSE OF ORGANIZATION

One of the fundamental first steps a nonprofit organization must necessarily take is identification of its *purposes*. This is not just dictated by the law; each organization simply, as a practical matter, must state its purpose or purposes for existence in writing. An organization's purposes are different than an organization's *activities*. Activities are undertaken to effectuate purposes.

An organization's statement of purposes must first be written to comport with the applicable state's nonprofit law. This usually is not too difficult to achieve, as long as the statement does not empower the organization to engage in substantial commercial activities.

Second, the statement of purposes needs to be prepared properly to enable the organization to qualify for tax-exempt status (assuming that classification is available and desired). This statement must be in the organization's *articles of organization,* which is the document creating the entity (and is discussed later in this chapter). The contents of this aspect of the statement are dependent on the type of tax-exempt organization the nonprofit entity intends to be.

The types of tax-exempt organizations are reviewed in Chapter 2. Generally, however, the choice will be one of the following:

- Charitable organization
- Social welfare (e.g., advocacy) organization
- Labor organization
- Business league (association)
- Social club
- Employee benefit fund
- Fraternal society
- Political organization

The organization's statement of purposes needs to be written so as to bring the entity into conformity with the appropriate category of exempt organization. The purposes of an organization may partake of more than one of these categories. Tax-exempt status will be dependent on which of the types of purposes is primary—this is the *primary purpose rule.*

The federal tax law on this point is the most refined in the case of charitable organizations. These organizations must adhere to a formal *organizational test.* Other types of tax-exempt organizations may, however, extrapolate appropriate elements from this test. Organizations need not expressly make reference to the specific Internal Revenue Code section that is the basis for the exemption where the statement of purposes is confined to those that are inherently exempt. Otherwise, the statement of purposes must state that the organization will not engage in any activities outside the scope of the selected category of exemption.

Note   The length and level of detail of an organization's statement of purposes will vary. The statement can be brief, such as "shall be operated for charitable and educational purposes" or "shall operate a social club." Conversely, the statement can entail considerable detail. This is largely a matter of judgment in each case; a balance needs to be struck between the big picture and specificity. Constant amendment of articles of organization should be avoided. The bylaws (discussed later) can be more effusive as long as the statement in them is not broader than that in the articles of organization.

The organizational test for charitable organizations, in addition to requiring a suitable statement of purposes, mandates a *dissolution clause*. This is a provision in the organizing document that dictates where the organization's net income and assets (if any) will be distributed should the organization liquidate or otherwise dissolve. Permissible recipients are one or more other charitable organizations or governmental agencies. No other type of tax-exempt organization is required by federal law to have a dissolution clause in its articles of organization.

Tip   Some nonprofit, tax-exempt organizations have additional operational tests to satisfy. These include supporting organizations and private foundations (see Chapter 3).

Note   Tax-exempt, charitable organizations must also comply with an *operational test*. This test concerns whether the organization is in fact operated for exempt purposes. Generally, defects in an entity's articles of organization cannot be cured by complete adherence to the operational test.

LOCATION OF ORGANIZATION

Those planning a nonprofit organization must ascertain its state of formation. That is, under which state's law should the organization be created? (In a rare situation, the entity is established by federal or state statute, or a local government's ordinance.) The state selected may or may not be the state in which the organization will conduct its operations.

The starting assumption is that the jurisdiction in which the organization is to be formed is the state in which the organization will be located. That is the state in which it will have its principal (usually sole) office, conduct its programs, and otherwise function. There may be, however, one or more compelling features of another state's law or administration of it, unavailable under the law of the home state, that dictate formation elsewhere. These are just a few of the possibilities:

- The intensity or type of regulation in the home state (with California and New York at the top of the high-regulation list)
- The form of the organization
- The number of directors or trustees required
- Whether state law permits the nonprofit organization to be formed as a stock-based corporation
- The element of *appearances*, in that those forming the organization may believe that it must be formed under the law of a particular state, such as New York (in the case of an internationally focused organization) or the District of Columbia (in the case of a public policy organization)

The difficulty with forming a nonprofit organization in a state different than the one in which the entity will operate is that the organization will have to comply with elements of the law of both states. The state in which the organization is formed is the *domestic* one; the state in which the organization is to operate (if different) is the *foreign* jurisdiction. The organization must qualify to *do business* in the foreign state.

With the dual-state approach, the organization may have to maintain a registered agent in both jurisdictions. Both states may require an annual report and an annual filing fee. Overall (including legal fees), it is usually more costly to form a nonprofit organization in one state and function in another. There are, therefore, financial and efficiency issues associated with the two-state approach. In the case of nearly all nonprofit entities, one state will do.

SELECTION OF ORGANIZATION FORM

Once the home state has been determined, the legal form of the nonprofit organization must be considered. This is, as noted, basically a matter of state law. (Again, this assumes that the organization is not formed by statute or ordinance.)

Tax-exempt, nonprofit organizations generally are of three types:

1. Corporation
2. Unincorporated association
3. Trust

There are other forms of tax-exempt organizations, such as a limited liability company or a professional corporation. These forms are, however, rare in the nonprofit world.

Generically, the document by which a tax-exempt organization is created is known, in the parlance of the federal tax law, as *articles of organization.* There usually is a separate document containing rules by which the organization conducts its affairs; this document is most often termed *bylaws.* The organization may develop other documents governing its operations, such as various policies and procedures, an employee handbook, a conflict-of-interest policy (although that may be part of the bylaws), and/or a code of ethics.

There are several types of articles of organization for each of the principal types of tax-exempt, nonprofit organizations:

- Corporation: articles of incorporation
- Unincorporated association: constitution
- Trust: declaration of trust or trust agreement

The contents of a set of articles of organization should include the following:

- The name of the organization (discussed in the next section)
- A statement of its purposes (previously discussed)

- The name(s) and address(es) of its initial directors or trustees
- The name and address of the registered agent (if a corporation)
- The name(s) and address(es) of its incorporator(s) (if a corporation)
- A statement as to whether the entity has members
- A statement as to whether the entity can issue stock (if a corporation)
- Provisions reflecting any other state law requirements
- Provisions reflecting any other federal tax law requirements
- A dissolution clause

The bylaws of a nonprofit organization (if any) will usually include provisions with respect to the following:

- The organization's purposes
- The origins (e.g., election) and duties of its directors
- The origins and duties of its officers
- The role of its members (if any)
- Meetings of members and directors, including dates, notice, quorum, and voting
- The role of executive and other committees
- The role of its chapters (if any)
- The organization's fiscal year
- A conflict-of-interest policy (if not separately stated)
- Reference to (any) affiliated entities
- Restatement of the federal tax law requirements

Several factors need to be considered in deciding which form a nonprofit organization should select, particularly if tax-exempt status is desired. Generally, the pivotal factor concerns the personal liability of the organization's trustees, directors, and officers. The corporate form is the only form that provides the advantage of shielding board members and officers (and perhaps key employees) from most types of personal liability. With the corporation, liability, if any, is generally confined to the corporation; that is, it does not normally extend to those who manage it.

Another factor is that the law of a state usually provides answers to many of the questions that inevitably arise when forming and operating a nonprofit organization. These answers are most likely found in the state's nonprofit corporation act.

A third factor is privacy. In exchange for the grant of corporate status, the state usually expects certain forms of compliance by the organization, such as adherence to rules of operations, an initial filing fee, annual reports, annual fees, and public disclosure requirements. There rarely are comparable filing requirements for trusts and unincorporated associations. Although articles of incorporation are public documents, trust documents and unincorporated association constitutions often are not.

In most cases, federal tax law is silent as to the form of tax-exempt organizations; most of them can select from among the three types. In a few instances, however, a specific form of organization is required to qualify under federal law as a tax-exempt organization.

Note   This choice of form is not immutable. A tax-exempt organization can change its form. (As a matter of state law, trusts are likely to be the most difficult of entities to change.) A common instance is conversion of an unincorporated association to a nonprofit corporation. (It is rare for a nonprofit corporation to unincorporate.) When this type of conversion is made, however, a new legal entity is created. This may require another filing with the IRS to procure a determination letter for the successor organization. (See Chapter 2.)

NAME OF ORGANIZATION

Those forming a nonprofit organization—particularly one that is to be tax-exempt—should give serious consideration to the entity's name. This is not a matter of law; it is an element of appearance. Certainly, the organizational test (discussed under the section "Purpose of Organization") is silent on the point.

The organization's name sets a tone that overshadows the evaluation that is accorded the entity, whether it is by the IRS, a court, the media, or the general public. Thus, the name should do more than convey what the entity's purposes and programs are about—it should be appropriate for a tax-exempt organization and, if applicable, an exempt charitable organization. Particularly in an instance of a putative charitable entity, as a matter of sheer presentation, and of imbuing the exemption application process with a positive start (from the applicant's viewpoint), more than passing thought should be given to this matter of the nonprofit organization's name.

A name can be clever and yet only provide a court with a basis for concluding that the undertaking was something less than serious, thereby tainting the entire cause; an example of this is Salvation Navy. If an organization is trying to qualify for tax exemption but probably is not entitled to it, it is not a good idea to select a name that conveys the individuals' true intentions in forming the entity (such as attempting to qualify an organization as a religious one because it conducts "worship services" on a yacht while floating around in a large bay); an example is the Southern Church of Universal Brotherhood Assembled (the acronym being SCUBA).

By contrast, one of the finest names ever assigned to a tax-exempt, nonprofit organization is this: the Vigilant Hose Company. The organization is a volunteer fire company.

COMPOSITION OF GOVERNING BODY

A nonprofit organization—irrespective of form—must have a governing body. These individuals generally are termed *trustees* or *directors*. State law will determine the minimum number of board members; the law typically mandates at least three of these individuals, particularly in the case of nonprofit corporations. Some states require only one. (The federal tax law is silent on this point.)

Some nonprofit organizations have large governing boards, often to the extent of being unwieldy. (State law does not set a maximum number of directors of nonprofit organizations.) The optimum size of a governing board of a nonprofit organization is dependent on many factors, including the type of organization, the extent of its program activities, the nature and size of the organization's constituency, the way in which directors are elected, and the role and effectiveness of an executive committee.

Nomenclature

State law generally refers to those who serve on the governing board of a nonprofit organization as *directors*. Some tax-exempt organizations use other terms, such as *trustees* or *governors*. Generally, organizations are free to use the terminology they want. Nonetheless, applicable state law should be reviewed.

The choice of term in this context usually is not a matter of law. Some organizations prefer to refer to their governing board as the *board of trustees* because it sounds more impressive. This is particularly the case with charitable entities (such as private foundations) and educational institutions (such as schools, colleges, and universities). (Technically, only a member of the governing board of a trust can be a trustee, but that formality has long disappeared.)

Where there are related organizations, this terminology can be employed to reduce confusion. For example, in an instance of a tax-exempt association and its related foundation, the board of the former may be termed the *board of directors* and the board of the latter the *board of trustees*.

Scope of Authority

The directors of a nonprofit organization are those who set policy for the organization and oversee its affairs. Implementation of plans and programs, and day-to-day management, are the functions of officers and employees. The foregoing is conceptual; in reality, it is difficult to mark precisely where the scope of authority of a particular board of directors stops and the authority of other managers begins. (In the parlance of the tax law, trustees, directors, officers, and key employees are *managers* of the organization.)

Frequently, authority of this nature (or territory or turf) is resolved in the political arena, not the legal one. It may vary, from time to time, as the culture of the entity changes. In some organizations, the directors do not have the time or do not want to take the time to micromanage. Others restrain themselves from doing so—and still others do not. Often, the matter comes down to the sheer force of personalities. In some organizations, the most dominant manager is the executive director rather than the president or chair of the board. Still, in the end, the principle of law is that the board of a nonprofit organization has the ultimate authority over the affairs of the organization, unless there is a voting membership, in which case the ultimate authority is vested in the larger group.

Emerging governance principles for nonprofit organizations are placing more emphasis on an active, participating governing board (see Chapter 12). The days of the passive, often-absent board member may be over. Emphasis is now on standards of *fiduciary responsibility*. Under evolving guidelines, board members are expected to be knowledgeable, involved, and making decisions as the full body, rather than deferring to the officers, an executive committee, or other smaller group.

Origins

The board of directors of a nonprofit organization can be derived in several ways. Indeed, there can be a blend of these ways. The basic choices are as follows:

- Election by a membership (including a sole member)
- Election by the other directors (a self-perpetuating board)
- Selection by the membership of another organization
- Selection by the governing board of another organization
- Ex officio positions

If there are bona fide members of the organization (such as an association or a social club), it is likely that these members will elect some or all of the members of the governing board of the entity. This election may be conducted by mail ballot or voting at the annual meeting. It is possible, however, for a nonprofit organization with a membership to have a governing board that is not elected by that membership.

In the absence of a membership or if the membership lacks a vote on the matter, the governing board of a nonprofit organization may be a *self-perpetuating board*. With this model, the initial board members (often named in the articles of organization) continue with those the board elects and those elected by subsequent boards.

Some governing boards have one or more *ex officio* positions. This means that an individual is a board member by virtue of another position he or she holds, such as an officer position or a board position with a related organization. (This term does not mean that the individual lacks the right to vote.) These other positions may be confined to the organization involved or be those of another organization or a blend of the two approaches. For example, the governing board of a supporting organization (see Chapter 3) is likely to have at least its majority appointed by the governing board of one or more supported organizations.

In the case of many nonprofit organizations, the source of the membership of the board is preordained. Examples include the typical membership organization that elects the board (such as, as noted, an association or social club); a hospital, college, or museum that has a governing board generally reflective of the community; or a private foundation (see Chapter 3) that has one or more trustees who represent a particular family or corporation.

Control

With the rare exception of the stock-based nonprofit organization, no one "owns" a nonprofit organization. *Control* of a nonprofit organization, however, is another matter. Certainly, the governing board of a nonprofit organization generally controls the organization, even in an instance of a membership entity.

There are other manifestations of this matter of control of the affairs of a nonprofit organization. One is the situation where an individual or a close-knit group of individuals wants to control, on an ongoing basis, an organization. This can be of particular consequence in the case of a single-purpose organization that was founded by an individual or this type of a group. Those who launch a nonprofit organization understandably do not want to put their blood, sweat, tears, and dollars into formation and growth of the organization, only to helplessly watch others garner control over it and freeze them out of the organization's affairs. Solutions to this dilemma include selection of a board the founders trust, long terms of office, formation of the entity in a state that allows only one or two directors, different classes of board members, the founders as sole members, the founders as stock owners of the organization, and use of an advisory committee rather than a large governing board. These techniques need to be tested against the rules of applicable state law.

The IRS is particularly suspicious about nonprofit organizations that have only members of one family as board members. The agency has said that, where an organization is totally controlled by its founder and his or her immediate family, the entity "bears a very heavy burden to be forthcoming and explicit about its plans for the use of [its] assets" for exempt purposes. Although the law does not preclude a closely controlled nonprofit organization from being tax-exempt, the IRS is of the view that this structure lacks "institutional protections," that is, a board of directors consisting of "active, disinterested persons." (The term *disinterested* means not being predominantly concerned with furthering private ends, not having a lack of interest in the affairs of the organization.) Thus, this IRS rule: "Small, closely controlled exempt organizations—and especially those that are closely controlled by members of one family—require thorough examination to insure that the arrangements serve charitable purposes rather than private interests."

Other Considerations

The board of directors of a nonprofit organization may decide to have a chair (designated chairperson, chairman, or chairwoman) of the board. This individual presides over board meetings. The chair position is not usually an officer position (although it can be made one). The position may (but need not) be authorized in the organization's bylaws.

Some organizations find it useful to stagger the terms of office so that only a portion of the board is up for election or reelection at any one time, thereby providing some continuity of service and expertise. A tidy model in this regard is the nine-person board, with three-year terms for members; one-third of the board is elected annually. The organization's bylaws should state the terms of the offices and address the matter of reelections to office (including any term limits).

A board of directors of a tax-exempt organization usually acts by means of in-person meetings, where a quorum is present. Where state law allows, the members of the board can meet by means of conference call (a call where all participants can simultaneously hear each other) or by unanimous written consent. These alternative procedures should be authorized in the organization's bylaws—indeed, that may be a requirement of state law. If there is to be one or more nonvoting directors, the bylaws should make that clear.

Unless there is authorization in the law (and there is not likely to be), the directors of a nonprofit organization may not vote by proxy, mail ballot, e-mail, or telephone call other than a qualified conference call.

Members of a nonprofit organization have more flexibility as to voting than members of the governing board of the organization. For example, usually they can vote by mail ballot and by use of proxies. Thus, some nonprofit organizations are structured as membership entities, with the organization's membership and the board membership identical, to facilitate maximum flexibility as to the conduct of meetings and voting.

A trustee of a nonprofit organization may be an institution (such as a bank or trust company). This is most common in the charitable organization context; for example, a private foundation may have an institutional trustee. An organization may have one or more individuals and an institutional trustee as the governing group.

Trustees and directors usually are disqualified persons for intermediate sanctions purposes and insiders for private inurement purposes (see Chapter 10).

OFFICERS AND KEY EMPLOYEES

Nearly every nonprofit organization has officers. A prominent exception may be the trust, which can have only one or more trustees.

Scope of Authority

As with the board of directors, the scope (or levels) of authority of the officers of a nonprofit organization is difficult to articulate. In the case of a nonprofit organization that has members, directors or trustees, officers, and employees (key or otherwise), setting a clear distinction as to who has the authority to do what is nearly impossible. General principles can be stated but will often prove nearly useless in practice.

For example, it can be stated that the members of the organization set basic policy and the members of the board of directors set additional policy, albeit within the parameters established by the membership. The officers thereafter implement the policies, as do the employees, although this is more on a day-to-day basis. Yet, the reality is that, at all levels, policy is established and implemented.

In a typical nonprofit organization, who decides what programs will be undertaken, who is hired and fired as employees? Who determines the nature of the retirement plan arrangements, who the lawyers and accountants for the organization will be, the type of fundraising program, and the organization's location(s)? Who chooses the style of the stationery, the design of the Web site, or the format of the journal? Depending on the circumstances, the answers may be the members, the governing board, the executive committee, the chair of the board, the president, the vice president, the executive director, and/or any number of others.

Positions and Duties

As a general proposition, the officers of a nonprofit organization, and their respective duties and responsibilities, are as follows:

- *President.* The president is the principal executive officer of the organization and in general supervises and controls all of the business and affairs of the entity. He or she presides at meetings of the governing board. The president signs, often with one other officer of the organization (usually, the secretary), any contracts (including leases) or other documents required to be executed on behalf of the organization (such as mortgages, deeds, or bonds). The bylaws of the organization should provide that the president is to perform all duties "generally incident to" the office of a president.
- *Vice president.* In the absence of the president, or in the event of the president's inability or refusal to act, the vice president performs the duties of the president. An organization may have more than one vice-president, with each assigned differing areas of responsibility.
- *President-elect.* Some organizations have, as an officer, the position of president-elect. This is the individual who is slated to succeed the president. He or she serves in an apprentice capacity, although this individual may also be given discrete responsibilities or projects.
- *Past-president.* A nonprofit organization may have, as an officer, the individual who was the immediate past president. This is done to leaven the change of board composition with continuity of experience.
- *Treasurer.* The treasurer has charge and custody of and is responsible for all funds, securities, and any other prop-

erty of the nonprofit organization. He or she receives and gives receipts for money due and payable to the organization, and deposits such money in the name of the organization in the banks, trust companies, or other depositories selected by the organization. The treasurer may make or oversee investments, pursuant to an overall investment policy developed by the organization's board. The bylaws of the organization should provide that the treasurer is to perform all duties "generally incident to" the office of treasurer. If required by the board, the treasurer has to provide a bond (at the organization's expense) for the faithful discharge of the treasurer's duties in such sum and with such surety or sureties as the board determines.

- *Secretary.* The secretary is responsible for the minutes of the meetings of the governing board of the nonprofit organization. He or she has the responsibility to give all notices in accordance with the organization's bylaws or as required by law. The secretary is custodian of the records and of the seal (if any) of the organization. The secretary is to keep a register of the addresses of each member of the board of the organization (and perhaps each member of the organization). The bylaws of the organization should provide that the secretary is to perform all duties "generally incident to" the office of secretary.

These individuals usually are disqualified persons for intermediate sanctions purposes and insiders for private inurement purposes (see Chapter 10).

Origins

The officers of a nonprofit organization are usually elected, either by a membership or by the organization's governing board. In some instances, the officers of an organization are ex officio with, or all selected by, another organization. Here are the basic choices:

- Election by a membership
- Election by the directors, who are elected by members
- Election by the directors, who are a self-perpetuating board

- Election (or appointment) by the board of another organization
- Ex officio positions
- A blend of two or more of the foregoing options

Governing Instruments

The governing instruments of the nonprofit organization (frequently the bylaws) should identify the officers of the organization, and state the duties and responsibilities of each position, provide for the manner of their election or other selection, state the terms of the offices, and address the matter of reelections to office (including any term limits).

For the most part, the law allows a nonprofit organization to use whatever governing structure it wants. In most states, a nonprofit corporations act contains rules (some mandatory, some optional) concerning officers, terms of office, and the like.

Particularly if the nonprofit organization is a corporation, state law usually requires at least certain officers. Quite likely, the minimum will be president, treasurer, and secretary. In general, the same individual can hold more than one office; the positions of secretary and treasurer are commonly combined. The president and secretary, however, should not be the same individual. (The law in many states prohibits this duality.) Frequently, legal documents will require these two officers' separate signatures.

Officers are officers of the nonprofit organization. They are not officers of the governing board. An exception to this can be the chairperson of the board, who may be considered an officer of the board.

Key Employees

The federal tax law recognizes that an individual can have significant duties and responsibilities with respect to a nonprofit organization, and not be a trustee, director, or officer. These individuals, the classification of whom can be controversial (more political than legal), are those who have responsibilities or powers "similar to" those of a trustee, director, or officer. One likely candidate for key employee status is the executive director of a nonprofit organization; other key employees are other chief management or finance individuals. There often are, for example, special reporting requirements as to these individuals (see Chapter 4). Also, they are usually disqualified persons for intermediate sanctions purposes and insiders for private inurement purposes (see Chapter 10).

MANAGEMENT COMPANIES

A nonprofit organization may utilize the services of a management company. This type of company—almost certainly a for-profit entity—does not supplant the need for directors and officers of the nonprofit organization, although it may substitute, in whole or in part, for the organization's employees.

Although there is nothing inherently inappropriate about a nonprofit organization's use of a management company, the IRS (when the organization is tax-exempt) tends to accord these arrangements particular scrutiny. For example, if members of the board of the management company also serve as members of the board of the nonprofit organization (and/or there are other business or family ties between the two entities), the agency may be even more sensitive to the potential for private inurement, private benefit, and/or excess benefit transactions (see Chapter 10). In some instances, the IRS may attempt to characterize a nonprofit organization's arrangement with a management company as a joint venture (see Chapter 9).

Some management companies perform only *back office* or other wholly administrative functions. Others are more involved, undertaking efforts such as fundraising or meetings planning. Some of these companies assist the organization in the operation of its programs. The more the management company is entrenched in the nonprofit, tax-exempt organizations operations, the greater will be the suspicions of the IRS.

MINUTES

The proceedings of most nonprofit organizations are (and should be) reflected in minutes. Essentially, there are two types of these minutes: *organizational minutes* and ongoing *directors' meetings minutes*. There can, of course, be other sets of minutes, such as those of an organization's meetings of members and/or committees.

Organizational Minutes

A document—in addition to articles of organization and bylaws—that is important when forming a nonprofit organization is the organizational minutes. The organization's initial board of directors, and any directors elected at the organizational meeting, adopts these minutes.

At a minimum, this document should reflect the following:

- Ratification of the articles of organization
- Adoption of the bylaws
- Election of any directors at that meeting
- Election of officers
- Passage of the requisite resolution for establishment of a bank account or any other accounts at financial institutions
- Passage of a resolution selecting legal counsel
- Passage of a resolution selecting an accountant or accounting firm
- Authorization or ratification of certain actions, such as preparation and filing with the IRS of an application for recognition of tax-exempt status
- Authorization of reimbursement of expenses incurred in establishment of the entity

Other actions of the board can be reflected in these minutes, such as discussion of program activities, development of one or more components of a fundraising program, or selection of a management or fundraising consultant.

These minutes can be a summary of actions taken by means of an in-person meeting or a meeting by conference call. An alternative is a written unanimous consent document.

Other Board Minutes

Each meeting of the board of directors of a nonprofit organization should be the subject of a set of minutes. These documents should not be veritable transcripts of the proceedings but instead should memorialize material developments and decisions formally made (as in resolutions). A current and complete minute book, reflecting explanation of important decisions and transactions, can go a long way in resolving disputes, shortening (or even forestalling) an IRS audit, satisfying an attorney general inquiry, and the like. The minutes should not be too long nor too short, and should be written with a certain amount of prescience, with the scrivener always thinking about how the document will look in the months and years to come.

Note A good practice is to have board meeting minutes drafted, then reviewed (and perhaps revised) by a lawyer, before they are circulated to the board for its review and adoption. In this way, inartful phraseologies can be eliminated and other potential problems minimized or eliminated. Some lawyers review and, if necessary, rewrite board meeting minutes with the view that each document will someday be an exhibit in a trial.

Minutes should be kept in a minute book, along with other important documents, such as the articles of organization, bylaws, and IRS determination letter. Minute books can be purchased commercially, although a simple ring binder will suffice. The point is to initiate and maintain a substantive history of the board's material decisions and the organization's progress toward the objective of achieving its mission (if tax-exempt, its exempt purposes).

As with organizational minutes, these minutes can reflect actions taken by means of an in-person meeting or a meeting by conference call. An alternative is a written consent document.

OTHER DOCUMENTS

A nonprofit organization may have other documents, beyond those discussed above, with legal import.

Mission Statement

It is becoming increasingly popular for nonprofit organizations to develop a full mission statement, explaining their purposes, programs, and objectives. This exercise often ties in with development of a business plan (see following section). There certainly is nothing inappropriate with this endeavor. Two cautions, nonetheless:

1. The mission statement should be consistent with the organization's articles of organization and bylaws.
2. The mission statement should not contain language that is inconsistent with the requirements for maintaining the organization's tax-exempt status (if applicable).

Business Plan

A nonprofit organization may be operating in conformity with a business plan. Again, this is a commendable practice. The same two cautions referenced in connection with a mission statement apply in this context.

Case Statement

A nonprofit organization, most likely a tax-exempt charitable one, may have a case statement, used in conjunction with its fundraising program. This document will summarize the purposes and programs of the organization, and explain why contributions are needed for discrete programs and projects. The statement may include elements of a capital campaign and/or appeal for funds for an endowment. Often, the case statement will include a solicitation for a specific amount of funds for specific purposes, such as individual programs, capital needs, and an endowment. Once again, the two cautions apply.

Caution   Statements made in a case statement (or, for that matter, a fundraising solicitation letter) can be interpreted as in substance a contract between the soliciting charitable entity and donors and grantors.

Code of Ethics

Membership and some other types of nonprofit organizations may have a code of ethics that they enforce and administer. This document will include criteria for membership and may be the basis for expulsion of an individual (or perhaps an organization) from membership. The organization may have an ethics committee that oversees and interprets application of the principles of this code.

Because of the heightened potential for legal liability (such as for defamation or violation of the antitrust or tax laws) in cases of membership exclusion and expulsion, and other applications of a code of ethics, it is essential that the code be reasonable and legal (tested, for example, against antitrust law principles), and enforced by means of a procedure that is fair (although the full panoply of due process rights need not be available).

Conflict-of-Interest Policy

It has become increasingly popular (fueled in part by IRS demands and in part by corporate governance developments (see Chapter 12)) for a nonprofit organization to have a conflict-of-interest policy. Although this type of policy is mandated by the federal tax law only in the health care setting, it can be useful in protecting the interests of the nonprofit (particularly tax-exempt, charitable) organization when it is contemplating a transaction or other arrangement that might benefit the financial interest of the organization's directors, officers, and/or other interested persons.

Pursuant to these policies, interested persons are identified, then required to disclose to the board of directors, with regard to actual or possible conflicts of interest, the existence of their financial interest in connection with a transaction or arrangement. The policy should include a procedure by which the board determines if, in fact, a conflict of interest exists and, if so, whether to proceed with the transaction or arrangement. Compensation paid to all interested parties should be identified and periodically tested against the standard of reasonableness (see Chapter 10).

Directors and officers (and perhaps others, such as full-time employees) should sign a statement that affirms that they understand and agree to comply with the conflict-of-interest policy. Thereafter, the policy should be annually executed by these interested persons, disclosing any conflict of interest, relationships with other organizations and suppliers of goods and services to the nonprofit organization involved, and places of employment of family members.

SUMMARY

This chapter provided basic information about nonprofit organizations and the law. The discussion started with the philosophical framework, then defined the term *nonprofit organization* and explained how to select the form and location of the organization. The chapter also analyzed the matter of the nonprofit organization's governing board, including its origins and scope of authority. The chapter further summarized the types and roles of a nonprofit organization's officers and key employees. It referenced the key documents a nonprofit organization must or may have, such as minutes, a conflict-of-interest policy, and a mission statement. These topics provide the reader with the fundamentals of nonprofit law. The balance of the book is devoted to an examination of specific law subjects, issues, and trends. This frame, coupled with the information provided in the balance of the book, provide the non-lawyer with a usable understanding of nonprofit law.

CHAPTER 2

Acquiring and Maintaining Tax-Exempt Status

The purpose of this chapter is to explain what *tax-exempt status* means, what the categories of eligible tax-exempt organizations are, and how to apply (ideally successfully) for recognition of exempt status. Specifically, this chapter will:

- Explain the meaning of *recognition* of tax-exempt status
- Explain how to select the appropriate category of exempt organization
- Identify the legal aspects of the application forms
- Address the matter of changes in form or operation
- Summarize the group exemption rules

CONCEPT OF TAX EXEMPTION

Commonly, when an organization is referred to as a *tax-exempt organization,* the reference is to its status as an entity that is not required to pay federal income tax. This is somewhat of a misnomer, however, inasmuch as most of these organizations are subject to (although they may not in fact pay) one or more taxes. Thus, for example, the unrelated business income rules (see Chapter 7) are applicable to nearly all tax-exempt organizations. Also, some exempt organizations must pay an income tax or an excise tax on their net investment income. Moreover, these organizations may be subject to other taxes, such as, in the case of public charities, excise taxes on excess lobbying expenditures and political campaign expenditures (see Chapter 10). Indeed, private foundations are subject to a battery of excise taxes (see Chapter 3).

There may be other federal taxes that a tax-exempt organization need not pay. Further, exemption from the federal income tax usually leads to exemption from state (and perhaps local) income tax. Depending on state law, an organization may be exempt from sales, use, tangible personal property, intangible personal property, real estate, and/or other taxes.

Note   An organization may be exempt from *payment* of a state's sales tax, yet be required to *collect* (and remit) sales tax when selling goods or services.

ELIGIBILITY FOR TAX-EXEMPT STATUS

Eligibility for tax-exempt status is established by law, almost always statutory law. With the emphasis on the federal income tax, nearly all organizations that are tax-exempt are expressly referenced in the IRC. Tax-exempt status at the federal law level is provided by IRC § 501(a). Most of the categories of exempt organizations (see following "Categories of Tax-Exempt Organizations" section) are the subject of IRC § 501(c). Other exempt organizations are referenced in IRC §§ 521 and 526 to 529. Tax exemption for governmental and quasi-governmental organizations is not provided by statutory law (although IRC § 115 provides for exclusion of gross income for certain political subdivisions).

There are other types of organizations that are tax-exempt by reason of federal law. Charitable remainder trusts are exempt; pooled income funds are essentially exempt (see Chapter 5). Certain entities often functioning in the for-profit world are (or can be) tax-exempt: partnerships, other joint ventures, limited liability companies, certain cooperatives, and small business (or S) corporations.

Thus, to be tax-exempt, it is not enough for the organization to be a nonprofit one (see Chapter 1). It must also meet the appropriate requirements stipulated in the law for exempt status.

RECOGNITION OF TAX-EXEMPT STATUS

As noted, eligibility for tax-exempt status is dictated by the provisions of (usually statutory) law. Thus, an organization either qualifies for a category of exemption or it does not (although judgment may have to be exercised on the point). Tax exemption is conferred on an organization by operation of law.

Recognition of tax-exempt status occurs when a governmental agency agrees with the applicant organization that the entity is eligible for exempt status. At the federal level, this is, of course, a function of the IRS. The IRS does not grant an organization tax-exempt status; the agency recognizes the exempt status that is inherent with the organization as a matter of law. The IRS's forms used by organizations to acquire recognition of exempt status are titled "Application for Recognition of Exemption."

CATEGORIES OF TAX-EXEMPT ORGANIZATIONS

There is no agreement as to the number of types of tax-exempt organizations authorized by the federal tax law; the number obtained depends on how the law is parsed. Suffice it to say that this number is well in excess of 50.

In order of IRC sections, the categories of tax-exempt organizations are as follows:

Instrumentalities of the United States—IRC § 501(c)(1) and (1)

Title-holding companies (exempt organizations that hold title to property for the benefit of one or more other exempt organizations)—IRC § 501(c)(2) and (25)

Charitable organizations (such as entities that provide relief to the poor or the distressed, lessen the burdens of government, promote health or social welfare, advance the arts or patriotism, protect the environment, or advance religion, science, or education)—IRC § 501(c)(3)

Educational organizations (such as colleges, universities, and schools, or entities that provide instruction or training to individuals or to the general public)—IRC § 501(c)(3)

Scientific organizations (such as entities that engage in scientific research or disseminate scientific information)—IRC § 501(c)(3)

Religious organizations (such as churches, synagogues, and mosques, and integrated auxiliaries of churches and religious orders)—IRC § 501(c)(3)

Social welfare organizations (such as advocacy entities and civic leagues)—IRC § 501(c)(4)

Local associations of employees—IRC § 501(c)(4)

Labor organizations (including unions)—IRC § 501(c)(5)

Agricultural organizations—IRC § 501(c)(5)

Horticultural organizations—IRC § 501(c)(5)

Business leagues (almost all of which are associations providing services to members)—IRC § 501(c)(6)

Social clubs (entities that provide social and recreational services to members)—IRC § 501(c)(7)

Fraternal organizations—IRC § 501(c)(8) and (10)

Voluntary employees' beneficiary associations—501(c)(9)

Teachers' retirement fund associations—IRC § 501(c)(11)

Benevolent or mutual organizations—IRC § 501(c)(12)

Cemetery companies—IRC § 501(c)(13)

Credit unions and mutual reserve funds—IRC § 501(c)(14)

Small insurance companies—IRC § 501(c)(15)

Crop operations finance corporations—IRC § 501(c)(16)

Supplemental unemployment benefit trusts—IRC § 501(c)(17)

Employee benefit trusts—IRC § 501(c)(18)

Veterans' organizations—IRC § 501(c)(19) and (23)

Black lung benefits trusts—IRC § 501(c)(21)

Multiemployer plan trusts—IRC § 501(c)(22)

Trusts described in the Employee Retirement Income Security Act—IRC § 501(c)(24)

High-risk individuals health care coverage organizations—IRC § 501(c)(26)

Workers' compensation reinsurance organizations—IRC § 501(c)(27)

National Railroad Retirement Investment Trust—IRC § 501(c)(28)

Religious or apostolic organizations—IRC § 501(d)

Farmers' cooperatives—IRC § 521

Ship owners' protection and indemnity associations—IRC § 526

Political organizations (including political parties, political action committees, and candidate funds)—IRC § 527

Homeowners' associations—IRC § 528

Qualified prepaid tuition programs—IRC § 529

States, political subdivisions, instrumentalities, and integral parts

Native American tribes

Some organizations are reflected in other provisions of the IRC, yet must also meet the requirements of IRC § 501(c)(3):

- Cooperative hospital service organizations—IRC § 501(e)
- Cooperative educational service organizations—IRC § 501(f)
- Child care organizations—IRC § 501(k)
- Charitable risk pools—IRC § 501(n)

SELECTION OF APPROPRIATE CATEGORY

The appropriate category of tax exemption for an eligible organization is dictated by application of the *primary purpose test*. Thus, those involved in the formation of an organization that will seek recognition of exemption must identify the entity's primary purpose (see Chapter 1). That exercise should guide the parties to the appropriate category of tax exemption. (Not all nonprofit organizations are eligible for tax-exempt status.) Also, an entity's primary purpose can change; an alteration of purpose may cause the organization to be transformed into a different type of exempt entity (or, worse, to lose exempt status).

Exempt organizations are generally divided into the following categories:

- Charitable
- Educational
- Religious
- Scientific
- Social welfare
- Labor
- Membership services
- Social and recreational services
- Advocacy (legislative or political)

It is common for an organization to have more than one of these (or other) purposes. Again, it is the primary purpose or purposes that must be ascertained in selecting the appropriate category of tax-exempt status. For example, an organization may have some charitable and educational purposes, yet its dominate ones are social and recreational; the entity will fail to qualify for exemption by reason of IRC § 501(c)(3) but satisfy the requirements of IRC § 501(c)(7).

Moreover, in some circumstances, distinctions as to purposes will dictate more than one tax-exempt organization. Often, one entity will control the other (parent and subsidiary relationship). One or more of these entities may be a supporting organization (see Chapter 3). The usual combinations are

- Business league parent and charitable organization subsidiary
- Social welfare organization parent and charitable organization subsidiary
- Other noncharitable exempt organization parent and charitable organization subsidiary
- Foreign charity parent and domestic charity subsidiary
- Charitable organization parent and charitable organization subsidiary
- Charitable organization parent and social welfare organization subsidiary
- Charitable organization parent and business league subsidiary

Other illustrations of bifurcations of this nature are the use of title-holding companies, political organizations, and employee benefit funds.

For that matter, this need for bifurcation (or trifurcation and so on) may entail the use of a for-profit organization or a limited liability company (see Chapter 9), a taxable nonprofit organization, and/or some other entity.

APPLICATION PROCESS

The seeking of recognition of tax-exempt status by the IRS is either mandatory or voluntary—this depends on the type of exempt organization involved. For most types of exempt organizations, recognition of exempt status is not required. This is the case, for example, for social welfare organizations, labor organizations, business leagues, social clubs, fraternal organizations, and veterans' groups.

By contrast, most charitable organizations are required—to be tax-exempt—to achieve recognition of exempt status. There are exceptions to this requirement, such as for churches, certain other religious organizations, and small organizations. Certain employee benefit funds are likewise required to obtain recognition of exempt status. Political organizations, while not required to secure recognition of exempt status, must (to be exempt) give notice of their formation to the IRS.

The leadership of many types of tax-exempt organizations thus must decide whether to pursue recognition of exemption for the entity. For some, the operative factor is the expense of the process. Another element of the decision may be aversion to interaction with the IRS—and to avoid it if it is not absolutely necessary. Or, the parties may be confident that the organization is eligible for exempt status, so that recognition of exemption is not needed. The countervailing (and often prevailing) factor is the comfort of an IRS ruling: knowing that the agency is in agreement with the view that the organization is a tax-exempt entity.

For the most part, the process of seeking recognition of tax-exempt status from the IRS entails the filing of a formal application for that status. The IRS has promulgated application forms:

- Form 1023, which is used to apply for IRS recognition of IRC § 501(c)(3) status
- Form 1024, which is used to apply for IRS recognition of most other categories of exempt status
- Form 1028, which is filed by farmers', fruit growers', and similar associations

For some types of exempt organizations, there is no formal application; recognition of exempt status is sought by the submission of a letter.

To state these requirements another way, the filing of the Form 1023 usually is mandatory, while the filing of the Form 1024 (or 1028 or letter) is voluntary. The word usually in this context reflects the fact that some organization that are not required to file a Form 1023 (yet can nonetheless be exempt by reason of IRC § 501(c)(3)) may elect to do so; an example of this type of organization is a church.

TIMING

An application for recognition of tax exemption filed on behalf of a charitable organization can, if successful, be retroactive to the date the organization was formed. This involves a *threshold notice rule.*

This threshold notice rule is of two parts. One rule is that the notice as to tax-exempt status (that is, the application) must be given to the IRS within 15 months from the end of the month in which the organization was organized. The IRS, however, provided an automatic 12-month period extension of time for this filing, thereby converting it to a 27-month period. The application is formatted to reflect which of these two threshold periods is being used. The point is that a successful application, if filed within this 27-month period, will be retroactive to the date of formation of the organization.

An organization is considered organized on the date it became an entity (a charitable one). In determining the date on which a corporation is organized for purposes of this exemption recognition process, the IRS looks to the date the entity came into existence under the law of the state in which it was incorporated, which usually is the date its articles of incorporation were filed in the appropriate state office. This date is not the date the organizational meeting was held, bylaws adopted, or actual operations began.

The IRS has general discretionary authority, on a showing of good cause, to grant a reasonable extension of time fixed by the tax regulations for making an election or application for relief in respect of the federal income tax law. This discretionary authority may be exercised where the time for making the election or application is not expressly prescribed by statute, the request for the extension is filed with the IRS within a period the agency considers reasonable under the circumstances, and it is shown to the satisfaction of the IRS that granting the extension will not jeopardize the interests of the federal government. The IRS acknowledged that it can exercise this discretionary authority to extend the time for satisfaction of the threshold notice period requirement (which is not fixed by statute). The IRS has outlined the information and representations that must be furnished and some factors that will be taken into consideration in determining whether an extension of this nature will be granted. The application is formatted to accommodate this request.

An organization's eligibility to receive deductible charitable contributions also is governed by the threshold notice rule. Thus, where a charitable organization timely files the application for recognition of tax exemption, and the determination letter or ruling ultimately is favorable, the ability to receive deductible charitable gifts is effective as of the date the organization was formed.

An organization that qualifies for tax exemption as a charitable organization but files for recognition of exemption after the applicable threshold notice period can be exempt as a social welfare organization for the period commencing on the date of its inception to the date tax exemption as a charitable entity becomes effective. Contributions to social welfare organizations, however, are rarely deductible as charitable gifts, so this approach is of little utility to charitable organizations that rely significantly on support in the form of contributions.

Timing is not an issue for other categories of tax-exempt organizations (other than political organizations; see "Notice Requirements for Political Organizations" section, later in this chapter). Inasmuch as these organizations are inherently exempt and need not file for recognition of exemption, they can file for recognition of exemption at any time. The determination letter generally will be silent as to the date of applicability of exemption because it is irrelevant.

EXCEPTIONS

The application process for charitable organizations is not required of these organizations:

- Churches, interchurch organizations of local units of a church, conventions, or associations of churches, and integrated auxiliaries of churches
- Organizations whose gross receipts in each tax year are normally not more than $5,000 (as long as they are not private foundations (see Chapter 3))
- Subordinate organizations covered by a group exemption letter where the central organization has submitted to the IRS the requisite notice covering the subordinates (see "Group Exemption" section later in this chapter)

For purposes of the second exception, the term *normally* embodies an averaging mechanism. That is, the gross receipts of an organization are normally not more than $5,000 if, during its first tax year, it received gross receipts of no more than $7,500; during its first two tax years, it received gross receipts of no more than $12,000; and, in the case of an organization that has been in existence for three tax years, the gross receipts received by it during its immediately preceding two tax years plus the current year are not more than $15,000.

The exception in these rules for organizations with gross receipts that are normally no more than $5,000 can operate to relieve a small organization from the requirement of filing an application for recognition of tax exemption during the initial years of its operation (yet still be tax-exempt) but expire as the organization receives greater amounts of financial support. Once an organization no longer qualifies for this exception, it is required to file the application within 90 days after the close of the year in which its gross receipts exceeded the amounts permitted under the exception. Thus, this notice period is used in this circumstance instead of the general threshold notice rule. An organization in this situation can, therefore, be tax-exempt as a charitable entity from its inception—no matter how many years have elapsed—as long as it files the application on a timely basis (that is, under the 90-day rule).

NOTICE REQUIREMENTS
FOR POLITICAL ORGANIZATIONS

Basically, for an organization to be treated as a tax-exempt political organization, it must give notice to the IRS of its existence. This notice must be transmitted no later than 24 hours after the date on which the organization is established, for the exemption to be available from the formation date. This notice must be submitted in writing and electronically. If this notice is provided after the 24-hour period, the exemption is only prospective.

This notice (Form 8871) must contain the following: the name and address of the organization and its electronic mailing address; the purpose of the organization; the names and addresses of its officers, highly compensated employees, contact person, custodian of records, and members of its board of directors; the name and address of, and relationship to, any related entities; and such other information the IRS may require. Any material change in the information provided in the initial notice must be reported to the IRS within 30 days of the change.

Where an organization fails to submit the requisite notice on a timely basis, it is taxable (unless exempt for other reasons). The taxable income of the organization, in this circumstance, is computed by taking into account any exempt function income and any directly related deductions.

This notice requirement does not apply in the case of a political organization that reasonably anticipates that it will not have gross receipts of $25,000 or more for the year. The requirement also does not apply to an entity that is required to report to the Federal Election Commission under the Federal Election Campaign Act as a political committee. Further, the requirement is not applicable to any other type of tax-exempt organization that is nonetheless subject to the political campaign activities tax (see Chapter 10).

PREPARATION OF APPLICATIONS

An applicant organization is expected to fully describe the activities in which it intends to engage, including the standards, criteria, procedures, or other means adopted or planned for carrying out the activities, the anticipated sources of receipts, and the nature of contemplated expenditures. An organization filing an application for recognition of exemption has the burden of proving that it satisfies all of the requirements of the particular tax exemption category.

The preparer of the application must make a judgment as to the extent of the contents of the document. Mere "vague generalizations" will not suffice, in that "meaningful explanations" must be provided along with "complete and candid" responses to any follow-up inquiries from the IRS.

At the same time, an organization is considered to have made the requisite "threshold showing" where it describes its activities in "sufficient detail" to permit a conclusion that the entity will meet the pertinent requirements, particularly when it answered all of the questions propounded by the IRS. A court observed that, although the law "requires that the organization establish reasonable standards and criteria for its operation as an exempt organization," this requirement does not necessitate "some sort of metaphysical proof of future events." It is within these boundaries, then, that the preparer of the application strives to present the most complete and favorable portrayal of the organization that is reasonably possible.

The proper preparation of an application for recognition of

exemption, therefore, involves far more than merely niggardly responding to questions on a government form. It is a process not unlike the preparation of a prospectus for a business in conformity with securities law requirements. Every statement made in the application should be carefully considered and tested against the applicable law. Indeed, some of the questions—on the application or in one or more follow-up letters from the IRS—may force the applicant organization to focus on matters that good management practices should cause it to consider, even in the absence of the application's requirements.

The prime objectives must be completeness and accuracy: it is essential that all material facts be correctly and fully disclosed. Of course, the determination as to which facts are material and the marshaling of these facts requires judgment. Also, the manner in which the answers are phrased can be significant; in this regard, the exercise can be more art than science. The preparer (or reviewer) of the application should be able to anticipate the concerns the contents of the application may cause the IRS and to see that the application is properly prepared, while simultaneously minimizing the likelihood of conflict with the agency.

Organizations that are entitled to tax-exempt status have been denied recognition of exemption, or at least have caused the process of gaining the recognition to be more protracted, because of inartful phraseologies in the application that motivated the IRS to muster a case that the organization did not qualify for exemption. Consequently, the application for recognition of tax exemption should be regarded as an important legal document and constructed accordingly. The fact that the application is available for public inspection and dissemination (see Chapter 6) only underscores the need for the thoughtful preparation of it.

The application for recognition of exemption seems to be a document that tax-exempt organizations misplace more than may other. The organization should endeavor to maintain copies of it. An exempt organization is required to provide a copy of the application to a requestor if it had a copy of the document on or after July 15, 1987.

RELIANCE ON DETERMINATION

In general, an organization can rely on a determination letter or ruling from the IRS recognizing its tax-exempt status. This is not the case, however, if there is a material change, inconsistent with exemption, in the character, purpose, or methods of operation of the organization (see "Material Changes" section later in this chapter).

Generally, others may rely on this determination letter or ruling as well. This is particularly important to donors and grantors (such as private foundations) to charitable organizations. Donors of large gifts want the protection of the ruling, to be assured that they are entitled to the maximum charitable contribution (see Chapter 5). Private foundations want the comfort of reliance, so that they will not inadvertently make a grant that requires expenditure responsibility or is for noncharitable purposes.

MAINTENANCE OF EXEMPT STATUS

Once an organization achieves tax-exempt status—recognized or not—that qualification is maintained as long as the entity does not materially change its character, purposes, or methods of operation. A change in an organization's form is likely to have tax consequences (discussed next). Of course, an organization's exempt status may be affected by a change in the law.

Those involved with a tax-exempt organization may, from time to time, have to make a judgment as to whether one or more material changes have occurred, and if so, whether the change or changes are inconsistent with the organization's tax-exempt status.

CHANGES IN ORGANIZATIONAL FORM

A change in organizational form generally is treated as the creation of a new legal entity, which may require the filing of an application for recognition of exemption for the successor entity, even though the organization's purposes, methods of operation, sources of support, and accounting period remain the same as they were in its predecessor form.

The common changes in form are

- Conversion of a trust to a corporation
- Conversion of an unincorporated association to a corporation
- Reincorporation of an organization, incorporated under the law of one state, pursuant to the law of another state

It is rare for an organization that is incorporated to become unincorporated. If that were to happen, however, another application might be required.

Generally, the tax-exempt status of the predecessor entity will, in effect, be transmitted to the successor entity. If the predecessor organization is a publicly supported charity (see Chapter 3), the public support received by the predecessor can be used in measuring the public support of the successor entity. If an application for recognition of status as a charitable entity is filed, a specific question about successor organizations must be answered.

MATERIAL CHANGES

An organization's tax-exempt status remains in effect as long as there are no substantial—that is, *material*—changes in the organization's character, purposes, or methods of operation. (This phraseology is from the tax regulations; the determination letter language adds sources of support to the list of changes involved.) The IRS must be notified of these material changes.

This matter of materiality can affect the timing of the communication of the change to the IRS. The agency is supposed to be notified of every one of an organization's fact changes. A material change should be communicated to the IRS as soon as possible after the change is made or becomes effective. In any event, each of these changes in the facts—material or not—should be reflected in due course in the organization's annual information return (see Chapter 4), unless the change was previously reported. Thus, the issue is not whether a change should be communicated to the IRS, but when.

A material change does not necessarily mean that the organization's tax-exempt status is imperiled. For example, a change in the facts may entail a substantial expansion or revision of exempt function activities. Or, the change could involve a modification of the organization's purposes, yet within the bounds of exempt status.

The foregoing considerations also apply to other changes in the organization's governing instruments. Although all of these changes are to be reported as part of the filing of an annual information return (unless previously reported), substantial changes should be communicated to the IRS when they occur.

GROUP EXEMPTION

In most instances, an organization is tax-exempt by operation of law, although in some cases (as discussed) recognition of that exemption by the IRS is required. Occasionally, however, tax exemption can be achieved by means of the *group exemption* procedure.

An organization (such as a chapter, local, post, or unit) that is affiliated with and is subject to the general supervision or control of a central organization (usually a state, regional, or national organization) may be recognized as a tax-exempt organization solely by reason of its relationship with the parent organization. Tax-exempt status acquired in this manner is referred to as tax exemption on a group basis. The advantage of the group exemption is that each of the organizations covered by a group exemption determination is relieved from filing its own application for recognition of tax exemption.

The procedures by which group exemption may be recognized by the IRS contemplate a functioning of the parent organization as, in effect, an agent of the IRS. This means that the parent organization must responsibly and independently evaluate the exempt status of the prospective group members from the standpoint of the organizational and operational tests applicable to them. A parent organization is required to annually file with the IRS a list of its qualifying group members; this listing amounts to an attestation by the parent organization that the members of the group qualify as exempt organizations so that the IRS need not carry out an independent evaluation as to the exempt status of these organizations.

Assuming that the general requirements for recognition of tax-exempt status are satisfied, a group exemption letter will be issued to a parent organization where these requirements as to affiliated organizations are met and each of the affiliated organizations has an organizing document (although they do not have to be incorporated). Also, the exemption to be recognized must be under the general exemption rules. That is, this procedure is not available to farmers' cooperatives, shipowners' protection and indemnity associations, political organizations, homeowners' associations, or prepaid tuition plan entities. Private foundations (see Chapter 3) may not be included in a group exemption arrangement, nor may an organization that is organized and operated in a foreign country.

Overall, an organization applying for a group exemption classification must (1) obtain recognition of its own tax-exempt status, (2) establish that all of the organizations to be included in the group exemption determination are affiliated with it, (3) demonstrate that all of the organizations in the group are exempt under the same section of the general exemption rules (although not necessarily the provision under which the parent organization is exempt), (4) be certain that none of the entities in the group are private foundations or foreign organizations, (5) show that the organizations in the group have the same accounting period as the parent organization (if they are not to be included in group returns), and (6) show that the entities in the group were formed within the 27-month period (see "Timing" section earlier in this chapter) prior to the date of submission of the group exemption application (assuming this is the case, these entities are claiming charitable status, and the organizations are subject to the requirements for application for recognition of tax exemption).

For example, with respect to this third requirement, a parent organization may be tax-exempt as a charitable entity with all of the affiliated organizations exempt as social welfare organizations. As to the sixth requirement, if one or more of the affiliates have not been organized within the 27-month period, the group exemption determination will be issued only if all of the affiliates agree to be recognized as exempt from the date of the application rather than the date of their formation.

Once a group exemption determination is issued, certain information must be submitted to the IRS annually by the parent organization at least 90 days before the close of its annual accounting period. This information must include notice as to any changes in the purposes, character, or method of operation of the subordinates. Also, this submission must include a list of any organizations that are no longer to be included in the group exemption and of other entities added to the group. Additional information is required.

An affiliated organization may, rather than file a separate annual information return (see Chapter 4), file in combination with the parent organization. For this option to be available, however, each of the affiliates must be tax-exempt under the same federal tax law provision.

A parent organization may be involved in more than one

group exemption arrangement. For example, a charitable parent organization may have, as noted, both charitable and social welfare organization affiliates. Also, a parent organization may be an affiliated organization with respect to another central organization, such as a state organization that has affiliated units and is itself affiliated with a national organization.

The principal advantage of the group exemption is that each of the organizations in the group is relieved from filing an application for recognition of exemption, irrespective of whether the filing is otherwise mandatory or voluntary (see "Application Process" section earlier in this chapter). Consideration should be given to the group exemption in circumstances where there are (or are expected to be) several chapters, locals, posts, units, or other affiliates of a tax-exempt organization. It is a useful procedure that can save the organizations (and the IRS) much time and effort.

There are difficulties with the group exemption procedure, however; they start with the terminology involved. The organization that is the one with which the others are affiliated is termed the *central organization*. Worse, the affiliates are referenced as *subordinate organizations*. Many who are associated with organizations do not care to be considered subordinated to and/or dominated by another organization.

There are other disadvantages to the group exemption approach, including the following:

- There is a fear of ascending liability—the worry that an affiliated organization will incur legal liability for a commission or omission and that liability will extend to the central organization.
- The members of the group do not individually possess determination letters as to their tax exemption, perhaps posing difficulties with respect to grantors and donors.
- State tax exemption(s) may be laborious to obtain, in that the state tax authorities usually expect submission of a federal determination letter as to tax-exempt status.
- In the case of charitable organizations, there is no separate assessment of their public charity status; indeed, the IRS assumes that a charitable affiliate has the same public charity status as the central organization (which in fact is not always the case).

Nonetheless, the group exemption generally is a most favorable technique for clusters of nonprofit organizations that are affiliated in some manner. This approach to tax exemption obviates, as noted, the need for each member entity in the group to file an application for recognition of exemption. (It does not, however, necessarily mean that each affiliate is relieved from the requirement of filing annual information returns (see Chapter 4).) In the proper set of circumstances, the group exemption arrangement is an effective, streamlined approach for the establishment of recognition of tax-exempt status.

SUMMARY

This chapter provided basic information as to the process for acquiring and maintaining tax-exempt status pursuant to the federal tax law. It explained what a tax-exempt organization is and how to select the appropriate category of exempt organization. The chapter discussed the concept of recognition of tax-exempt status, the application process with the IRS, and the effective date of recognition of exempt status. It described the appropriate approach to preparation of applications for recognition of exemption. Also, the chapter explained what should be done to maintain tax-exempt status. The chapter concluded with a summary of the group exemption procedure.

CHAPTER 3

Public Charities and Private Foundations

The purpose of this chapter is to describe the rules differentiating between private foundations and public charities, offer some planning tips, summarize the private foundation rules, and discuss alternatives to private foundations. Specifically, this chapter will:

- Define the term *private foundation*
- Define the term *public charity*
- Focus on the measurement of public support
- Discuss the uses of supporting organizations
- Summarize the private foundation rules
- Discuss the donor-advised fund

DEFINING PRIVATE FOUNDATION

Oddly, the federal tax law does not define the term *private foundation*. This is the case even though IRC § 509 is captioned "Private Foundation Defined." This section should be titled "Public Charity Defined" because that is what it really does. That is, the section defines what a private foundation is not. Another perspective on the point is that, technically, a private foundation is any tax-exempt charitable entity that is not a public charity.

Nonetheless, a private foundation generally is an organization that has the following characteristics:

- It is, as noted, a tax-exempt, charitable, educational, scientific, or like organization (and is thus subject to the rules applicable to charitable organizations generally).

47

- It is funded (often on only one occasion) from a single source (such as an individual, a family, or a business).
- Its ongoing revenue is income from investment assets (so that a foundation operates much like an endowment fund).
- It does not have its own program but, rather, makes grants in furtherance of the charitable ends of other organizations (and sometimes individuals).

It is because of this second characteristic that an organization is considered to be private. (That term does not pertain to an organization's board, although a board can be private in the sense that it consists of representatives of a single corporation or a single family. Yet, a public charity can likewise have a private board.)

Every tax-exempt, charitable organization is presumed to be a private foundation. This presumption can be rebutted by a showing that the organization is a form of public charity.

DEFINING PUBLIC CHARITY

There are three fundamental types of public charities:

1. Institutions
2. Publicly supported charities
3. Supporting organizations (so classified because of their nexus to one or more other tax-exempt organizations)

Institutions

The *institutions* are not private foundations because of their functions. They are churches (including synagogues and mosques) and certain other religious organizations; colleges, universities, and schools; hospitals and other providers of health care; medical research organizations; and governmental units.

Publicly Supported Charities

A *publicly supported charity* is the antithesis of a private foundation. While, as noted, a private foundation is a charity that is privately funded, a publicly supported charity is a charitable organization that receives financial support on an ongoing basis from the general public. Thus, this public charity status is dependent on the nature of the organizations' funding. Most of the elements of the definition of the term *publicly supported charity* focus on the meaning, in the appropriate context, of the term *general public.*

There are two types of publicly supported charities:

1. The *donative* type
2. The *service provider* type

Donative Publicly Supported Charity

A donative publicly supported charity is an organization that *normally* receives a *substantial part* of its financial support from direct or indirect contributions from the *general public* and/or from one or more governmental units in the form of grants.

Most donative publicly supported charities must derive at least one-third of their financial support (the *support ratio*) from eligible governmental and/or public sources. Except for new entities, the normal time span for measuring the organization's support is its most recent four tax years (the *support computation period*).

Public support can come from individuals, corporations, trusts, other charitable organizations, or other legal entities. The total amount of contributions or grants from any one donor or grantor during the support computation period generally is not public support to the extent that the amount exceeds 2 percent of the organization's allowable total support received during that period. The 2 percent limitation, however, does not apply to support in the form of grants from other donative publicly supported organizations or from governmental units. All grant support from these two sources is public support.

Donors who have certain relationships with one another (such as spouses or individuals and controlled businesses) must share a single 2 percent limitation. Multiple contributions or grants from any one source are aggregated over the support computation period and treated as a single gift or grant.

In the computation of its support ratio, a donative publicly supported organization cannot include amounts received from the exercise or performance of its tax-exempt functions (*program service revenue*). An organization cannot, however, meet this *public support test* if it receives almost all of its support from its related activities and only an insignificant amount of support from the general public and/or governmental units in the form of grants.

Service Provider Publicly Supported Charity

A service-provider publicly supported charitable organization normally must receive more than one-third of its financial support in the form of gifts and grants, membership fees, and/or gross receipts in the form of program service revenue. Amounts that are eligible as public support are those derived from *permitted sources*. These sources are governmental agencies, the other types of institutions, donative publicly supported charities, and persons who are not *disqualified persons* with respect to the organization (see the "Disqualified Persons" section later in this chapter).

Like the law concerning donative publicly supported charitable organization, the service-provider organization rules take into account financial support received over the organization's most recent four tax years (the meaning of the word *normally*) and utilize a one-third support fraction.

Exempt function revenue can count as public support for the service-provider organization, but only to the extent that the revenue from any one source does not exceed the greater of $5,000 or 1 percent of the organization's support during the support computation period involved. Also, support of this nature, to constitute public support, cannot come from disqualified persons.

Thus, these rules place limits on qualifying gifts and grants to service-provider publicly supported charitable organizations. As noted, public support cannot come from *disqualified persons*. These persons are an organization's directors (or trustees) and officers, members of their families, persons controlled by disqualified persons (such as businesses, trusts, and estates), and substantial contributors. A *substantial contributor* is a person who contributes or bequeaths an aggregate amount of more than $5,000 to a charitable organization, where that amount is more than 2 percent of the contributions and bequests received by the organization over the totality of its existence.

To qualify as a service-provider publicly supported charitable organization, the entity may not receive more than one-third of its financial support in the form of investment income.

Supporting Organizations

The third category of charitable organization that is not a private foundation is the *supporting organization*. This is an entity that is related, structurally or operationally, to one or more institutions and or publicly supported organizations (or, in some instances, other organizations). A supporting organization must be organized, and at all times operated, in an active relationship with one or more eligible supported organizations.

This relationship must be one of three types, with the interaction between the organizations different for each type:

1. *Operated, supervised, or controlled by one or more eligible supported organization(s).* This is a parent–subsidiary relationship, where the parent maintains a significant degree of direction over the policies, programs, and other activities of the supporting organization.
2. *Supervised or controlled in connection with one or more eligible supported organization(s).* This is a brother–sister relationship, where there is common supervision or control by the persons heading both the supporting and supported organizations.
3. *Operated in connection with one or more eligible supported organization(s).* This means that the supporting organization is responsive to and significantly involved in the operation of one or more supported organizations.

Most supported organizations are charitable, educational, religious, and like entities. Nonetheless, it is possible to structure a relationship where the supported organization is a tax-exempt social welfare, agricultural, horticultural, labor, or trade, business, or professional organization (see Chapter 2). The basic requirement is that this type of supported organization must satisfy the public support test applicable to service-provider publicly supported organizations.

There is no limitation as to the number of organizations that can be supported by a supporting organization. Moreover, there is no limitation as to the number of supporting organizations that a supported organization may have.

A supporting organization may not be controlled directly or indirectly by one or more disqualified persons with respect to it.

WHAT DIFFERENCE DOES IT MAKE?

As noted, a tax-exempt charitable organization is either a public charity or a private foundation. From a law perspective, it is usually important for the organization to qualify as a public charity. That is, there is no law advantage to private foundation status.

Here are the disadvantages to classification as a private foundation:

- The need to comply with a battery of onerous rules, namely, prohibitions on self-dealing, insufficient grants for charitable purposes, excess business holdings, jeopardizing investments, and certain types of grants and other expenditures (see "Private Foundation Rules" section later in this chapter)
- A tax on net investment income
- Extensive record-keeping and reporting responsibilities
- Narrow limitations on gift deductibility
- The reality that private foundations are highly unlikely to make grants to other private foundations

The biggest advantage to the use of a private foundation is that the donor or donors can retain control over the funds and property they have contributed (and taken a deduction for) to the organization. Also, under certain circumstances, donors and their family members can be compensated for services rendered to the foundation.

DISQUALIFIED PERSONS

Often, the private foundation rules and the rules as to public support (see following "Determining Public Support—Tricks of the Trade" section) require a private foundation to avoid or take into account relationships or arrangements with those who are *disqualified persons* with respect to it. Disqualified persons fall into one of these categories:

- Substantial contributors to the foundation (see Chapter 4)
- Foundation managers (i.e., trustees, directors, officers, and those with similar powers and responsibilities)
- Owners of more than 20 percent of an interest in a business entity that is a substantial contributor to the foundation
- A member of the family of any of the foregoing individuals

- Corporations, partnerships, trusts, or estates in which disqualified persons own or hold more than 35 percent of the voting power, profits interest, or beneficial interest
- Other private foundations (but only for purposes of the excess business holdings rules)
- Government officials (but only for purposes of the self-dealing rules)

DETERMINING PUBLIC SUPPORT— TRICKS OF THE TRADE

Determining the amount of public support of a publicly supported organization, or one that wants to be so classified, can be an easy task—or it can be a difficult one.

Basic Planning Considerations

An organization that can expect to receive nearly all of its support in the form of many, relatively small gifts will have no trouble in achieving either donative or service-provider status. An organization that is essentially dues-based will be a service provider publicly supported charity. Likewise, an organization that anticipates receiving most of its financial support as program service revenue must look to the category of service-provider organization, for relief from private foundation classification. The reverse is likely true for an organization that is relying largely on government grants (not contracts) for support; it would look to the donative organization category, although classification as a service provider entity may also be available.

Many charitable organizations, particularly during their formative years, rely on just a few sources of financial support (such as some private foundations and/or makers of large gifts). For these entities, compliance with either the donative organization rules or the service-provider rules—particularly during the advance ruling period (see "Rules for New Organizations" section later in this chapter)—can be difficult (perhaps impossible). Under the service-provider rules, because the sources of support are likely to be substantial contributors, none of their support is eligible for treatment as public support. The outcome will be more favorable where the donative organization rules are applied: At least the amount received from each of these sources up to the 2 percent threshold can count as public support.

Compliance with either the donative organization rules or the service-provider organization rules at any point in time (including as of the close of the advance ruling period) is all that is required. An organization is not locked in to one set of these rules or the other (despite language in the determination letter); it can if necessary drift from one category to the other.

Gifts, Grants, and Contracts

As noted, support in the form of program service revenue is omitted from the public support ratio of donative publicly supported organizations. Almost always, it is not difficult to ascertain whether a payment is a *gift*. Conversely, what may appear to be a *grant* may in fact be a payment pursuant to a contractual arrangement that causes the amount to be program service revenue (in the parlance of this aspect of the law, *gross receipts*). In these circumstances, an organization may find that its public support ratio is improved if the amount is eliminated from the fraction.

A grant is normally made to encourage the grantee organization to carry on its exempt function programs. The grant arrangement may entail certain terms and conditions imposed by the grantor to ensure that the grantee's programs are conducted in a manner that is compatible with the grantor's programs and policies. The grantee may also perform a service or produce a work product that incidentally benefits the grantor. Because of the imposition of terms and conditions, the frequent similarity of public purposes of grantor and grantee, and the possibility of benefit resulting to the grantor, amounts received as grants *for* the carrying on of exempt activities are sometimes difficult to distinguish from amounts received as gross receipts *from* the carrying on of exempt functions.

The term *gross receipts* means amounts received from an activity (which is not an unrelated business (see Chapter 7)) if a specific service, facility, or product is provided to serve the direct and immediate needs of the payor, rather than primarily to confer a direct benefit on the general public. In general, payments made primarily to enable the payor to realize or receive some economic or physical benefit as a result of the service, facility, or product obtained will be treated as gross receipts with respect to the payee. The fact that a profit-making organization would, primarily for its own economic or physical betterment, contract with a nonprofit organization for the rendition of a comparable service, facility, or product from such organization is evidence that any payments received by the nonprofit payee organization for the services, facilities, or products are primarily for the economic or physical needs of the payor, and thus considered gross receipts (rather than grants).

Grant from Donative Entity

A charitable organization that is attempting to qualify, or continue to qualify, as a donative publicly supported entity may receive a grant from a charitable organization that is a donative publicly supported entity. In this situation, the grant is not limited by the 2 percent limitation; that is, the grant amount constitutes public support in full. This type of support is considered *indirect public support* (see Chapter 4). This means that donors to the grantor organization are deemed to be indirectly contributing to the grantee organization. This rule may enable an organization to enhance its public support ratio.

Moreover, this exception can be available where the grantor is not a donative publicly supported organization in the sense that it has been so recognized by the IRS. That is, it is sufficient if the grantor entity is *described in* the donative publicly supported organization rules. For example, a grant from a church to a charitable organization may qualify for this exception from the 2 percent limitation.

Unusual Grants

In some instances, a substantial contribution (including a bequest) or grant can be excluded from the numerator and the denominator of the public support ratio, thus usually enhancing the ratio. This exception is available in the case of both donative publicly supported organizations and service-provider publicly supported organizations.

For this exception to be available, the payment

- Must be attracted by reason of the publicly supported nature of the organization
- Must be unusual or unexpected with respect to its amount
- Would adversely affect the status of the organization as

normally meeting the applicable one-third public support test

All pertinent facts and circumstances are taken into consideration in applying this unusual grant rule. No single factor is determinative. These factors should be considered:

- Whether the contribution was made by a person (or related persons) who created the organization, previously contributed a substantial part of its support or endowment, or stood in a position of authority with respect to the organization (A contribution made by any other person ordinarily is given more favorable consideration.)
- Whether the contribution was a bequest or transfer during lifetime (The former is favored.)
- Whether the contribution was in the form of money, readily marketable securities, or assets that further the exempt purposes of the organization
- Whether, prior to the receipt of the contribution, the organization has carried on a program of public solicitation and exempt activities, and has been able to attract a significant amount of public support (This factor is thus inapplicable in the case of a new organization.)
- Whether the organization may reasonably be expected to attract a significant amount of public support subsequent to the contribution (Continued reliance on unusual grants is a negative factor.)
- Whether, prior to the year in which the contribution was received, the organization met the applicable one-third public support test, without the benefit of the unusual grant exclusion
- Whether the contributor or a related person continues directly or indirectly to exercise control over the organization
- Whether the organization has a representative governing body
- Whether material restrictions or conditions have been imposed by the transferor on the transferee in connection with the transfer

An unusual grant generally consists of *substantial contributions* (or grants) from disinterested parties. Also, as noted, a contribution from a person who created the organization is ordinarily given less favorable consideration in this regard than contributions from unrelated persons. Nonetheless, the IRS has been known to regard financial support provided by a tax-exempt organization to a related exempt organization as an unusual grant.

Facts-and-Circumstances Test

Some organizations generically are not private foundations, yet they come within the broad reach of that term under the federal tax law. These organizations can include museums, libraries, and other entities that have substantial endowment funds (so that they cannot achieve a one-third public support ratio). Some of these organizations may nonetheless be able to gain nonprivate-foundation status by means of the *facts-and-circumstances test.*

To meet this test, an organization must demonstrate the following:

- The total amount of public support it receives (using the donative publicly supported organization rules) is at least 10 percent of its total support.
- It has a continuous and bona fide program for the solicitation of funds from the general public, governmental units, and/or other public charities.
- It has other attributes of a public organization.

Among its other attributes, an organization may cite the composition of its governing board (showing how it is representative of the general public), the extent to which its facilities or programs are publicly available, its membership dues rates, and how its activities are likely to appeal to persons having some broad common interest or purpose.

The higher the percentage of public support, the easier the burden of establishing the publicly supported nature of the organization through the other factors. A main point to be emphasized, however, is that under this test the organization's public support need only be as little as 10 percent of its total support, rather than having to be at least one-third of the total support under the general rules. (This facts-and-circumstances test is only available for donative publicly supported charities; it is not available in connection with the service-provider organization rules.)

Use of Supporting Organization

There may be a circumstance where a charitable organization that is striving to be publicly supported is offered a contribution or grant that would, if accepted, cause the organization to no longer be publicly supported. This contribution or grant may not be from a donative publicly supported charity, the prospective recipient may not qualify under the facts-and-circumstances test, and the amount involved may not qualify as an unusual grant. What to do? (An unacceptable option is to decline the payment.)

The solution would be to establish a supporting organization to receive the large gift or grant. The transfer would not upset the supported organization's public support ratio. Once in the supporting organization, the gift or grant amount could be paid to the supported organization in increments so as to preserve the public charity status of the parent.

FOCUS ON SUPPORTING ORGANIZATIONS

As noted, supporting organizations are among the most versatile of planning vehicles in the law of tax-exempt organizations; indeed, they may be the most useful of all of them. They can be established by an exempt organization or by a donor or donors.

Uses by Charitable Organizations

There are at least nine reasons for use of a supporting organization by a public charity. Some public charities utilize several supporting organizations.

1. *Fundraising.* Many charitable organizations choose to house their fundraising activities in a separate entity. This organization is often termed a *foundation*, although it is not a private foundation (being a public charity). This is not done for tax reasons; these foundations are established for management purposes. In this fashion, the fundraising efforts can be separated from the charitable organization's general governance. The point is to concentrate the fundraising function in a separate organization. The foundation supports the parent entity by making grants to or for the benefit of that entity. A sup-

porting organization is an ideal vehicle for achievement of this objective.

2. *Endowment.* Some charitable organizations prefer to place their endowment fund (or funds) in a separate entity. Again, this is done for management, not tax, reasons. There may be concern about liability issues; thus, the endowment is maintained in a separate corporation. A board of directors of a charitable organization may want access to the endowment fund to be as difficult as possible; this goal is furthered when the fund is in a separate entity (with a separate, albeit controlled, board). The assets comprising the endowment fund(s) are not reflected on the parent organization's annual information return. If wanted, income generated by the endowment fund can be transferred to or for the benefit of the parent entity. A supporting organization is the perfect entity for this purpose. The holding of the fund and the payment of income is provision of the requisite support.

3. *Property.* There may be a reason to have property that would otherwise be owned by a charitable organization, titled and held by another entity. Usually, that reason is concern about legal liability (such as real property with potential environmental hazards). Again, this separate entity would be a corporation. A supporting organization can serve in this role. (Alternatives are a title-holding company (see Chapter 2) or a single-member limited liability company (see Chapter 9).) Holding of the property is the necessary support function.

4. *Program.* There may be a reason why a charitable organization may choose to have one or more programs in a separate entity. Again, the underlying reason for this may be management, not tax, objectives. A supporting organization can be used in this regard. The conduct of the program(s) is in itself provision of the requisite support.

5. *Public support ratio.* As discussed, a supporting organization can be used to attract and hold large contributions and grants of money or property, in circumstances where receipt of the money or property directly by the supported organization would cause the donee or grantee to lose its status as a publicly supported charity.

6. *Conversions.* A supporting organization can be invaluable

in saving the day for a charitable organization. For example, an organization may have tried to achieve the requisite public support during its advance-ruling period (see "Rules for New Organizations" section later in this chapter) and is failing. If it is converted to a supporting organization before the period ends, it will be a public charity from its inception and on an ongoing basis. Likewise, a private foundation can be converted to a supporting organization. This may be done to avoid the private foundation rules or to sidestep the other disadvantages of being a private foundation. Indeed, a private foundation may have inadvertently violated (or be on the brink of violating) one or more of the private foundation rules; conversion to a supporting organization may be the only path to avoidance or minimization of penalties.

7. *Joint venture.* A public charity may want to participate in a joint venture with a for-profit organization but be concerned about an adverse impact on its tax-exempt status (see Chapter 9). A solution is to create a supporting organization and have it be the exempt organization participant in the venture. Then, if something goes amiss, the adverse consequences are confined to the supporting organization. (Again, a single-member limited liability company is an alternative.)

8. *Holding company.* Some clusters of tax-exempt organizations require a coordinating entity. This is common, for example, in the health care field, where a group of hospitals, clinics, other health care providers, a fundraising foundation, and the like are managed by what is loosely termed a *holding company.* A supporting organization can be used for this purpose.

Uses by Noncharitable Organizations

One of the most curious provisions of the Internal Revenue Code reads as follows: "For purposes of paragraph (3), an organization described in paragraph (2) shall be deemed to include an organization described in section 501(c)(4), (5), or (6) which would be described in paragraph (2) if it were an organization described in section 501(c)(3)." Translated, this means that a tax-exempt social welfare organization, labor organization, or business league (see Chapter 2) can have one or more supporting organizations if the supported organization meets the public support test imposed on service-provider publicly supported charities. These organizations almost always meet that test, if only because dues are a form of gross receipts.

This rule is of considerable significance. It is one of the several places in the Code where bifurcation involving different categories of tax-exempt organizations is reflected. This provision enables an eligible noncharitable supported organization to transfer its charitable, educational, and/or scientific activities to a separate (charitable) entity, where they can be funded by means of grants and deductible contributions. As an alternative, organizations of this nature can use a supporting organization as a fundraising vehicle, with the supporting organization making grants to the supported organization in support of the latter's charitable, educational, and/or scientific activities.

Activities that are suitable for conduct and/or financial support by supporting organizations in this context are conferences and seminars, research, publishing, library maintenance, scholarships and fellowships, awards, and community outreach.

Note   Other types of tax-exempt organizations can have related charitable entities. These organizations include social clubs, fraternal organizations, and veterans' groups (see Chapter 2). These charitable affiliates cannot, however, be supporting organizations. (They usually are publicly supported charities.)

Use by Donors

Donors to charitable organizations may be the impetus for formation of supporting organizations. This may occur where a donor wants to provide major support for a charitable organization, yet be directly involved in the particular charitable endeavor. Another reason for this is that the charitable deduction involved may be greater (perhaps far greater) where the donee is a supporting organization rather than a private foundation. For example, a gift of appreciated property may be deductible based on its full fair market value when made to a supporting organization, whereas the same gift made to a private foundation may yield a charitable deduction confined to the donor's basis in the property (see Chapter 5).

Thus, a supporting organization is an alternative to a private foundation. A third option is the donor-advised fund (see "Donor-Advised Funds" section later in this chapter). The pivotal factor in the decision as to which vehicle to use is likely to be *control*. Donors to supporting organizations and donor-advised funds cannot maintain control over the gift funds or property. Of the choices, only a private foundation enables a donor to have a charitable deduction and ongoing control over the gifted items.

HYBRID FOUNDATIONS

The foregoing discussion of private foundations centered on the typical, grant-making foundation. There are, however, two other types of private foundations that are hybrid entities: part private foundation and part public charity. They are the *private operating foundation* and the *exempt operating foundation*.

Private Operating Foundation

The major activity of a typical private foundation is the making of grants, which are usually used by grantee organizations to further their exempt purposes (see "Gifts, Grants, and Contracts" section earlier in this chapter). Thus, the more a private foundation engages in program activities itself (rather than funding those of others), the greater the likelihood that it will be classified as something other than a standard private foundation.

Because of this distinction between grant-making and program administration, a hybrid entity has evolved, one that has some of the characteristics of a private foundation and some of those of a public charity. This is the private operating foundation—a foundation that devotes most of its earnings and much of its assets directly for the conduct of its charitable, educational, and/or similar purposes.

To be a private operating foundation, the organization must meet an *income test*. Annually, it must expend directly, for the active conduct of its exempt activities, an amount equal to substantially all of the lesser of its adjusted net income or its minimum investment return. The phrase *substantially all* means at least 85 percent. The *minimum investment return* is equal to 5 percent of the foundation's assets that are not used for charitable purposes.

To qualify as an operating foundation, an organization must satisfy at least one of three other tests:

1. The *assets test.* At least 65 percent of the foundation's assets must be devoted directly to the active conduct of its charitable activities.
2. The *endowment test.* The organization must normally expend its funds directly for the active conduct of its charitable activities in an amount equal to at least two-thirds of its minimum investment return $(2/3 \times (5 + 31/3))$.
3. The *support test.* At least 85 percent of its support (other than investment income) must be normally received from the general public and/or at least five tax-exempt organizations (that are not disqualified persons); no more than 25 percent of its support can be derived from any one exempt organization; and no more than one-half of its support can be normally received in the form of gross investment income.

Because of these rules, a private operating foundation is not subject to the minimum payout requirements imposed on standard private foundations. Contributions to a private operating foundation are deductible to the full extent permitted for gifts to public charities (see Chapter 5). That is, the percentage limitations that can restrict the deductibility of contributions to standard private foundations do not apply to gifts to private operating foundations.

Exempt Operating Foundations

A hybrid of a hybrid is the *exempt operating foundation.* The word *exempt* in this context does not mean exempt from federal income taxes (which private foundations generally are anyway).

Exempt operating foundations are presumably otherwise private operating foundations, but they enjoy two characteristics that other private foundations lack:

1. Grants to them are exempt from the expenditure responsibility requirements otherwise imposed on grantor foundations.
2. They do not have to pay the excise tax imposed on the net investment income of most private foundations.

To be an exempt operating foundation, an organization must (in addition to satisfaction of the requirements for private operating foundations) meet three tests:

1. It must have been publicly supported (under the donative charity or service-provider charity rules for at least 10 years or have qualified as an operating foundation as of January 1, 1983.
2. It must have a board of directors that, during the year involved, consisted of individuals at least 75 percent of whom are not *disqualified individuals* and was broadly representative of the general public (presumably using the facts-and-circumstances test rules.
3. It must not have an officer who was a disqualified individual at any time during the year involved.

Note   An organization that is able to qualify as an exempt operating foundation often is also able to qualify under the facts-and-circumstances test—and thereby avoid private foundation status altogether.

RULES FOR NEW ORGANIZATIONS

A newly created organization, by definition, lacks a suitable financial history as proof of public support. For these newcomers, the IRS will provide a classification as a publicly supported charitable organization on the basis of a proposed budget, submitted as part of the application for recognition of tax exemption (see Chapter 2).

Where a new organization's nonprivate foundation status is based on a classification linked to what it is programmatically or structurally—an institution or supporting organization (see "Focus on Supporting Organizations" section earlier in this chapter)—the IRS will issue a *definitive ruling.* Where, however, the nonprivate foundation classification depends on the organization's prospective ability to function as a publicly supported organization (i.e., a donative charitable organization or a service-provider charitable organization), the IRS will issue an *advance ruling,* which protects the organization from private foundation status during an *advance ruling period.* This period consists of the organization's first five tax years. If the organization meets one of the public support tests as of the close of the advance ruling period, the IRS will issue a definitive ruling as to its public charity status.

PRIVATE FOUNDATION RULES

There is a battery of complex, stringent, and onerous rules imposed on private foundations. These rules are underlain with penalties in the form of excise taxes.

Rules

Self-Dealing

The term *self-dealing* means a transaction that occurs, directly or indirectly, between a private foundation and a disqualified person. Generally, self-dealing transactions include sale or exchange of property; lease of property; lending of money or other extension of credit; furnishing of goods, services, or facilities; payment of unreasonable compensation; and transfer to, or use by or for the benefit of, disqualified persons of the income or assets of a private foundation. There are, however, many exceptions to and subtleties within the self-dealing rules. For example, a private foundation can pay reasonable compensation to a disqualified person (employee or independent contractor), but the services provided must be necessary to carrying out the exempt purposes of the payor private foundation and constitute *personal services.*

Minimum Payout

A private foundation must annually expend for charitable purposes an amount equal to 5 percent of the value of its investment assets. This *distributable amount* is determined by calculating the foundation's *minimum investment return.* If a private foundation does not achieve at least a 5 percent return on its principal, it must use part of its assets to satisfy this payout requirement. The amounts expended must constitute *qualifying distributions,* which essentially are grants for charitable purposes (including *set-asides*) and reasonable administrative expenditures. These rules thus require valuation of the investment assets (which do not include assets held for charitable purposes).

Business Holdings

Generally, a private foundation and its disqualified persons may not have combined holdings of more than 20 percent of a business enterprise. This rule applies to voting stock in a corporation, units in a partnership, and other forms of holdings in a business venture. Holdings are termed *permitted holdings* or, if not allowable, *excess business holdings*. If effective control of a business rests with unrelated parties, however, a private foundation and its disqualified persons may hold as much as 35 percent of a business enterprise. For these purposes, the term *business enterprise* does not include a *functionally related business* or an activity that derives at least 95 percent of its income from passive sources.

Investments

A private foundation may not invest any amount in a manner that will jeopardize the fulfillment of any of its charitable purposes. The law does not define *jeopardizing investments* but in this context it means highly speculative investments. There is no investment form that is per se jeopardizing. The rule, however, does not apply to *program-related investments*.

Expenditures

A private foundation is expected to avoid making taxable expenditures. Generally, a *taxable expenditure* is an amount paid or incurred to carry on propaganda, influence legislation, promote a particular outcome of a public election, make grants to individuals in connection with a program not preapproved by the IRS, make grants to organizations where the foundation has failed to exercise *expenditure responsibility*, or for any other noncharitable purpose. These rules entail a range of exceptions, involving such matters as voter registration drives, eligible scholarship and fellowship grants, and circulation of the results of nonpartisan analysis, study, or research. Because of these rules, most private foundations are forced to confine their grant-making to public charities.

Investment Income Tax

A private foundation must pay an excise tax equal to 2 percent of its net investment income for each of its years. (In a few instances, where the payout amount is appropriately increased, this tax rate is 1 percent.) *Net investment income* means interest, dividends, rents, royalties, and the like, less allowable deductions. In this context, the concept of *income* includes capital gain. As discussed earlier in this chapter, certain operating foundations are excused from payment of this tax.

Taxes

The private foundation rules have as their underpinning, as noted, sanctions in the form of excise taxes. There are *initial* (first-tier taxes) and *additional* (second-tier) taxes. The additional taxes are payable when an offense has occurred, one or more initial taxes have been imposed, and the offense is not timely corrected (see following "Corrections" section). A *termination tax* (see "Termination of Status" section later in this chapter) serves as a third-tier tax, enabling the IRS to confiscate the income and assets of a private foundation in the case of willful repeated acts (or failures to act) or a willful and flagrant act (or failure to act) giving rise to liability for a private foundation tax.

Self-Dealing

In the case of an act of self-dealing, the initial tax is 5 percent of the amount involved and is payable by the disqualified person who participated in the wrongful act. (Good faith is not a defense.) If this initial tax is imposed on a self-dealer, the foundation manager who participated in the act is subject to an initial tax (not to exceed $10,000) of 2½ percent of the amount involved, where he or she knew that the act was self-dealing and where the participation was willful and was not due to reasonable cause. The additional tax on the self-dealer is 200 percent of the amount involved. The additional tax (not to exceed $10,000) on the participating foundation manager, who refused to agree to part or all of a correction, is 50 percent of the amount involved. Two or more individuals may be jointly and severally liable for these taxes.

Payout

If a private foundation (other than an operating foundation) fails to satisfy the minimum payout requirements, it is subject to a tax equal 15 percent of the undistributed income. The additional tax is 100 percent of the undistributed amount.

Business Holdings

A private foundation must annually pay a tax equal to 5 percent of its excess business holdings. The additional tax is 200 percent of these holdings.

Investments

If a private foundation makes a jeopardizing investment, it must pay a tax equal to 5 percent of the investment. If that initial tax is imposed, a foundation manager who participated in the investment is subject to a tax (not to exceed $5,000) equal to 5 percent of the investment, where he or she knew that the investment was a jeopardizing one and where the participation was willful and not due to reasonable cause. The additional tax on the foundation is 25 percent of the amount of the investment. The additional tax (not to exceed $10,000) on a manager, who refused to agree to part or all of the removal from jeopardy, is 5 percent of the amount of the investment. Two or more individuals may be jointly and severally liable for these taxes.

Expenditures

The initial tax on a private foundation that makes a taxable expenditure is 10 percent of the amount involved. An initial tax (not to exceed $5,000 per taxable expenditure) is also imposed on every foundation manager who agreed to the taxable expenditure, where he or she knew it was a taxable expenditure, where the making of the taxable expenditure was willful, and where it was not due to reasonable cause. The additional tax on a private foundation is 100 percent of the expenditure. The additional tax (not to exceed $10,000 per expenditure) on a manager of a private foundation, where he or she refused to agree to part or all of the correction, is 50 percent of the amount of the taxable expenditure. Again, two or more individuals may be jointly and severally liable for these taxes.

Other than the self-dealing taxes, the IRS has the authority to abate, where reasonable cause is shown, a private foundation excise tax.

Correction

Thus, it is not enough, in the case of a violation of one of these rules, for the offending party to pay a tax and move on. The transaction or other arrangement involved must be *corrected*, that is, undone.

Self-Dealing

With respect to an act of self-dealing, correction means undoing the transaction to the extent possible, but in any case placing the private foundation in a financial position not worse than that in which it would be if the disqualified person were dealing under the highest fiduciary standards.

Payout

In the case of an insufficient payout for a year, the matter is corrected when the foundation makes the requisite qualifying distributions for the year (thereby reducing the amount of the undistributed income to zero).

Business Holdings

In the case of an excess business holding, the matter is corrected when the foundation disposes of the unlawful holding (thereby reducing the amount of the excess business holdings to zero).

Investments

In the case of a jeopardizing investment, the matter is corrected by changing the nature of the investment (known as removing the investment from jeopardy).

Expenditures

In the case of a taxable expenditure, the matter is corrected by recovering part or all of the expenditure to the extent recovery is possible; where full recovery is not possible, correction means taking appropriate corrective action. In some instances, correction is accomplished by obtaining or making a report.

TERMINATION OF STATUS

A private foundation can *terminate* its private foundation status. (This is often different than termination of the organization itself, such as by dissolution.) A private foundation can cease to be classified as a private foundation under the following circumstances:

- A private foundation transfers all of its net income and assets to one or more public charities, and then goes out of existence.
- A private foundation becomes qualified as a public charity, by revising the nature of its financial support and/or the nature of its activities.
- A private foundation transfers all or some of its assets to one or more other private foundations.

Fundamentally, there are two types of these terminations: voluntary and involuntary.

Voluntary Termination

As the term indicates, *voluntary terminations* of private foundation status take place when a private foundation takes the initiative to become a public charity, transform into two or more private foundations, and the like. In some instances, notice of termination to the IRS is required. The prospective termination tax is usually abated in these circumstances.

The type of termination that is favored in the law is the distribution of all of a private foundation's assets to one or more public charities, each of which has been in existence for a continuous period of at least 60 calendar months immediately preceding the distribution. These charities must, however, be either one of the types of institutions and/or donative publicly supported charitable organizations. Notification to the IRS is not required, nor is a ruling; there is no need for abatement of any tax.

If the distributee public charity (or charities) has been in existence for fewer than 60 calendar months, or the distributee public charity is a service-provider publicly supported organization or a supporting organization, the status of the private foundation is not terminated until it gives notice to the IRS. Thereafter, although the distributing foundation technically becomes subject to the termination tax, if it does not have any net assets on the day it provides the notice (undoubtedly because the notice is given after distribution of net assets), the tax is zero.

Involuntary Terminations

A private foundation's private foundation status may be involuntarily terminated if the IRS notifies the organization that, because of willful, flagrant, or repeated acts or failures to act giving rise to one or more of the private foundation excise taxes, the organization is liable for the termination tax.

The phrase "willful repeated acts (or failures to act)" means at least two acts or failures to act that are voluntary, conscious, and intentional. This type of act (or failure to act) is one that is voluntarily, consciously, and knowingly committed in violation of any of the private foundation rules and that appears to a reasonable person to be a gross violation of the rules. An act or failure to act may result in this type of termination, with the tax imposed on the foundation's managers. A failure to timely correct the act or acts, or failures to act, that gave rise to liability for tax under any of the private foundation rules, may be a willful and flagrant act (or failure to act).

A motive to avoid legal restrictions or the incurrence of tax is not necessary to make an act or failure to act willful. A private foundation's act or failure to act is not willful, however, if the private foundation, or its manager if applicable, did not know that the act or failure to act was an act of self-dealing, a taxable expenditure, or other act or failure to act giving rise to liability for one or more of the private foundation taxes.

The *termination tax* is equal to the lower of the aggregate tax benefits resulting from the tax-exempt status of the private foundation or the value of its net assets. The *aggregate tax benefit* essentially means the sum of the value of the foundation's tax exemption (going back to 1912), the value of the charitable deductions (income, estate, and gift) resulting from contributions made by substantial contributors (going back to 1913), and interest. This tax thus can amount to IRS confiscation of a foundation's assets, although the tax is rarely imposed.

DONOR-ADVISED FUNDS

An alternative to the private foundation is the donor-advised fund. Although this term is not formally defined, a *donor-advised fund* is a segregated fund or account maintained by a public charity for contributions received from a donor (or donors) for which there is an agreement that the donor (or the donor's designee) may advise (make recommendations to) the charity regarding the distribution of amounts held in the fund. The account (fund) usually is named after the donor(s) (or, in some instances, grantor(s)).

Donor-advised funds are controversial. Some contend that the maintenance of these funds is not a charitable activity. An extension of this assertion is that an organization that has maintenance of these funds as its primary or sole activity cannot qualify for tax exemption as a charitable organization. Critics argue that the process is akin to a commercial bank account holding deposits for the private benefit of customers. The courts reject this argument.

Another contention is that these transfers are not *gifts* (and thus are not deductible). The ostensible reason: The *donor* has not, by reason of the agreement with the charity, parted with all of his, her, or its right, title, and interest in the gift money or property. To assess this, the IRS applies a set of *material restrictions* rules that were promulgated in the private foundation setting to test whether a private foundation has properly terminated its status when granting its assets to one or more public charities.

Still another issue is whether these charities are public. The gifts (assuming that is what they are) to the charity (assuming that is what it is) are forms of public support for purposes of both types of publicly supported charitable organizations. Almost always, however, these entities are the donative type of publicly supported charity. Then, when a grant is made from an account within the public charity to another charity, it can also be public support for the grantee. (See the discussion of indirect public support in the "Grant from Donative Entity" section earlier in this chapter.) Some in the IRS and elsewhere are uncomfortable with the view that a gift (or a portion of it) can constitute public support for two charities. That is, nonetheless, in fact the case.

SUMMARY

This chapter defined the types of tax-exempt charitable organizations that are known as public charities and private foundations. This analysis focused on publicly supported charities and supporting organizations. It also provided a description of disqualified persons. The matter of determining public support can be difficult; the chapter included an inventory of "tricks of the trade" for doing this. It contains a description of the rules for qualification as a private operating foundation and an exempt operating foundation. The chapter provided a summary of the law regulating private foundations. The chapter concluded with a look at the controversial subject of donor-advised funds. Knowledge of the public charity/private foundation dichotomy is essential to an understanding of the federal tax law of charitable organizations.

CHAPTER 4

Reporting Requirements

The purpose of this chapter is to summarize the various federal and state reporting requirements imposed on nonprofit, usually tax-exempt, organizations. It is amply clear that, nonprofit status notwithstanding, these organizations are required to engage in a considerable amount of reporting. This aspect of nonprofit law is compounded when the various disclosure requirements are taken into account (see Chapter 6). Specifically, this chapter will:

- Describe the principal federal law filing requirements for tax-exempt organizations
- Inventory the legal aspects of the annual information return
- Provide a perspective on the preparation of these returns
- Summarize the federal law penalties
- Review the basic state law filing requirements

FEDERAL LAW BASICS

Nearly every organization that is exempt from federal income taxation must file an information return with the IRS. This return, consisting of six pages plus two schedules amounting to another 14 pages, calls for a plethora of information, some of it financial and some in prose form. This document, being an *information return*, rather than a *tax return*, is available for public inspection (see Chapter 6). For most exempt organizations, this information return that must be filed annually is Form 990.

Annual Information Returns

The general annual information return for tax-exempt organizations (Form 990) requires the filing organization to report its
items of revenue. This entails gifts, grants, dues, program service
revenue, revenue from the sales of assets, rents, and investment
income. The term *gifts* does not include the value of donated
services or items such as the free use of materials, equipment, or
facilities. The return differentiates between *direct support*—
amounts received from individuals, corporations, trusts, estates,
foundations, and other grantor tax-exempt organizations—and
indirect support—amounts received from federated fundraising
agencies and similar entities. *Program service revenue* is revenue derived from the performance of services or sale of items that are
related to the organization's tax-exempt purposes. Examples of
this type of revenue are tuition received by a school, patient fees
paid to a hospital, and revenue from admissions to a conference
or from sales of publications.

The return also must reflect disbursements (grants awarded,
compensation, employee benefits, professional fundraising fees,
legal and accounting fees, occupancy, travel, conferences, and
supplies). Expenses must be categorized by function: program
services, management/general and administrative, and fundraising. Expenses that relate to more than one functional category
may be allocated on a reasonable basis. The four largest *program
service accomplishments* (measured by the total expenditures incurred) and their related expenses must be identified.

The return includes a balance sheet showing assets, liabilities, and net worth (net assets or fund balances). The directors'
and officers' names, addresses, time expended, and compensation must be listed.

The reporting organization must provide an analysis of its
income-producing activities. These revenues include program
service revenue (related income), membership dues, government contract income, interest, dividends, rent, and net income
from special events. If an item of income is unrelated business
income (see Chapter 7), the amount must be identified along
with a corresponding business code. (Thus, unrelated income
must be reflected on the annual information return as well as
on the unrelated business income tax return (Form 990-T).) If
the income is not related income but is excluded by statute, the

amount must be shown along with the corresponding exclusion code.

If the revenue is reported as income from a related business, the organization must explain how the activity that generated the income contributed importantly to the accomplishment of the organization's exempt purposes. The fact that the net income was used for exempt purposes is not relevant to this characterization.

The annual information return includes a list of questions about the organization's activities:

- Has the organization engaged in any activities not previously reported to the IRS?
- Have any changes been made in the organizing or governing documents and not previously reported to the IRS?
- Was there a liquidation, dissolution, termination, or substantial contraction during the year?
- Is the organization related to any tax-exempt or nonexempt organization?
- Did the organization receive donated services or the use of materials, equipment, or facilities at no charge or at substantially less than fair rental value?
- Did the organization comply with the public disclosure requirements concerning applications for recognition of exemption and annual information returns (see Chapter 6)?
- Did the organization comply with the disclosure requirements relating to quid pro quo contributions (see Chapter 8)?
- Did the organization pay any excise taxes because of lobbying or political campaign expenditures (see Chapter 10)?
- Did the organization engage in an excess benefit transaction during the year, or did it become aware of such a transaction from a prior year (see Chapter 10)?

The annual information return filed by a tax-exempt charitable organization (see Chapter 2) must include the following information (in Schedule A):

- The compensation of the five highest compensated employees paid more than $50,000
- The total number of other employees paid more than $50,000

- The compensation of the five persons who received the highest payment for professional services of more than $50,000
- The total number of others receiving more than $50,000 for professional services
- A description of any legislative or political campaign activities
- An explanation of any acts of self-dealing between the organization and its directors and officers (see Chapter 3)
- If a public charity, the reason for the organization's non-private-foundation status and, if applicable, details as to the extent of its public support
- If a school, certain information concerning policies that may involve discrimination
- Information concerning legislative activities if the organization has elected to come within special lobbying rules for public charities (see Chapter 10)
- Information on direct or indirect transfers to, and other direct or indirect transactions and relationships with, tax-exempt organizations other than charitable ones (such as lobbying and political campaign entities)

The organization is required to provide its address, identification number, accounting method, and group exemption number (if applicable) (see Chapter 2), as well as the federal tax law provision describing its tax exemption.

Charitable organizations must provide certain information about contributions made to them (on Schedule B).

Information on the annual information return for private foundations (see Chapter 4) (Form 990-PF) is required to include the following:

- An itemized statement of the foundation's support, expenses, assets, and liabilities
- A report of capital gains and losses
- A calculation of the excise tax on net investment income
- An information statement concerning any legislative or political campaign activities
- An information statement concerning any acts of self-dealing, mandatory distributions, excess business holdings, jeopardy investments, or taxable expenditures

- A list of directors, officers, highly paid employees, and contractors
- A list of the five persons who received the highest payment for professional services
- A computation of the minimum investment return and distributable amount
- An itemized list of all grants made or approved, showing the amount of each grant, the name and address of each recipient, any relationship between a grantee and the foundation's managers or substantial contributors, and a concise statement of the purpose of each grant
- The address of the principal office of the foundation and (if different) of the place where its books and records are maintained.
- The names and addresses of the foundation's managers who are substantial contributors or who own 10 percent or more of the stock of any corporation of which the foundation owns 10 percent or more, or corresponding interests in partnerships or other entities.

A private foundation must divulge, on Form 990-PF, a schedule of relevant statistical information regarding its principal direct charitable activities and program-related investments. It must also reveal organizations and other beneficiaries served, conferences convened, or research papers produced. The foundation must provide information demonstrating conformance with the public inspection and document dissemination requirements (see Chapter 6).

Exceptions

An annual information return must be filed by nearly all tax-exempt organizations whose annual gross receipts are normally in excess of $25,000. Organizations with less gross receipts should file only the information portion of the return. This entails no more than providing the IRS with the organization's name and address, and an indication, by marking a box on the first page of the return, that its gross receipts are under the $25,000 threshold. (Technically, this filing is not required; but if it is not done, the IRS does not know whether the organization is not filing because it is not required to do so or because it is avoiding the requirement.) All private foundations must file an annual information return.

As to the $25,000 filing threshold, generally, an organization's annual gross receipts are the total amount it received during its annual accounting period, without subtraction of any expenses. The form, however, allows an organization, in computing its total revenue, to net certain income items and related expenses: receipts and associated expenses from rents, revenue from asset sales, revenue from special fundraising events, and certain other gross sales. An organization's gross receipts can be more than $25,000, even though the total revenue shown on the return is less than $25,000.

Moreover, $25,000 filing threshold normally means a four-year average. An organization is not necessarily excused from filing an annual information return for any year in which its gross receipts are less than $25,000. In fact, depending on its circumstances, an organization can have more than $25,000 in gross receipts in a year and not be required to file an information return. An organization's gross receipts are considered to be $25,000 or less if the organization meets one of three conditions:

1. It is up to one year old and has received, or holds pledges for, $37,500 or less during its first tax year.
2. It is between one and three years old and has averaged $30,000 or less in gross receipts during each of its first two tax years.
3. It is three or more years old and has averaged $25,000 or less in gross receipts for the immediately preceding three tax years (including the year for which the return is to be filed).

The requirement for the filing of an annual information return does not apply to the following:

- Churches (including interchurch organizations of local units of a church)
- Integrated auxiliaries of churches
- Conventions or associations of churches
- Financing, fund management, or retirement insurance program management organizations functioning on behalf of the foregoing organizations

- Certain other entities affiliated with a church or convention or association of churches
- Most religious orders (to the exclusive extent of their religious activities)
- State institutions
- Certain schools and mission societies
- Governmental units
- Affiliates of governmental units (which can include nonprofit, tax-exempt organizations)
- As noted, organizations (other than private foundations) that have gross receipts that normally are not in excess of $25,000 annually
- Foreign organizations (other than private foundations) that normally do not receive more than $25,000 in gross receipts annually from sources within the United States and that do not have any significant activity (including lobbying or political activity) in the United States

Just because an organization is exempt from filing an annual information return does not mean a return should not be filed. Preparation of the return may be a good discipline for keeping the organization's financial records up to standards, and a rehearsal for when gross receipts go over the filing threshold and filing of the return becomes mandatory. In addition, filing a return starts the statute of limitations running—a protection against IRS audits for years long passed.

Filing Due Dates

The annual information return is due on or before the fifteenth day of the fifth month following the close of the organization's tax year. Thus, the return for a calendar year organization should be filed by May 15 of each year. One or more extensions may be obtained. These returns are filed with the IRS service center in Ogden, Utah.

The filing date for an annual information return may fall due while the organization's application for recognition of tax-exempt status (see Chapter 2) is pending with the IRS. In that instance, the organization should nonetheless file the information return (rather than a tax return) and indicate on it that the application is pending.

Penalties

Failure to timely file the annual information return, without reasonable cause or an exception, can generally give rise to a $20-per-day penalty. The organization must pay for each day the failure continues, up to a maximum of $10,000. For larger organizations (those with annual gross receipts in excess of $1 million), the per-day penalty is $100 and the maximum penalty is $50,000.

An additional penalty can be imposed, at the same rate and up to the same maximum, on the individual(s) responsible for the failure to file, absent reasonable cause. Other fines and even imprisonment can be imposed for willfully failing to file returns or for filing fraudulent returns and statements with the IRS.

A MULTITUDE OF FORMS

As noted, most tax-exempt organizations are required to annually file the information return that is the Form 990. Some exempt organizations, however, file other returns:

- *Form 990-EZ.* This return, consisting of two pages, may be filed by small organizations, that is, entities that have gross receipts that are less than $100,000 and total assets that are less than $250,000 in value at the end of the reporting year.
- *Form 990-PF.* This return is the one filed by private foundations (see Chapter 3).
- *Form 990-BL.* This return is filed by black lung benefit trusts.
- *Form 1120-POL.* This return, which is a tax return, is filed by political organizations. These organizations also, however, may file Form 990 or 990-EZ.
- *Schedule A.* This schedule must be filed by all tax-exempt charitable organizations, other than private foundations.
- *Schedule B.* This schedule of contributions must be filed by every filing organization that has received contributions and/or grants.
- *Form 990-T.* This is the tax return by which unrelated business income is reported and any tax due is paid.
- *Form 990-W.* This is the form by which any estimated tax on unrelated business taxable income of tax-exempt organizations, payable in installments, is calculated.

FORM 990 GLOSSARY

The law pertaining to the annual information return includes several terms of art (in addition to *annual information return* and *gross receipts*):

Contribution. This is a payment, or the part of any payment, for which the donor does not receive full fair market value from the donee organization. The usual sources of contributions are individuals, corporations, partnerships, limited liability companies, estates, and trusts.

Grant. A grant has the attributes of a contribution. This is a payment (by a grantor) that encourages the organization receiving the grant (grantee) to carry on programs that further its tax-exempt purposes. The usual sources of grants are public charities, private foundations, other exempt organizations, government agencies, and trusts.

Contract revenue. A payment made to a tax-exempt organization is not a grant if the arrangement requires the recipient to provide the payor with a service, facility, or product (as opposed to providing a direct benefit to the general public or a segment of the public). This, instead, is contract-for-service (program service or related business) revenue.

Direct public support. The term *direct public support* means the gross amount of contributions and grants the organization received from members of the public. Gifts, subject to limitations (see Chapter 3), are usually forms of public support. A grant may be direct or indirect (see following bullet) public support, depending on the tax status of the source. Contract revenue is never direct public support for this purpose. (By contrast, see the rules for service-provider publicly supported charities.)

Indirect public support. There are several forms of indirect public support. Generically, this type of support is provided in the form of a grant, with the donors who contributed directly to the grantor considered as having indirectly contributed to the grantee. One type of indirect public support is funding from federated fundraising agencies and similar fundraising organizations (such as a United Way organization and certain sectarian federations). Another type is funding from an organization closely associated with the recipient organization, such as financial support from a parent organization, a subordinate organization, or another organization with the same parent. Funding from a supporting organization (see Chapter 3) thus may be public support. A third type of indirect public support is funding in the form of a grant from one donative publicly supported organization (see Chapter 3) to another such organization, or from an organization that meets the definition of a donative publicly supported organization (such as a church) to a donative publicly supported organization (irrespective of whether the organizations are closely associated).

Exempt function income. The phrase *exempt function income* means income derived from the conduct of a related business (see Chapter 7). Essentially, a business is an activity carried on to produce revenue from the sale of goods or services. For this purpose, the terms *related business, exempt function,* and *program* are identical.

Dues. The term *dues* (including other member assessments and fees) means payments by the organization's members (and perhaps affiliates) in exchange for a package of membership benefits and other services. The concept is that the value of the dues paid is equivalent to the value of services received. This is the case even if a benefit provided is not used. Thus, dues are a form of exempt function income, program service revenue, contract revenue, and related business income.

Special event. A special event is an event, usually conducted by a charitable organization, for fundraising purposes. The revenue raised is not always in the form of contributions, however; often there are fees paid for the acquisition of goods and/or services. The amount paid may be part charitable gift and part payment for a good or service. From the charity's viewpoint, the purpose of the event may go beyond revenue-raising and extend to community relations and outreach. It is designed to increase public awareness of the organization and its programs (what some in the fundraising profession label *friend-raising*). Examples of special events are dinners, dances, theater outings, sports tournaments, carnivals, auctions, raffles, and bingo games and other forms of gambling.

Functional accounting. Once a tax-exempt organization's expenses have been designated by object classification (such as salaries or supplies), they must then be allocated across the functions of program, management and general, and fund-raising.

Program services. The term program services means activities that the organization was created to conduct and which, along with any activities commenced subsequently, form the basis of the organization's tax exemption. Thus, program services are exempt functions, related businesses, and sources of contract revenue.

Management and general. This phrase pertains to the organization's overall function and management. Thus, the distinction is between expenses for that type of management activity and expenses for the direct conduct of program services or fundraising activities. Overall management usually includes the salaries and expenses of the chief officer of the organization and that individual's staff. Other expenses of this category include those for meetings of the governing board, committee and staff meetings, general legal services, accounting services, general liability insurance, office management, personnel and other centralized services, preparation and distribution of annual reports, and investment expenses.

Fundraising. Fundraising expenses are outlays incurred in the solicitation of contributions, grants, and perhaps other payments. This includes the conduct of fundraising campaigns, solicitation of grants from private foundations and government agencies, participation in federated fundraising campaigns, distribution of fundraising materials, and the conduct of special events. This includes allocable overhead costs.

Primary purpose. A tax-exempt organization, to be and remain exempt, must operate primarily in furtherance of its exempt purposes; this is the primary purpose test, which is most developed in conjunction with charitable organizations. The activities of an exempt organization are to be evaluated in light of its primary purpose or purposes.

Program service accomplishments. These are the accomplishments achieved by an organization resulting from the conduct of program services, also known as exempt functions, related businesses, and activities generating contract revenue.

Trustee. A trustee is a person (usually an individual) who is a member of the organization's governing body (when it is termed a board of trustees).

Director. An organization most likely terms its governing body the board of directors; a director, then, is a person (almost always an individual) who is a member of that governing body.

Officer. An officer is an individual (who may also serve as a trustee or director) who serves an organization in the capacity of president, vice president, secretary, treasurer, and the like.

Creator. The creator of an organization is the organization's founder (or one of the founders).

Substantial contributor. A substantial contributor is a person who contributed, granted, or bequeathed to an organization an aggregate amount of more than the higher of (1) 2 percent of the total contributions, grants, and bequests received by the organization before the close of its tax year in which the amount is received by the organization from that person or (2) $5,000.

Key employee. A key employee is an individual having responsibilities or powers, in connection with an organization, that are similar to those of trustees, directors, or officers. The term includes the chief management and administrative officials of an organization (such as an executive director or chancellor) but does not include the heads of separate departments or smaller units within an organization. A chief financial officer and the officer in charge of administration or program operations are key employees if they have the authority to control the organization's activities, finances, or both. The phrase *heads of separate departments* means individuals such as the head of the radiology department or coronary care unit of a hospital or the head of the chemistry, history, or English department at a college. These individuals are managers within their specific areas but not for the organization in its entirety and, therefore, are not key employees.

Member of the family. An individual is a member of the family if he or she is related to a disqualified person, such as by being a parent, child, grandchild, or great-grandchild.

Program service revenue. The phrase program service revenue means revenue (income) derived from the conduct of a program, also known as an exempt function or a related business. Program service revenue, exempt function income, related business income, and contract-for-service revenue are thus essentially the same.

Disregarded entity. A disregarded entity is a limited liability company that has only one member. For federal tax purposes, the income and activity of the company is treated as if it was received and conducted by the member. That is, the company is disregarded for tax purposes. When the sole member of a limited liability company, then, is a tax-exempt organization, the activities, income, and assets of the company are reflected on the exempt organization's annual information returns, just as if these elements were conducted, received, and held by the exempt organization.

Personal benefit contract. The term *personal benefit contract* generally means any life insurance, annuity, or endowment contract that benefits, directly or indirectly, a transferor of money or property to a charitable organization, a member of the transferor's family, or any other person designated by the transferor, other than a charitable organization.

Unrelated business income. Income is derived from an unrelated business when it is from a business that is regularly carried on and is not substantially related to the exempt purposes of the reporting organization. Thus, it is income that is not from a related business or from an activity or income type that is sheltered by statute from taxation.

ANNUAL INFORMATION RETURN—A LAW PERSPECTIVE

The Form 990 is a remarkable document. There are those who criticize it as not containing sufficient information about the reporting tax-exempt organization and not being user-friendly. Yet, if the return is properly prepared, it can amount to a wealth of information about the organization that filed it.

The IRS states the point this way: "Some members of the public rely on Form 990, or Form 990-EZ, as the primary or sole source of information about a particular organization. How the public perceives an organization in such cases may be determined by the information presented on its return. Therefore, please make sure the return is complete and accurate and fully describes the organization's programs and accomplishments."

Note The reader may find it convenient to have a copy of this return at hand to refer to in connection with the following discussion of the contents of the form.

The primary purpose rule requires that an organization's initial and ongoing eligibility for tax-exempt status be evaluated in light of its purposes. Again, a particular activity can be an exempt function or not an exempt function, depending on the context in which it is conducted. The scope of the organization's purpose or purposes provides that evaluative framework.

Therefore, when reviewing a Form 990 (and after reading the organization's name and address), the first step is to go to page 2, Part III. The first question there is: "What is the organization's primary exempt purpose?" The answer ideally sets the stage for the subsequent review of the return.

Once the primary exempt purpose of the organization is understood, the reviewer should return to the beginning of the form. At the top, the reviewer will find such information as the accounting method used in preparation of the return; the category of tax exemption involved; whether the return is the initial, amended, or final one; whether the organization's application for recognition of exemption (if any) is pending; the organization's Web site address (if any); and whether the return is being filed by a central organization as a group return for affiliates or the return of an organization covered by a group exemption ruling (see Chapter 2).

The balance of page 1, consisting of Part I, has the attributes of a conventional income tax return. Part IV, on page 3, is a balance sheet, much like one found on a typical financial statement. Unlike a tax return, however, an exempt organization must also, in Part II, on page 2, report its expenses on a functional basis. Certain joint costs must also be reported.

Part III of Form 990 is where the organization describes its program service accomplishments. This obviously is one of the most important components of the return. Part V, on page 4 of the return is where the organization reports the compensation paid (if any) to the organization's trustees, directors, officers, and/or employees. For some organizations, this is a sensitive aspect of the return. Part VI of Form 990, occupying page 5, contains a list of questions. Part VII, on page 6, is where the organization is expected to report all of its income, and classify it as related business income, unrelated business income, or income that is not related but is shielded from taxation by statute (see Chapter 7). Part VIII, on page 6, is where the organization explains why it believes the income it has reported as exempt function income qualifies as such.

Part IX, on page 6, is where the organization reports as to any taxable subsidiaries and/or disregarded entities (see Chapter 9) it may have. Part X, on page 6, is where the organization provides information concerning any transfers associated with personal benefit contracts.

Thus, a properly prepared Form 990 can yield an enormous amount of useful information about the filing organization.

LAW PERSPECTIVE ON PREPARATION OF RETURNS

The Form 990, not surprisingly, reflects many aspects of the law concerning nonprofit, tax-exempt organizations. Its significance is enhanced by the fact that it is open to public inspection and dissemination (see Chapter 6).

Part I

In Part I of Form 990, the filing tax-exempt organization is required to report, on line 1, its total amount of revenue received in the form of contributions and grants. The organization is also required to report, on line 2, its program service revenue. This distinction between grants and program service revenue is not always an easy one. For example, the funding of an exempt organization by means of a contract may be program service revenue, rather than a grant, even though the document is labeled a *grant*.

As to contributions and grants, the organization is required to distinguish between direct public support and indirect public support. This differentiation is made in the context of donative publicly supported charities (see Chapter 3).

The reporting of revenue from a special event is one of the few instances on the annual information return where the netting of revenue is permitted in the revenue portion of the return. Thus, in computing gross revenue from a special event, the organization must strip out any portion of the revenue that is considered contributions.

Part II

In addition to conventional reporting of a tax-exempt organization's expenses (in Part I), the organization must report these expenses on a functional basis. The IRS and other readers of the return are sensitive to the matter of the reporting of fundraising expenses. Many large charitable organizations that clearly engage in fundraising activities report little or no fundraising expenses.

Another subject of some sensitivity is the matter of joint costs. The Form 990 includes a question as to whether any joint costs from a combined educational campaign and fundraising solicitation are reported in the amount of program services. If the answer to this question is yes, the following must be reported: the aggregate amount of these joint costs, the amount allocated to program services, the amount allocated to management and general, and the amount allocated to fundraising.

Part III

The Form 990 requires the filing organization to inventory and report its program service accomplishments. This should be the most delectable portion of the annual information return for the exempt organization, because it offers a marvelous opportunity for it to showcase its programs. This is the place to "tell the story" for the benefit of not only the IRS but also prospective funders, the media, other government agencies, and many others.

Part V

The exempt organization is required to list each of its trustees, directors, officers, and key employees. Also to be reported is the average number of hours devoted, on a weekly basis, to the position(s).

The return calls for reporting the compensation paid to these individuals. This term means more than simply a salary or wage. It includes all benefits paid, including nontaxable benefits. Separate reporting is required of contributions to employee benefit plans, deferred compensation, and expense accounts and similar allowances.

Most tax-exempt organizations need to be concerned about the reasonableness of the compensation they pay, particularly when it is paid to insiders and/or disqualified persons. If the compensation is excessive, the organization's tax-exempt status may be endangered, either because of private inurement or other form of private benefit. There may also be a problem by application of the intermediate sanctions rules (see Chapter 10).

If a trustee, director, officer, or key employee of a tax-exempt organization received compensation of more than $100,000 from the exempt organization and one or more related organizations, an explanatory statement must be attached where the compensation provided by one or more related organizations was more than $10,000. A related organization is any entity (tax-exempt or taxable) that the filing organization directly or indirectly owns or controls, or that directly or indirectly owns or controls the filing organizations. The word *owns* means holding, directly or indirectly, 50 percent or more of the voting membership rights, voting stock, profits interest, or beneficial interest.

The instructions accompanying the annual information return state: "If you [the filing organization] pay any other person, such as a management services company, for the services provided by any of your officers, directors, trustees, or key employees, report the compensation and other items in Part V as if you had paid the officers, etc., directly." In most instances involving the use of a management company, this rule will not apply because the services being provided are not those of the organization's officers and the like. (Even in situations where this rule is applicable, it is not clear how the filing organization is to obtain this information, where the management company is being paid a fee for its services.)

Part VI

The first of the questions in this part of the return inquires as to whether the organization engaged, during the reporting year, in any activity not previously reported to the IRS. Although the form refers to *any* activity, the rule is tempered in the instructions to pertain to any *significant* activity. The concept is that significant alterations in activities (additions and discontinuations) will be reported, in an attached statement, incrementally over the years.

A comparable question pertains to any changes made in the organizing or governing documents of the organization. This question literally relates to any change in these documents, which usually are articles of incorporation, constitution, trust agreement, declaration of trust, or bylaws.

The organization is questioned as to whether it had gross unrelated business income of $1,000 or more in the reporting year. The question is framed in this fashion because there is a

$1,000 standard deduction in this context. If the question is answered yes, the IRS expects the filing of the unrelated business income tax return (see Chapter 7).

An explanatory statement is to be attached to the annual information return if, as to the organization, there was a liquidation, dissolution, termination, or substantial contraction during the year. The statement must indicate whether the assets of the organization have been distributed and, if so, the date of distribution. The IRS also wants (1) a certified copy of any resolution, or plan of liquidation or termination, with all amendments or supplements not previously filed and (2) a schedule listing the names and addresses of all persons who received the assets distributed in liquidation or termination, the kinds of assets distributed to each one, and each asset's fair market value.

A substantial contraction is a partial liquidation or other major disposition of assets, other than transfers for full consideration (usually, sales) or distributions from current income (such as grants). A major disposition of assets means any disposition for the tax year that is (1) at least 25 percent of the fair market value of the organization's net assets at the beginning of the tax year, or (2) one of a series of related dispositions commenced in prior years that add up to at least 25 percent of the net assets the organization had at the beginning of the tax year when the first disposition in the series was made.

The organization is required to report whether it is related to one or more organizations. These other organizations (if any) are to be identified by name; the reporting organization is required to indicate whether the other organization(s) are tax-exempt. This definition of relatedness is broad, including arrangements such as common membership, common governing boards, and/or common officers. The instructions state that there has to be more than a 50 percent overlap for relatedness to exist.

The return inquires as to whether the organization made, during the year, any direct or indirect political expenditures and requires insertion of any such amount. This question relates to political expenditures and not just political campaign expenditures (see Chapter 10). The form also reflects the fact that the organization may have to file a tax return (Form 1120-POL) to report these expenditures and collect any tax.

There is a question as to whether the organization received contributions of services or the use of materials, equipment, or facilities, either at no charge or at substantially less than fair market value. Although these items cannot be treated as revenue (for purposes of Part I) or taken into account by charitable organizations in computing public support (see Chapter 3), they can be valued and reflected on the return.

The form asks the organization to indicate whether it complied with the public inspection requirements and disclosure requirements that apply with respect to applications for recognition of exemptions and annual information returns (see Chapter 6). (The appropriate answer to this question is yes, inasmuch as the law mandates such compliance.) A similar question is asked about compliance with the disclosure requirements pertaining to quid pro quo contributions (see Chapter 5). (Again, the law mandates compliance.)

Tax-exempt charitable organizations are required to enter the amount of tax (if any) imposed on them for engaging in excessive legislative activity or any political campaign activity. Any amount of these taxes imposed on organization managers or disqualified persons during the year must be disclosed, along with any amount of the tax that the exempt organization reimbursed.

Tax-exempt charitable and social welfare organizations are asked whether they engaged in an excess benefit transaction (see Chapter 10) during the year or became aware of such a transaction that took place in a prior year. If the answer to either question is yes, an explanatory statement must be attached.

Part VII

This part of the annual information return requires the filing exempt organization to tally each of its sources of *income*. (Contributions and grants, not being income, are not listed here.) Once all of these income-producing activities have been identified and the associated amounts determined, each item must be classified as income from a related business, income from an unrelated business, or income not from a related business but sheltered from unrelated business income taxation by statute.

Part VIII

This part is devoted to recitation(s) as to why the activity underlying each income item that is being reported as from a related business contributes importantly to the furtherance of the organization's exempt purpose(s).

Part IX

The filing exempt organization is required to identify any corporation, partnership, or disregarded entity in which is has an ownership interest (see Chapter 9).

Part X

The filing organization is asked whether, during the year involved, it received any funds, directly or indirectly, to pay premiums on a personal benefit contract.

Schedule A

Schedule A, as already noted, is a supplemental form, accompanying Form 990 (or Form 990-PF), that must be filed by every tax-exempt charitable organization that is required to file an annual information return. This schedule is used to report compensation arrangements, any transactions with insiders and/or noncharitable exempt organizations, public charity status, policies and activities of private schools, and lobbying activities.

This schedule should cover the same period of time as that for the annual information return it accompanies. The schedule is part of the annual return and, therefore, the penalties applicable with respect to the annual information return also are applicable with respect to this schedule.

Schedule B

Schedule B, as already noted, also is a supplemental form to accompany the annual return. The purpose of this schedule is to collect certain information about contributions the organization received during the filing period.

STATE LAW REQUIREMENTS

The states impose filing requirements on nonprofit entities. Usually these requirements are the most defined for corporations, although there often is somewhat similar law for trusts.

If the entity is a corporation, its articles of incorporation (and perhaps its bylaws) must be filed with the state. There may be an annual reporting requirement, such as an annual report required of corporations. If the organization is doing business in more than one state, each state involved will have a filing requirement. A charitable organization may be required to adhere to the filing requirements of one or more state charitable solicitation acts (statutes regulating the fundraising process). There may be filing rules under local ordinances.

Some states and local governments accept a copy of the federal annual information return in place of all or part of their own financial report forms. This may be the case if the filing is pursuant to a charitable solicitation law or a doing business requirement.

State or local filing rules may require the organization to attach to the annual information return one or more elements of information, including additional financial statements (such as a complete analysis of functional expenses or a statement of changes in net assets), notes to financial statements, additional financial schedules, a report on the financial statements by an independent accountant, and/or answers to additional questions.

WATCHDOG AGENCIES

A public charity may be subject to scrutiny by one or more *watchdog organizations*. These are self-anointed nonprofit entities that hold themselves out as "voluntary" agencies (although they are nothing of the sort), with the competence and expertise to evaluate the programs and practices of charities, particularly those that engage in public fundraising.

This type of nongovernmental regulatory function is undertaken in three ways. One is the establishment and application of standards applicable to philanthropic groups. The second is the distribution of ratings of these organizations, based on the extent of their compliance with the standards. The third of these regulatory functions is the preparation and public dissemination of reports on charitable organizations.

The watchdog agencies will require charitable organizations to periodically file information with them, which the agency often will use to create or update a report. This information is also used to determine whether the organization is to be, or is to continue to be, favorably rated. Failure to fully comply with these demands for information is itself a violation of the standards—and can lead to a negative assessment by the watchdog group.

SUMMARY

This chapter summarized the various federal and state reporting requirements imposed on nonprofit organizations. It included a review of the contents of the annual information return, the exceptions to the filing requirements, and the due dates. The chapter provided a glossary of the technical terms employed in connection with that return. The chapter described a law perspective on the annual information return and its preparation. The chapter concluded with a summary of the state law reporting requirements. Proper preparation of these returns and other forms is important—if only because most of them are publicly accessible.

CHAPTER 5

Charitable Giving

The purpose of this chapter is to summarize the federal tax law rules concerning deductible charitable giving. A seemingly simple subject, the law pertaining to the making of and deductibility of gifts to charitable organizations is complex. This is particularly the case with respect to planned giving. Specifically, this chapter will:

- Analyze the elements of a gift
- Discuss the advantages of gifts of property
- Summarize the percentage limitations on deductibility
- Discuss the planned giving techniques
- Address the techniques of the day

BASIC CONCEPTS

The basic concept of the federal income tax deduction for a charitable contribution is this: Corporations and individuals who itemize their deductions can deduct on their annual tax return, within certain limits, an amount equivalent to the amount contributed (money) or to the value of a contribution (property) to a qualified donee. A *charitable contribution* for income tax purposes is a gift to or for the use of one or more qualified donees.

Deductions for charitable gifts are also allowed under the federal gift tax and estate tax laws. Donors and the charitable organizations they support commonly expect gifts to be in the form of outright transfers of money or property. For both parties (donor and donee), a gift is usually a unilateral transaction, in a financial sense: the donor parts with the contributed item; the charity acquires it.

The advantages of charitable donation to the donor generally are the resulting charitable deduction and the gratification derived from the giving. Planned giving (discussed later in this chapter) provides additional financial and tax advantages to the donor. Overall, these are the economic advantages that can result from a charitable gift:

- A federal, state, and/or local tax deduction
- Avoidance of capital gains taxation
- Creation of or an increase in cash flow
- Improved tax treatment of income
- Free professional tax and investment management services
- Opportunity to transfer property between the generations of a family
- Receipt of benefits from the charitable donee

DEFINING CHARITABLE GIFT

A fundamental requirement of the charitable contribution deduction law is that the cash or property transferred to a charitable organization must be transferred in the form of a *gift*. Just because money is paid or property is transferred to a charity does not necessarily mean that the payment or transfer is a gift. When a tax-exempt university's tuition, an exempt hospital's health care fee, or an exempt association's dues are paid, there is no gift and thus no charitable deduction for the payment.

Basically, a gift has two elements: it involves a transfer that is *voluntary* and is motivated by something other than *consideration* (something being received in return for a payment). Where payments are made to receive something in exchange (education, health care, and the like), the transaction is a purchase. The law places more emphasis on what is received by the payor than on the payment or transfer. The income tax regulations state that a transfer is not a contribution when made "with a reasonable expectation of financial return commensurate with the amount of the transfer." A single transaction, however, can be partially a gift and partially a purchase (see "Partial Interest Gifts" section later in this chapter); when a charity is the payee, only the gift portion is deductible.

The U.S. Supreme Court, in a famous pronouncement, observed that a gift is a transfer motivated by "detached or disinterested generosity." The Court also characterized a gift as a transfer stimulated "out of affection, respect, admiration, charity, or like impulses." Thus, the focus in this area for the most part has been an objective analysis, comparing what the "donee" parted with and what (if anything) the "donor" received net in exchange.

Another factor, that of donative intent, is sometimes taken into consideration. A set of tax regulations states that, for any part of a payment made in the context of a charity auction to be deductible as a charitable gift, the patron must have donative intent. More broadly, a congressional committee report contains this statement:

> The term "contribution or gift" is not defined by statute, but generally is interpreted to mean a voluntary transfer of money or other property without receipt of adequate consideration and with donative intent. If a taxpayer receives or expects to receive a quid pro quo in exchange for a transfer to charity, the taxpayer may be able to deduct the excess of the amount transferred over the fair market value of any benefit received in return provided the excess payment is made with the intention of making a gift.

A federal court of appeals described the matter as to what is a gift this way: It is a "particularly confused issue of federal taxation." The statutory law on the subject, said this court, is "cryptic," and "neither Congress nor the courts have offered any very satisfactory definitions" of the terms gift and contribution (which are, for these purposes, basically synonymous).

QUALIFIED DONEES

Qualified donees are charitable organizations (including educational, religious, and scientific entities), certain fraternal organizations, certain cemetery companies, and most veterans' organizations. Contributions to both private and public charities are deductible, but the law favors gifts to public charities.

Federal, state, and local governmental bodies are charitable donees. State or local law, however, may preclude a governmental entity from accepting charitable gifts. In most jurisdictions, a charitable organization can be established to solicit deductible contributions for and make grants to governmental bodies. This is a common technique for public schools, colleges, universities, and hospitals.

An otherwise nonqualifying organization may be allowed to receive a deductible charitable gift in cases where the gift property is used for charitable purposes or received by an agent for a charitable organization. An example of the former is a gift to a trade association that is earmarked for a charitable fund within the association. Examples of an agent for a charity is a title-holding company that holds a property for charitable purposes and a for-profit company that acquires and disposes of vehicles as part of a charity's used vehicle donation program.

GIFTS OF PROPERTY

Aside from the eligibility of the gift recipient, the other basic element in determining whether a charitable contribution is deductible is the nature of the property given. Basically, the distinctions are between outright giving and planned giving, and between gifts of cash and gifts of property. In many instances, the tax law differentiates between personal property and real property, and tangible property and intangible property (securities).

The federal income tax treatment of gifts of property is dependent on whether the property is capital gain property. The tax law makes a distinction between long-term capital gain and short-term capital gain. Property that is not capital gain property is ordinary income property. These three terms are based on the tax classification of the type of revenue that would be generated on sale of the property. Short-term capital gain property is generally treated the same as ordinary income property. Therefore, the actual distinction is between capital gain property (really long-term capital gain property) and ordinary income property.

Capital gain property is a capital asset that has appreciated in value and, if sold, would give rise to long-term capital gain. To result in long-term capital gain, property must be held for at least 12 months. Most forms of capital gain property are securities and real estate.

The charitable deduction for capital gain property is often equal to its fair market value—or at least, is computed using that value. Gifts of ordinary income property generally produce a deduction equivalent to the donor's cost basis in the property. The law provides exceptions to this basis-only rule; an example is a gift by a corporation out of its inventory (see "Twice-Basis Deductions" section later in this chapter). A charitable deduction based on the full fair market value of an item of appreciated property (with no recognition of the built-in capital gain) is a critical feature of the federal tax law incentives for charitable giving.

LIMITATIONS ON DEDUCTIBILITY

The extent of charitable contributions that can be deducted for a particular tax year is limited to a certain amount, which for individuals is a function of the donor's *contribution base*—essentially, an amount equal to the individual's adjusted gross income. This level of allowable annual deductibility is determined by five percentage limitations. They are dependent on several factors, principally the nature of the charitable recipient and the nature of the property contributed. The examples used here assume an individual donor with an annual contribution base of $100,000.

The first three limitations apply to gifts to public charities and to private operating foundations.

First, there is a percentage limitation of 50 percent of the donor's contribution base for gifts of cash and ordinary income property. A donor with a $100,000 contribution base may, in a year, make deductible gifts of these items up to a total of $50,000. If an individual makes contributions that exceed the 50 percent limitation, the excess generally may be carried forward and deducted in one to five subsequent years. Thus, if this donor gave $60,000 to public charities in year 1 and made no other charitable gifts in that year, he or she would be entitled to a deduction of $50,000 in year 1, and the remaining $10,000 would be available for deductibility in year 2.

The second percentage limitation is 30 percent of the donor's contribution base for gifts of capital gain property. A donor thus may, in a year, contribute up to $30,000 of qualifying stocks, bonds, real estate, and like property, and receive a charitable deduction for that amount. Any excess (more than 30 percent) of the amount of these gifts is subject to the carryforward rule. If a donor gave $50,000 in capital gain property in year 1 and made no other charitable gifts that year, he or she would be entitled to a charitable contribution deduction of $30,000 in year 1 and the $20,000 would be available in year 2.

A donor who makes gifts of cash and capital gain property to public charities (and/or private operating foundations) in any one year generally is limited by a blend of these percentage limitations. For example, if the donor in year 1 gives $50,000 in cash and $30,000 in appreciated capital gain property to a public charity, his or her charitable deduction in year 1 is $30,000 of capital gain property and $20,000 of the cash (to keep the deduction within the overall 50 percent ceiling); the other $30,000 of cash would be carried forward to year 2 (or to years 2 through 5, depending on the donor's circumstances).

The third percentage limitation allows a donor of capital gain property to use the 50 percent limitation, instead of the 30 percent limitation, where the amount of the contribution is reduced by all of the unrealized appreciation in the value of the property. This election is usually made by donors who want a larger deduction in the year of the gift for an item of property that has not appreciated in value to a great extent. Once made, this election is irrevocable.

The fourth and fifth percentage limitations apply to gifts to private foundations and certain other charitable donees (other than public charities and private operating foundations). These donees are generally veterans' and fraternal organizations.

Under the fourth percentage limitation, contributions of cash and ordinary income property to private foundations and other entities may not exceed 30 percent of the individual donor's contribution base. The carryover rules apply to this type of gift. If the donor gives $50,000 in cash to one or more private foundations in year 1, his or her charitable deduction for that year (assuming no other charitable gifts) is $30,000, with the balance of $20,000 carried forward into subsequent years (up to five).

The carryover rules blend with the first three percentage limitations. For example, if in year 1 a donor gave $65,000 to charity, of which $25,000 went to a public charity and $40,000 went to a private foundation, his or her charitable deduction for that year would be $50,000: $30,000 for the gift to the private foundation and $20,000 for the gift to the public charity. The remaining $10,000 of the gift to the foundation and the remaining $5,000 of the gift to the public charity would be carried forward into year 2.

The fifth percentage limitation is 20 percent of the contribution base for gifts of capital gain property to private foundations and other charitable donees. There is a carryforward for any excess deduction amount. For example, if a donor gives appreciated securities, having a value of $30,000, to a private foundation in year 1, his or her charitable deduction for year 1 (assuming no other charitable gifts) is $20,000; the remaining $10,000 may be carried forward.

Deductible charitable contributions by corporations in any tax year may not exceed 10 percent of pretax net income. Excess amounts may be carried forward and deducted in subsequent years (up to five). For gifts by corporations, the federal tax laws do not differentiate between gifts to public charities and gifts to private foundations. As an illustration, a corporation that grosses $1 million in a year and incurs $900,000 in expenses in that year (not including charitable gifts) may generally contribute to charity and deduct in that year an amount up to $10,000 (10 percent of $100,000); in computing its taxes, this corporation would report taxable income of $90,000. If the corporation contributed $20,000 in that year, the numbers would remain the same, except that the corporation would have a $10,000 charitable contribution carryforward.

A corporation on the accrual method of accounting can elect to treat a contribution as having been made in a tax year if it is actually donated during the first 2½ months of the following year. Corporate gifts of property are generally subject to the deduction reduction rules, discussed next.

A business organization that is a flow-through entity generates a different tax result when it comes to charitable deductions. (These organizations are partnerships, other joint ventures, small business (S) corporations, and limited liability companies.) Entities of this nature, even though they may make charitable gifts, do not claim charitable contribution deductions. Instead, the deduction is passed through to the partners, members, or other owners on an allocable basis, and they claim their share of the deduction on their tax return.

DEDUCTION REDUCTION RULES

A donor (individual or corporation) who makes a gift of *ordinary income property* to a charitable organization (public or private) must confine the charitable deduction to an amount equal to the donor's cost basis in the property. The deduction is not based on the fair market value of the property; it must be reduced by the amount that would have been gain (ordinary income) if the property had been sold. As an example, if a donor gave to a charity an item of ordinary income property having a value of $1,000, for which he or she paid $600, the resulting charitable deduction would be $600.

Any donor who makes a gift of capital gain property to a public charity generally can compute the charitable deduction using the property's fair market value at the time of the gift, regardless of the basis amount and with no taxation of the appreciation (the capital gain inherent in the property). Suppose, however, a donor makes a gift of capital gain tangible personal property (such as a work of art) to a public charity and the use of the gift property by the donee is unrelated to its tax-exempt purposes (see Chapter 7). The donor must reduce the deduction by an amount equal to all of the long-term capital gain that would have been recognized had the donor sold the property at its fair market value as of the date of the contribution.

Generally, a donor who makes a gift of capital gain property to a private foundation must reduce the amount of the otherwise allowable deduction by all of the appreciation elements (built-in capital gain) in the gift property. An individual, however, is allowed full fair market value for a contribution to a private foundation of certain publicly traded stock (known as qualified appreciated stock).

TWICE-BASIS DEDUCTIONS

As a general rule, when a corporation makes a charitable gift of property from its inventory, the resulting charitable deduction cannot exceed an amount equal to the donor's cost basis in the donated property. In most instances, this basis amount is rather small, being equal to the cost of producing the property. Under certain circumstances, however, corporate donors can receive a greater charitable deduction for gifts out of their inventory. Where the tests are satisfied, the deduction can be equal to cost basis plus one-half of the appreciated value of the property. The charitable deduction may not, in any event, exceed an amount equal to twice the property's cost basis.

Five requirements have to be met for this twice-basis charitable deduction to be available:

1. The donated property must be used by the charitable donee for a related use.

2. The donated property must be used solely for the care of the ill, the needy, or infants.
3. The property may not be transferred by the donee in exchange for money, other property, or services.
4. The donor must receive a written statement from the donee representing that the use and disposition of the donated property will be in conformance with these rules.
5. Where the donated property is subject to regulation under the U.S. Food, Drug, and Cosmetic Act, the property must fully satisfy the Act's requirements on the date of transfer and for the previous 180 days.

For these rules to apply, the donee must be a public charity; that is, it cannot be a private foundation or a private operating foundation (see Chapter 3). An S corporation—the tax status of many businesses—cannot utilize these rules.

Similarly computed charitable deductions are available for contributions of scientific property used for research and contributions of computer technology and equipment for educational purposes.

CONTRIBUTIONS OF VEHICLES

The IRS has, in recent years, become greatly troubled over the matter of contributions to charity of used vehicles, to the point of dubbing these fundraising programs *suspect vehicle donation plans.* One of the principal issues in this regard is valuation of the gift property; the IRS has issued considerable guidance in this regard. The agency has ruled that, where a charitable organization uses the services of a for-profit company to receive and process the donated vehicles, a charitable contribution deduction is available where the company is designated the agent of the charity. For unrelated business purposes, the charity is not taxable on the resulting income because of the *donated goods exception* (see Chapter 7). The IRS has warned that it will apply the private inurement doctrine, the private benefit doctrine, and the intermediate sanctions rules in this setting (see Chapter 10). Also potentially applicable are penalties for aiding and abetting understatements of tax liability, and for promoting abusive tax shelters.

CONTRIBUTIONS OF INTELLECTUAL PROPERTY

A person may contribute intellectual property, by means of transfer of a patent, a license to use a patent, or otherwise, to a charitable organization and obtain a charitable deduction. Where, however, a contribution to a charity of a license to use a patent involves retention by the person of a substantial right in the patent (such as the right to license the patent to others or the right to use the patent or license in certain geographical areas), the transaction constitutes a nondeductible transfer of a partial interest (discussed next). The IRS has issued guidance as to valuation of this type of property and rules by which the value for deduction purposes must be reduced because of consideration provided to the donor. The agency also announced that it may impose penalties on those claiming inappropriate charitable deductions for these gifts, as well as on promoters and appraisers involved in improper deductions.

PARTIAL INTEREST GIFTS

Most charitable gifts are of all ownership of a property: the donor parts with all right, title, and interest in the property. A gift of a *partial interest*, however, is also possible—a contribution of less than a donor's entire interest in the property.

As a general rule, charitable deductions for gifts of partial interests in property, including the right to use property, are not available. The exceptions, which are many, include the following:

- Gifts made in trust form (using a *split-interest trust*)
- Gifts of an outright remainder interest in a personal residence or farm
- Gifts of an undivided portion of the donor's entire interest in an item of property
- Gifts of a lease on, option to purchase, or easement with respect to real property granted in perpetuity to a public charity exclusively for conservation purposes
- A remainder interest in real property granted to a public charity exclusively for conservation purposes

Contributions of income interests in property in trust are basically confined to the use of charitable lead trusts. Aside from a charitable gift annuity and gifts of remainder interests, there is no charitable deduction for a contribution of a remainder interest in property unless it is in trust and is one of three types: a charitable remainder annuity trust, a charitable remainder unitrust, or a pooled income fund (see "Planned Giving"section later in this chapter).

Defective charitable split-interest trusts may be reformed to preserve the charitable deduction where certain requirements are satisfied.

GIFTS OF INSURANCE

Another type of charitable giving involves life insurance. To secure an income tax charitable deduction, the gift must include all rights of ownership in a life insurance policy. Thus, an individual can donate a fully paid-up life insurance policy to a charitable organization and deduct (for income-tax purposes) its value. Or, an individual can acquire a life insurance policy, give it to a charity, pay the premiums, and receive a charitable deduction for each premium payment made.

For the donation of an insurance policy to be valid, the charitable organization must be able to demonstrate that it has an insurable interest in the life of the donor of the policy (unless state statutory law eliminates the requirement). From an income tax deduction standpoint, it is not enough for a donor to simply name a charitable organization as the or as a beneficiary of a life insurance policy. There is no income tax charitable contribution deduction for this philanthropic act. Although the life insurance proceeds become part of the donor's estate, however, there will be an offsetting estate tax charitable deduction.

There is a use of life insurance in the charitable giving context that essentially has been outlawed and thus is to be avoided. This use is embodied in the charitable split-interest insurance plan (see Chapter 6).

PLANNED GIVING

Planned giving is the most sophisticated form of charitable giving. For the most part, planned gifts are partial interest gifts. In a broader sense, planned giving encompasses contributions made via decedent's estates and by use of life insurance.

Introduction

There are two basic types of planned gifts. One type is a legacy: under a will, a gift comes out of an estate (as a bequest or a devise). The other type is a gift made during a donor's lifetime, using a trust or other agreement.

These gifts once were termed *deferred gifts* because the actual receipt of the contribution amount by the charity is deferred until the happening of some event (usually the death of the donor or subsequent death of the donor's spouse). This term, however, has fallen out of favor. Some donors (to the chagrin of the gift-seeking charities) gained the impression that it was their tax benefits that were being deferred.

A planned gift usually is a contribution of a donor's interest in money or an item of property, rather than an outright gift of the money or property in its entirety. (The term usually is used because gifts involving life insurance do not neatly fit this definition and because an outright gift of property, in some instances, is treated as a planned gift.) Technically, this type of gift is a conveyance of a partial interest in property; planned giving is (usually) partial interest giving.

An item of property conceptually has within it two interests: an income interest and a remainder interest.

The income interest within an item of property is a function of the income generated by the property. A person may be entitled to all of the income from a property or to some portion of the income—for example, income equal to 6 percent of the fair market value of the property, even though the property is producing income at the rate of 9 percent. This person is said to have the (or an) income interest in the property. Two or more persons (such as spouses or siblings) may have income interests in the same property; these interests may be held concurrently or consecutively.

The remainder interest within an item of property is equal to the projected value of the property, or the property produced by reinvestments, at some future date. Put another way, the remainder interest in property is an amount equal to the present value of the property (or its offspring) when it is to be received at a subsequent point in time.

These interests are measured by the value of the property, the age of the donor(s), and the period of time that the income interest(s) will exist. The actual computation is made by means of actuarial tables, usually those promulgated by the Department of the Treasury.

An income interest or a remainder interest in property may be contributed to charity, but a deduction is almost never available for a charitable gift of an income interest in property. (This is more of an estate planning technique.) By contrast, the charitable contribution of a remainder interest in an item of property will—assuming all of the technical requirements are satisfied—give rise to a (frequently sizable) charitable deduction.

When a gift of a remainder interest in property is made to a charity, the charity will not acquire that interest until the income interest(s) in the property have expired. The donor receives the charitable contribution deduction for the tax year in which the recipient charity's remainder interest in the property is established. On the occasion of a gift of an income interest in property to a charity, the charity acquires that interest immediately and retains it until such time as the remainder interest commences.

Basically, under the federal tax law, a planned gift must be made by means of a trust if a charitable contribution deduction is to be available. The trust used to facilitate a planned gift is known as a split-interest trust because it is the mechanism for satisfying the requirements involving the income and remainder interests. In other words, this type of trust is the medium for—in use of a legal fiction—splitting the property into its two component categories of interests. Split-interest trusts are charitable remainder trusts, pooled income funds, and charitable lead trusts. There are some exceptions to the general requirements as to the use of a split-interest trust in the planned giving context. The principal exception is the charitable gift annuity, which entails a contract rather than a trust. Individuals may give a remainder interest in their personal residence or farm to charity and receive a charitable deduction without utilizing a trust. Other exceptions are listed in the discussion of partial interest gifts.

A donor, although desirous of financially supporting a charity, may be unwilling or unable to fully part with property, either because of a present or perceived need for the income that the property generates and/or because of the capital gains taxes that would be experienced if the property were sold. The planned gift is likely to be the solution in this type of situation: The donor may satisfy his or her charitable desires and yet continue to receive income from the property (or property that results from reinvestment). The donor also receives a charitable deduction for the gift of the remainder interest, which will reduce or eliminate the tax on the income from the gift property. There is no tax imposed on the capital gain inherent in the property. If the gift property is not throwing off sufficient income, the trustee of the split-interest trust may dispose of the property and reinvest the proceeds in more productive property. The donor may then receive more income from the property in the trust than was received prior to the making of the gift.

The various planned giving vehicles are explored next.

Charitable Remainder Trusts

The most widespread form of planned giving involves a split-interest trust known as the charitable *remainder trust*. The term is nearly self-explanatory: The entity is a trust by which a remainder interest destined for charity has been created. Each charitable remainder trust is designed specifically for the particular circumstances of the donor(s), with the remainder interest in the gift property designated for one or more charities. (Occasionally, because of miscommunication with the donor(s), lack of skill in use of a word processor, or incompetence, a remainder trust will be drafted that is the wrong type. The IRS generously characterizes these trusts as the product of *scrivener's error*, and will recognize the qualification of the corrected trust, which must be undertaken by court-supervised reformation.)

A qualified charitable remainder trust must provide for a specified distribution of income, at least annually, to or for the use of one or more beneficiaries (at least one of which is not a charity). This flow of income must be for life or for a term of no more than 20 years, with an irrevocable remainder interest to be held for the benefit of the charity or paid over to it. The beneficiaries are the holders of the income interests, and the charity has the remainder interest.

How the income interests in a charitable remainder trust are ascertained depends on whether the trust is a charitable remainder annuity trust (income payments are in the form of a fixed amount, an annuity) or a charitable remainder unitrust (income payments are in the form of an amount equal to a percentage of the fair market value of the assets in the trust, determined annually). (Recently promulgated tax regulations have changed the concept of trust income, doing away with the traditional precepts of income and principal, with as yet-unknown consequences for some charitable remainder unitrusts.)

There are four types of charitable remainder unitrusts. The one just described is known as the standard charitable remainder unitrust or the fixed percentage charitable remainder unitrust. There are two types of unitrusts that are known as income exception charitable remainder unitrusts. One of these types enables income to be paid to the income interest beneficiary once there is any income generated in the trust; this is the net income charitable remainder unitrust. The other type of income-exception unitrust is akin to the previous one, but can make catch-up payments for prior years' deficiencies once income begins to flow; this is the net income make-up charitable remainder unitrust. The fourth type of unitrust is allowed to convert (flip) once from one of the income exception methods to the fixed percentage method for purposes of calculating the unitrust amount; this is the flip charitable remainder unitrust.

The income payout of both of these types of trusts is subject to a 5 percent minimum. That is, the annuity must be an amount equal to at least 5 percent of the value of the property initially placed in the trust. Likewise, the unitrust amount must be an amount equal to a least 5 percent of the value of the trust property, determined annually. These percentages may not be greater than 50 percent. Also, the value of the remainder interest in the property must be at least 10 percent of the value of the property contributed to the trust.

Nearly any kind of property can be contributed to a charitable remainder trust. Typical gift properties are cash, securities, and/or real estate. Yet, a charitable remainder trust can accommodate gifts of artworks, collections, and just about any other forms of property. One of the considerations must be the ability of the property (or successor property, if sold) to generate sufficient income to satisfy the payout requirement with respect to the income interest beneficiary or beneficiaries.

All categories of charitable organizations—public charities and private foundations—are eligible to be remainder interest beneficiaries of as many charitable remainder trusts as they can muster. The amount of the charitable deduction will vary for different types of charitable organizations, however, because of the percentage limitations (see "Limitations on Deductibility" section earlier in this chapter).

Often, a bank or other financial institution serves as the trustee of a charitable remainder trust. The financial institution should have the capacity to administer the trust, make appropriate investments, and timely adhere to all income distribution and reporting requirements. It is not unusual, however, for the charitable organization that is the remainder interest beneficiary to act as trustee. If the donor or a related person is named the trustee, the grantor trust rules may apply: The gain from the trust's sale of appreciated property is taxed to the donor.

Conventionally, once the income interest expires, the assets in a charitable remainder trust are distributed to the charitable organization (or organizations) that is the remainder interest beneficiary. If the assets (or a portion of them) are retained in the trust, the trust will be classified as a private foundation, unless it can qualify as a public charity (most likely, a supporting organization) (see Chapter 3).

There have been some abuses in this area in recent years. One problem has been the use of short-term (such as a term of two years) charitable remainder trusts to manipulate the use of assets and payout arrangements for the tax benefit of the donors. Certain of these abuses were stymied by legislation creating some of the previously referenced percentage rules. The tax regulations were revised in an attempt to prevent transactions by which a charitable remainder trust is used to convert appreciated property into money while avoiding tax on the gain from the sale of the assets. (Some of these arrangements were so audacious that the vehicles garnered the informal name *chutzpah trust.*)

Inasmuch as charitable remainder trusts are split-interest trusts, they are subject to at least some of the prohibitions that are imposed on private foundations, most notably the rules concerning self-dealing and taxable expenditures (see Chapter 3). For example, the IRS has an informal procedure for the premature termination of a charitable remainder trust, where the termination does not give rise to self-dealing because the procedure devised for allocation of the trust's assets to beneficiaries is reasonable.

A qualified charitable remainder trust generally is exempt from federal income taxation. In any year, however, in which it has unrelated business taxable income (see Chapter 7), the trust loses its tax-exempt status.

Pooled Income Funds

Another planned giving technique involves gifts to charity via a *pooled income fund*. Like a charitable remainder trust, a pooled income fund is a form of split-interest trust.

A donor to a qualified pooled income fund receives a charitable deduction for giving the remainder interest in the donated property to charity. The gift creates income interests in one or more noncharitable beneficiaries; the remainder interest in the gift property is designated for the charity that maintains the fund.

The pooled income fund's basic instrument (a trust agreement or a declaration of trust) is written to facilitate gifts from an unlimited number of donors, so the essential terms of the transactions must be established in advance for all participants. The terms of the transfer cannot be tailored to fit any one donor's particular circumstances (as is done with the charitable remainder trust). The pooled income fund constitutes, literally, a pool of gifts.

Contributions to a pooled income fund may be considerably smaller than is practical for those to a charitable remainder trust. Gifts to pooled income funds are generally confined to cash and readily marketable securities (other than tax-exempt bonds).

Each donor to a pooled income fund contributes an irrevocable remainder interest in the gift property to (or for the use of) an eligible charitable organization. Each donor creates an income interest for the life of one or more beneficiaries, who must be living at the time of the transfer. The properties transferred by the donors must be commingled in the fund (thereby creating the necessary pool of gifts).

Each income interest beneficiary must receive income at least once each year. The pool amount is determined by the rate of return earned by the fund for the year. Beneficiaries receive their proportionate share of the fund's income. The dollar amount of the income share is based on the number of units owned by the beneficiary; each unit must be based on the fair market value of the assets when transferred. Thus, a pooled income fund is essentially an investment vehicle whose funding is motivated by charitable intents.

A pooled income fund must be maintained by one or more charitable organizations. Usually, there is only one charity per fund. The charity must exercise control over the fund; it does not have to be the trustee of the fund (although it can be), but it must have the power to remove and replace the trustee. A donor or an income beneficiary of the fund may not be a trustee. A donor may be a trustee or officer of the charitable organization that maintains the fund, however, as long as he or she does not have the general responsibilities with respect to the fund that are ordinarily exercised by a trustee.

Unlike other forms of planned giving, a pooled income fund is restricted to only certain categories of charitable organizations. Most types of public charities can maintain a pooled income fund; private foundations and some other charities cannot.

The same general tax advantages that are available as the result of gifts to charitable remainder trusts are available for gifts to pooled income funds. The advantages are particularly solid when the gift consists of fully marketable and appreciated securities. If fixed income is an important consideration, however, a charitable remainder annuity trust or a charitable gift annuity will be preferable to a gift to a charitable remainder unitrust or a pooled income fund.

Pooled income funds are subject to at least some of the prohibitions that are imposed on private foundations, most particularly the rules concerning self-dealing and taxable expenditures (see Chapter 3).

A qualified pooled income fund is not treated as an association for tax purposes, nor does such a fund have to be a trust under local law. Generally, a pooled income fund is subject to federal income taxation. In actuality, however, a pooled income fund usually is not taxable, because it receives a deduction for amounts paid out to income interest beneficiaries and a set-aside deduction for the remainder interests reserved for the charitable beneficiary.

Pooled income funds currently are somewhat out of favor due to declines in interest rates and bond yields. This is causing a reduction in the investment return of these funds and, thus, a reduction in the amount of income paid to the income beneficiaries. Donors are avoiding pooled income funds, thereby increasing the costs to the charities of maintaining them. Some charities have terminated their pooled income fund(s), although many funds at the larger institutions continue to perform adequately.

Charitable Lead Trusts

Most forms of planned giving have a common element: The donor transfers to a charitable organization the remainder interest in an item of property, and one or more noncharitable beneficiaries retain the income interest. A reverse sequence may occur, however—and that is the essence of the *charitable lead trust.*

The property transferred to a charitable lead trust is apportioned into an income interest and a remainder interest. Like the charitable remainder trust and the pooled income fund, this is a split-interest trust. An income interest in property is contributed to a charitable organization, either for a term of years or for the life of one individual (or the lives of more than one individual). The remainder interest in the property is reserved to return, at the expiration of the income interest (the lead period), to the donor or pass to some other noncharitable beneficiary or beneficiaries. Often, the property passes from one generation (the donor's) to another.

The tax regulations limit the types of individuals whose lives can be used as measuring lives for determining the period of time the charity will receive the income flow from a charitable lead trust. The only individuals whose lives can be used as measuring ones are those of the donor, the donor's spouse, and/or a lineal ancestor of all the remaining beneficiaries. This regulation project is designed to eliminate the practice of using the lives of seriously ill individuals to move assets and income away from charitable beneficiaries prematurely and, instead to private beneficiaries. These trusts are sometimes referred to as *vulture trusts* or *ghoul trusts.*

The charitable lead trust can be used to accelerate into one year a series of charitable contributions that would otherwise be made annually. There can be a corresponding single-year deduction for the "bunched" amount of charitable gifts.

In some circumstances, a charitable deduction is available for the transfer of an income interest in property to a charitable organization. There are stringent limitations, however, on the deductible amount of charitable contributions of these income interests.

Charitable Gift Annuities

Still another form of planned giving is the *charitable gift annuity*. It is not based on use of a split-interest trust. Instead, the annuity is arranged in an agreement between the donor and the charitable donee. The donor agrees to make a gift and the donee agrees, in return, to provide the donor (and/or someone else) with an annuity.

With one payment, the donor is engaging in two transactions: the purchase of an annuity and the making of a charitable gift. The contribution gives rise to the charitable deduction. One sum is transferred; the money in excess of the amount necessary to purchase the annuity is the charitable gift portion. Because of the dual nature of the transaction, the charitable gift annuity transfer constitutes a bargain sale.

The annuity resulting from the creation of a charitable gift annuity arrangement (like an annuity generally) is a fixed amount paid at regular intervals. The exact amount paid depends on the age of the beneficiary, which is determined at the time the contribution is made. Frequently, the annuity payment period begins with the creation of the annuity payment obligation. The initiation of the payment period can be postponed to a future date; this type of arrangement is termed the *deferred payment charitable gift annuity*.

A portion of the annuity paid is tax-free because it is a return of capital. Where appreciated securities (or other capital gain property) are given, there will be capital gain on the appreciation that is attributable to the value of the annuity. If the donor is the annuitant, the capital gain can be reported ratably over the individual's life expectancy. The tax savings occasioned by the charitable contribution deduction may, however, shelter the capital gain (resulting from the creation of a charitable gift annuity) from taxation.

Inasmuch as the arrangement is by contract between the donor and donee, all of the assets of the charitable organization are subject to liability for the ongoing payment of the annuities. (With most planned giving techniques, the resources for payment of the income are confined to those in a split-interest trust.) That is why some states impose a requirement that charities must establish a reserve for the payment of gift annuities—and why many charitable organizations are reluctant to embark on a gift annuity program. Charities that are reluctant to commit to the ongoing payment of annuities can eliminate the risk by reinsuring them.

SUMMARY

This chapter provided a summary of the federal tax charitable giving rules, including definition of the term gift, identification of the nonprofit organizations that are eligible to receive a deductible charitable contribution, special rules as to gifts of property, and the limitations on deductibility of charitable contributions. Federal tax law in this context is additionally complicated because of the deduction reduction rules and the twice-basis deduction rules. The subjects of current controversy are addressed—contributions of used vehicles and of intellectual property. The chapter also summarized the rules as to planned giving, including underlying principles and the use of charitable remainder trusts, pooled income funds, charitable lead trusts, and charitable gift annuities. The nonlawyer may be surprised to find that something as seemingly simple as giving to charity can spawn these exceedingly complex bodies of law.

CHAPTER 6

Disclosure Requirements

The purpose of this chapter is to summarize the law imposing various forms of disclosure requirements on nonprofit organizations. This is an area frequently visited by Congress, as manifested in many forms of enacted and pending legislation. The prevailing view is that the operations of nonprofit organizations, as a price of tax-exempt status, must be *transparent*. Specifically, this chapter will summarize the disclosure requirements pertaining to

- Applications for recognition of tax exemption
- Annual information returns
- Charitable gift substantiation
- Quid pro quo contributions
- Noncharitable exempt organizations
- Gifts of property
- Dispositions of contributed property
- Appraisals
- Tax shelters

APPLICATIONS FOR RECOGNITION OF EXEMPTION

Nearly all charitable organizations are required, to be tax-exempt, to file an application for recognition of exemption with the IRS; other categories of exempt organizations may file an application (see Chapter 2). In either case, once the application is filed and the IRS has issued a favorable determination letter, the application becomes a public document, subject to disclosure by the exempt organization. A question on the annual information return (discussed in the next section) inquires as to whether the organization has complied with this disclosure requirement.

Tax-exempt organizations that have a determination letter from the IRS recognizing their tax-exempt status (see Chapter 2) are required to provide a copy of their application for recognition of exemption to requesting members of the public. This must be done, without charge, at the organization's principal, regional, and district offices during regular business hours. Generally, the copy must be provided to a requestor on the business day the request is made. In the case of an in-person request, where unusual circumstances exist so that fulfillment of the request on the same day places an unreasonable burden on the exempt organization, the copy must be provided on the next business day following the day on which the unusual circumstances cease to exist or the fifth business day after the date of the request, whichever occurs first. A tax-exempt organization that receives a written request for a copy of the application must mail the copy within 30 days from the date it receives the request.

A tax-exempt organization is not required to comply with requests for copies of its application for recognition of exemption if the organization has made the document widely available. The application is made widely available by posting the document on a Web site that the organization establishes and maintains. It can also satisfy the exception if the document is posted as part of a database of similar documents of other exempt organizations on a Web site established and maintained by another entity.

If the IRS determines that a tax-exempt organization is the subject of a harassment campaign and that compliance with the requests that are part of the campaign would not be in the public interest, the organization is not required to fulfill a request for a copy that it reasonably believes is part of the campaign.

If a tax-exempt organization denies an individual's request for a copy of an application for recognition of exemption, and the individual wishes to alert the IRS to the possible need for enforcement action, he or she may send a statement to the appropriate IRS district office, describing the reason why the individual believes the denial was in violation of these requirements. There is no private right of action in this setting.

There is a penalty for failure to comply with this disclosure requirement, amounting to $20 per day.

ANNUAL INFORMATION RETURNS

Just about every nonprofit, tax-exempt organization is required to file annual information returns with the IRS (see Chapter 4). These returns are public documents that are subject to disclosure by the exempt organization. A question on the annual information return inquires as to whether the organization has complied with this disclosure requirement.

Tax-exempt organizations are required to provide copies of their annual information returns (if any) to members of the requesting public. This requirement pertains to the most recent three annual information returns. The same rules, as previously summarized with respect to the disclosure and dissemination of applications for recognition of exemption, apply with respect to annual information returns. This includes the exception for returns that are posted on the Internet and the harassment campaign exception.

There is a penalty for failure to comply with this disclosure requirement, amounting to $20 per day ($10,000 per return).

GIFT SUBSTANTIATION REQUIREMENTS

The federal tax law contains charitable gift substantiation rules. Pursuant to this body of law, a donor who makes a separate charitable contribution of $250 or more (in amount or value) in a year, for which a charitable contribution deduction is claimed, must obtain written substantiation from the donee charitable organization.

More specifically, the rule is that the charitable deduction is not available for a separate charitable contribution of $250 or more unless the donor has obtained written substantiation from the charitable donee of the contribution in the form of a contemporaneous written acknowledgment. Thus, donors cannot rely solely on a cancelled check or similar documentation as substantiation for a gift of at least $250. Such documentation suffices as substantiation for smaller gifts.

An acknowledgment meets this requirement if it includes the following information: (1) the amount of money and a description (but not value) of any property other than money that was contributed; (2) whether the donee organization provided any goods or services in consideration, in whole or in part, for any money or property contributed; and (3) a description and good-faith estimate of the value of any goods or services involved or, if the goods or services consist solely of intangible religious benefits, a statement to that effect. The phrase *intangible religious benefit* means an intangible benefit provided by a religious organization that generally is not sold in a commercial transaction outside the donative context. An acknowledgment is considered to be contemporaneous if the contributor obtains the acknowledgment on or before the earlier of (1) the date on which the donor filed a tax return for the tax year in which the contribution was made or (2) the due date (including extensions) for filing the return.

There are other defined terms. The phrase *goods or services* means money, property, services, benefits, and privileges. Certain goods or services, however, are disregarded for these purposes—those that have insubstantial value and certain annual membership benefits offered to an individual in exchange for a payment of $75 or less a year. A charitable organization provides goods or services in consideration for a donor's transfer if, at the time the donor makes the payment to the charity, the donor receives or expects to receive goods or services in exchange for the payment. Goods or services a charitable organization provides in consideration for a payment by a donor include goods or services provided in a year other than the year in which the payment was made. A *good-faith estimate* means a charitable organization's estimate of the fair market value of any goods or services, without regard to the manner in which the organization in fact made the estimate.

As noted, this substantiation rule applies in connection with separate payments. Separate payments are generally treated as separate contributions and are not aggregated for the purpose of applying the $250 threshold. In cases of contributions paid by withholding from wages, the deduction from each paycheck is treated as a separate payment. The IRS has the authority to issue anti-abuse rules in this area (addressing practices such as the writing of multiple checks to the same charity on the same date) but has not done so.

The written acknowledgment of a separate gift is not required to take any particular form. Thus, these acknowledgments may be made by letter, postcard, e-mail, or computer-generated form. A donee charitable organization may prepare a separate acknowledgment for each contribution or may provide donors with periodic (such as annual) acknowledgments that set forth the required information for each contribution of $250 or more made by the donor during the period.

A court made the administration of this area of the law considerably more difficult. This is because it held that these rules apply with respect to verbal (unwritten) expectations or understandings a donor may have of the charitable recipient when making a contribution. This court thus equated, for these purposes, expectations with goods or services. How representatives of charitable organizations are supposed to divine their donors' inner thoughts when giving is not clear.

It is the responsibility of a donor to obtain the written substantiation and maintain it in his or her records. (Again, the allowability of the charitable contribution deduction is dependent on compliance with these rules.) A charitable organization that knowingly provides a false written substantiation to a donor may be subject to a penalty for aiding and abetting an understatement of tax liability.

These substantiation rules do not apply to transfers of property to charitable remainder trusts or to charitable lead trusts. The requirements are, however, applicable to transfers to pooled income funds (see Chapter 5). In the case of these funds, the contemporaneous written acknowledgment must state that the contribution was transferred to the charitable organization's pooled income fund and indicate whether any goods or services (in addition to the income interest) were provided in exchange for the transfer. The contemporaneous written acknowledgment, however, need not include a good-faith estimate of the income interest.

QUID PRO QUO CONTRIBUTIONS

Among the practices that entail payments that are partially gifts and partially payments for goods or services are special event programs, whereby the patron receives something of value (such as a ticket to a theater performance or a dinner, the opportunity to play in a sports tournament, and auctions), yet makes a payment in excess of that value amount. In these circumstances, the amount paid that is in excess of the value received by the patron is a charitable gift.

In an analogous area, the IRS held that payments by corpo-

rate sponsors of college and university bowl games are not charitable gifts to the bowl game associations, but must be treated by
the associations as forms of unrelated business income because
the corporate sponsors received a valuable package of advertising
services. This controversial ruling led to IRS and congressional
hearings, proposed regulations, and finally legislation. This statutory law shields qualified sponsorship payments from taxation. A
payment of this nature is one made by a person engaged in a
trade or business, from which the person did not receive a substantial return benefit other than the use or acknowledgment of
the name or logo (or product lines) of the person's trade or business in connection with the organization's activities. This use or
acknowledgment does not include advertising of the person's
products or services. Advertising entails qualitative or comparative language, price information or other indications of savings or
value, or an endorsement or other inducement to purchase, sell,
or use the products or services (see Chapter 7).

The federal tax law imposes certain disclosure requirements
on charitable organizations that receive quid pro quo contributions. A question on the annual information return inquires as to
whether the organization has complied with these disclosure requirements.

A quid pro contribution is a payment made partly as a contribution and partly in consideration for goods or services provided to the payor by the donee organization. The term does not
include a payment made to an organization, operated exclusively
for religious purposes, in return for which the donor receives
solely an intangible religious benefit that generally is not sold in a
commercial transaction outside the donative context.

Specifically, if a charitable organization (other than a state, a
possession of the United States, a political subdivision of a state
or possession, the United States, and the District of Columbia) receives a quid pro quo contribution in excess of $75, the organiza-
tion must, in connection with the solicitation or receipt of the
contribution, provide a written statement which (1) informs the
donor that the amount of the contribution that is deductible for
federal income tax purposes is limited to the excess of the
amount of any money and the value of any property other than
money contributed by the donor over the value of the goods or
services provided by the organization, and (2) provides the donor
with a good-faith estimate of the value of the goods or services.

In other words, this law is designed to cause a donor or patron to know that the only amount deductible in these circumstances as a charitable gift (if any) is the amount paid to the charity in excess of any benefits provided by the charity. A charitable organization may use any reasonable methodology in making this good-faith estimate as long as it applies the methodology in good faith. A good-faith estimate of the value of goods or services that are not generally available in a commercial transaction may be determined by reference to the fair market value of similar or comparable goods or services. Goods or services may be similar or comparable even though they do not have the unique qualities of the goods or services that are being valued. Where the goods or services are available on a commercial basis, the commercial value is used.

For purposes of the $75 threshold, separate payments made at different times of the year with respect to fundraising events generally will not be aggregated. The IRS has the authority to promulgate anti-abuse rules in this area (addressing practices such as the writing of multiple checks to the same charity on the same date) but has not done so.

These rules do not apply where only de minimis, token goods or services (such as key chains and bumper stickers) are provided to the donor. In defining these terms, prior IRS announcements are followed. Nor do these rules apply to transactions that lack a donative element (such as the charging of tuition by a school, the charging of health care fees by a hospital, or the sale of items by a museum).

The law in this area is meager on the matter of celebrity presence. If a celebrity is present at an event and does nothing, or does something that is different from that for which he or she is celebrated, the value of the celebrity presence is zero. (An example of the latter is a tour of a museum conducted by an artist whose works are on display; the artist is renowned for the art work, not for being a tour guide.) Presumably, if the celebrity performs as such, the charitable organization must utilize the commercial value of the performance.

No part of a payment can be considered a contribution unless the payor intended to make a payment in an amount that is in excess of the fair market value of the goods or services received. This requirement of donative intent has particular application in the instance of auctions conducted by charitable organizations. The procedure preferred by the law is that a charity holding an auction will publish a catalog that meets the requirements for a written disclosure statement, including the charity's good-faith estimate of the value of items that will be available for bidding.

A penalty is imposed on charitable organizations that do not satisfy these disclosure requirements. For failure to make the required disclosure in connection with a quid pro quo contribution of more than $75, there is a penalty of $10 per contribution, not to exceed $5,000 per fundraising event or mailing. An organization may be able to avoid this penalty if it can show that the failure to comply was due to reasonable cause.

In general, a person can rely on a contemporaneous written acknowledgment provided in the gift substantiation context (see "Gift Substantiation Requirements" section earlier in this chapter) or a written disclosure statement provided in the quid pro quo transaction setting. An individual might not, however, treat an estimate of the value of goods or services as their fair market value if he or she knows, or has reason to know, that the treatment is unreasonable.

DISCLOSURE BY NONCHARITABLE ORGANIZATIONS

A set of disclosure rules is applicable to all types of tax-exempt organizations—other than charitable ones. These rules are targeted at social welfare organizations (see Chapter 2). The rules are intended to prevent noncharitable exempt organizations from engaging in gift-solicitation activities under circumstances in which donors will assume, or be led to assume, that the contributions are tax-deductible as charitable gifts. Exempt organizations that file annual information returns are required to respond to a question as to whether they have complied with the law requiring adherence to these rules (see Chapter 4).

This law applies in general to any organization to which contributions are not deducible as charitable gifts and that (1) is tax-exempt under the general rules, (2) is a political organization, (3) was either type of organization at any time during the five-year period ending on the date of the solicitation, or (4) is a successor to one of these organizations at any time during this five-year period. The IRS has the authority to treat any group of two or more organizations as one entity for these purposes where necessary to prevent the avoidance of these rules by means of use of multiple organizations.

Under these rules, each fundraising solicitation by or on behalf of a tax-exempt noncharitable organization must contain an express statement, in a "conspicuous and easily recognizable format," that gifts to it are not deductible as charitable contributions for federal income tax purposes. The term *fundraising solicitation* is defined as any solicitation of gifts made in written or printed form, and/or by television, radio, or telephone (although there is an exclusion for letters or calls that are not part of a coordinated fundraising campaign soliciting more than 10 persons during a calendar year). Despite this clear reference in the statute to "contributions and gifts," the IRS interprets this rule to mandate the disclosure when any tax-exempt organization (other than a charitable one) seeks funds, such as dues from members.

The IRS promulgated rules in amplification of this law, particularly the requirement of a disclosure statement. These rules, which include guidance in the form of "safe-harbor" provisions, address the format of the disclosure statement in instances of use of print media, telephone, television, and radio. They provide examples of acceptable disclosure language and methods, and of included and excluded solicitations. They also contain guidelines for establishing the $100,000 threshold.

This disclosure requirement applies to solicitations for contributions as well as solicitations for attendance at testimonials and like fundraising events. The disclosure must be made in the case of solicitations for contributions to political action committees.

An organization that has annual gross receipts that are normally not more than $100,000 is not subject to these rules. Where all of the parties being solicited are tax-exempt organizations, the solicitation does not have to include the disclosure statement (inasmuch as these grantors have no need for a charitable contribution deduction).

Exempt from these disclosure rules are the billing of those who advertise in an organization's publications, billing by social clubs for food and beverages, billing of attendees of an exempt organization's conference, billing for insurance premiums of an insurance program operated or sponsored by an exempt organization, billing of members of a community association for mandatory payments for police and fire (and similar) protection, and billing for payments to a voluntary employees' beneficiary association, as well as similar payments to a trust for pension and/or health benefits.

Material generally discussing the benefits of membership in a tax-exempt organization, such as an association or labor organization, does not have to include the disclosure statement. The statement is required, however, where the material requests payments and specifies the amount requested as membership dues. If a person responds to the general material discussing the benefits of membership, the follow-up material requesting the payment of a specific amount of membership dues (such as an association billing statement for a new member or a union check-off card) must include the disclosure statement.

Material discussing a candidate for public office and requesting individuals to vote for the candidate or to support the candidate does not need to include the disclosure statement, unless the material specifically requests either a contribution of funds or a contribution of volunteer services in support of the candidate.

Failure to satisfy this disclosure requirement can result in imposition of a penalty of $1,000 per day (maximum of $10,000 per year), albeit with a reasonable cause exception. In an instance of intentional disregard of these rules, however, the penalty for the day on which the offense occurred is the greater of $1,000 or 50 percent of the aggregate cost of the solicitations that took place on that day (the $10,000 limitation is inapplicable). For these purposes, the days involved are those on which the solicitation was telecast, broadcast, mailed, otherwise distributed, or telephoned.

DISCLOSURE OF GIFTS OF PROPERTY

A donor to a charitable organization is required to disclose to the IRS, by means of the appropriate federal income tax return, certain information in the case of a claimed deduction for noncash contributions in excess of $500. This filing requirement is applicable in the case of contributions by individuals, partnerships, personal service corporations, closely held corporations, and other corporations. C corporations (that are not personal service corporations or closely held corporations) are required to make this disclosure only if the amount claimed as a charitable deduction is more than $5,000.

This disclosure is made by means of IRS Form 8283. The form consists of Sections A and B. A donor may need to complete one of these sections or the other, or both, depending on the type of property contributed and the amount claimed as a charitable deduction. This form is filed with the donor's tax return for the year of the gift.

The donor includes in Section A only references to items (or groups of similar items) for which the donor claimed a deduction of $5,000 or less per item (or group of similar items). The following information is required in Part I: the name and address of the donee organization, a description of the donated property in sufficient detail, the date of the contribution, the date the donated property was acquired by the donor, how the property was acquired by the donor, the donor's cost or adjusted basis in the property, the fair market value of the property, and the method used to determine this fair market value.

Also, the donor is required to list the following publicly traded securities even if the claimed deduction is more than $5,000: securities listed on an exchange in which quotations are published daily, securities regularly traded in national or regional over-the-counter markets for which published quotations are available, and securities that are shares of a mutual fund for which quotations are published on a daily basis in a newspaper of general circulation throughout the United States.

The donor must respond to questions in Part II about any partial interest gifts (see Chapter 5) and/or any conditions placed on contributed property. If this part applies to more than one item of property, a separate statement must be attached to the return, providing the required information for each property.

The donor references in Section B (appraisal summary, discussed shortly, under "Appraisal Requirements") only items (or groups of similar items) for which the donor claimed a deduction of more than $5,000 per item (or group). (This rule does not apply with respect to publicly traded securities that are reportable in Section A.) Generally, the donor must have a written appraisal from a qualified appraiser that supports the information provided in Section B, Part I. If the total deduction for art is $20,000 or more, the donor must attach a complete copy of the signed appraisal; a photograph of the artwork must be provided to the IRS on request.

A separate qualified appraisal and a separate Form 8283 are

required for each item of property, except for an item that is part of a group of similar items. If the donor gave similar items to more than one charitable donee for which the donor claimed a total deduction of more than $5,000, the donor must attach a separate form for each donee.

The donor should complete Part II of Section B for each item included in Part I of the section that has an appraised value of $500 or less. Because the donor does not have to show the value of these items in Part I of the donee's copy of the Form 8283, these items should be identified for the donee in Part II. Then, the donee does not have to file with the IRS if the property is sold within two years of the gift (see next section).

If the donor was required to obtain an appraisal, the appraiser must complete Part III of Section B to be qualified. The charitable organization that received the property is required to complete Part IV of the section. The donor must provide a copy of Section B of Form 8283 to the donee.

DISPOSITIONS OF CONTRIBUTED PROPERTY

Charitable organizations that dispose of certain charitable deduction property within two years of the gift must disclose the transaction to the IRS. This is accomplished by filing Form 8282. The charitable donee is required to file the form within 125 days after the date of disposition of the property.

This form does not have to be filed if, at the time the original donee signed the appraisal summary, the donor signed a statement on Form 8283 that the appraised value of the specific item was not more than $500. If the Form 8283 references more than one similar item, this rule applies only to those items that are clearly identified as having a value of $500 or less. Also, the charitable donee is not required to file this form if an item is consumed or distributed, without consideration, in fulfillment of its exempt purpose or function.

If the gift property is transferred by the donee charitable organization (the original donee) to another charitable organization (the successor donee) within the two-year period, the original donee must provide the successor donee with the name, address, and tax identification number of the organization; a copy of the appraisal summary; and a copy of the Form 8282 involved, within 15 days of filing by the original donee.

The first two of these items must be furnished to the successor donee within 15 days after the latest of the date the original donee transferred the property, the original donee signed the appraisal summary, or the original donee received a copy of the appraisal summary from the preceding donee if the charity is also a successor donee.

A successor donee must provide the original donee with the successor organization's name, address, and tax identification number within 15 days after the later of the date the property was transferred by the original organization or the date the successor organization received a copy of the appraisal summary.

A charitable organization must provide a copy of the completed Form 8282 to the original donor of the property.

A charitable organization may be subject to a penalty if it fails to timely file Form 8282, fails to include all of the information required to be shown on the form, or fails to include correct information on the form. Generally, this penalty is $50.

APPRAISAL REQUIREMENTS

There are disclosure requirements in connection with the substantiation of deductions claimed by an individual, a closely held corporation, a personal service corporation, a partnership, or an S corporation for charitable contributions of certain property.

Property to which these rules apply is termed *charitable deduction property*. If the contributed property is a partial interest in an item of property (see Chapter 5), the appraisal must be of the partial interest. These requirements apply to contributions of property (other than money and publicly traded securities) if the aggregate claimed or reported value of the property—and all similar items of property for which deductions for charitable contributions are claimed or reported by the same donor for the same tax year whether donated to the same charitable donee—is in excess of $5,000.

The phrase *similar items of property* means property of the same generic category or type, such as stamp collections, coin collections, lithographs, paintings, photographs, books, nonpublicly traded securities, parcels of land, buildings, clothing, jewelry, furniture, electronic equipment, household appliances, toys, everyday kitchenware, china, crystal, or silver.

For this type of gift, the donor must obtain a qualified appraisal and attach an appraisal summary to the federal income tax return on which the deduction is claimed. In the case of non-publicly traded stock, however, the claimed value of which does not exceed $10,000 but is greater than $5,000, the donor is not required to obtain a qualified appraisal but must attach a partially completed appraisal summary form to the federal income tax or information return on which the deduction is claimed.

A *qualified appraisal* is an appraisal document that relates to an appraisal that is made not earlier than 60 days prior to the date of contribution of the appraisal property; is prepared, signed, and dated by a qualified appraiser (or appraisers); contains the requisite information; and does not involve a prohibited type of appraisal fee.

The qualified appraisal must include a description of the property in sufficient detail for a person who is not generally familiar with the type of property to ascertain that the property that was appraised is the property contributed; the physical condition of the property (in the instance of tangible property); the date of contribution of the property; the terms of any agreement between the parties relating to any subsequent disposition of the property, including restrictions on the charitable organization's use of the gift property; the name, address, and tax identification number of the appraiser; the qualifications of the qualified appraiser (or appraisers); a statement that the appraisal was prepared for income tax purposes; the date or dates on which the property was appraised; the appraised fair market value of the property on the date of contribution; the method of valuation used to determine the fair market value of the property; and the specific basis for the valuation.

The qualified appraisal must be received by the donor before the due date (including extensions) of the return on which the deduction for the contributed property is first claimed or, in the case of a deduction first claimed on an amended return, the date on which the amended return is filed.

A separate qualified appraisal is required for each item of property that is not included in a group of similar items of property. One qualified appraisal is required for a group of similar items of property contributed in the same tax year, as long as the appraisal includes all of the required information for each item. The appraiser may select any items the aggregate value of which is appraised at $100 or less, for which a group description (rather than a specific description of each item) is adequate.

The tax regulations provide that the appraisal must be retained by the donor "for so long as it may be relevant in the administration of any internal revenue laws."

The appraisal summary must be made using Section B of Form 8283, signed and dated on behalf of the charitable donee and by the qualified appraiser (or appraisers), and attached to the donor's federal income tax return on which a deduction with respect to the appraised property is first claimed or reported. The signature by the representative of the charitable donee does not represent concurrence by the donee in the appraised value of the contributed property.

The appraisal summary must include the name and taxpayer identification number of the donor (such as the social security number of an individual); a description of the donated property in requisite detail; a brief summary of the condition of the property at the time of the gift (in the case of tangible property); the manner and date of acquisition of the property by the donor; the cost basis of the property; the name, address, and taxpayer identification number of the charitable donee; the date the donee received the property; a statement explaining whether the charitable contribution was made by means of a bargain sale and amount of any consideration received from the donee for the contribution; the name, address, and taxpayer identification number of the qualified appraiser (or appraisers); the appraised fair market value of the property on the date of contribution; and a declaration by the appraiser.

The rules pertaining to separate appraisals also apply with respect to appraisal summaries. A donor who contributed similar items of property to more than one charitable donee must, however, attach a separate appraisal summary for each donee.

Every donor who presents an appraisal summary to a charitable organization for signature must furnish a copy of the appraisal summary to the charitable organization. If the donor is a partnership or S corporation, the donor must provide a copy of the appraisal summary to every partner or shareholder who receives an allocation of a deduction for a charitable contribution of property described in the appraisal summary. The partner or shareholder must attach the appraisal summary to the partner's or shareholder's federal income tax return. If a donor (or partner or shareholder of a donor) fails to attach the appraisal summary to the return, the charitable deduction will not be disal-

lowed if the donor (or partner or shareholder of a donor) sub-
mits an appraisal summary within 90 days of being requested to
do so by the IRS, as long as the failure to attach the appraisal
summary was a good-faith omission and certain other requirements are met (including timely completion of the appraisal).

An appraisal summary on Section B of Form 8283 must be
filed by contributors where the total value of all noncash contributions exceeds $500 and is less than $5,000. This portion of the
form must also be used to report contributions of publicly traded
securities, even where the value of them is in excess of $5,000.

The term *qualified appraiser* means an individual who includes on the appraisal summary a declaration that (1) he or she
holds himself or herself out to the public as an appraiser to perform appraisals on a regular basis, (2) because of the appraiser's
qualifications as described in the appraisal, he or she is qualified
to make appraisals of the type of property being valued, (3) the
appraiser is not one of the persons excluded by these rules from
being a qualified appraiser, and (4) the appraiser understands
that an intentionally false or fraudulent overstatement of the
value of the property described in the qualified appraisal or appraisal summary may subject the appraiser to a civil penalty for
aiding and abetting an understatement of tax liability, and consequently the appraiser may have appraisals disregarded.

Notwithstanding these requirements, an individual is not a
qualified appraiser if the donor had knowledge of facts that
would cause a reasonable person to expect the appraiser to falsely
overstate the value of the donated property. Also, the donor,
donee, or certain other related persons cannot be a qualified appraiser of the property involved in the gift transaction.

More than one appraiser may appraise the donated property, as long as each appraiser complies with these requirements,
including signing the qualified appraisal and appraisal summary.
If more than one appraiser appraises the property, the donor
does not have to use each appraiser's appraisal for purposes of
substantiating the charitable deduction.

Generally, no part of the fee arrangement for a qualified appraisal can be based on a percentage of the appraised value of
the property. If a fee arrangement is based, in whole or in part,
on the amount of the appraised value of the property that is allowed as a charitable deduction, after an IRS examination or otherwise, it is treated as a fee based on a percentage of the ap-

praised value of the property. (This rule does not apply in certain circumstances to appraisal fees paid to a generally recognized association that regulates appraisers.)

In any situation involving a gift of property, the charitable organization that is the recipient of the gift must value the property for its own record keeping, reporting, and (if applicable) financial statement purposes. The charitable donee, however, is not required to share that valuation amount with the donor.

These rules are subject to the doctrine of substantial compliance. Pursuant to this doctrine, where the rules involved are procedural or directory in nature, strict adherence to them is not required; substantial compliance is sufficient. It has been held that in this context, the requirement that certain documentation be attached to the donor's federal income tax return is directory rather than mandatory.

A separate set of rules applies appraisal requirements to regular corporations (i.e., corporations other than those referenced above; termed C corporations). These rules, in general, require these corporations to obtain a qualified independent appraisal to validly claim a charitable contribution deduction for gifts of most items of property, other than money, having a value in excess of $5,000.

There are special rules concerning contributions of inventory. C corporations are required to include summary information in their annual federal income tax return, such as a description of the inventory contributed and the valuation method used. This information is to be embodied in a partially completed appraisal summary.

These substantiation requirements must be complied with if the charitable contribution deduction is to be allowed.

OFFERING OF INFORMATION OR SERVICES

A tax-exempt organization is required to adequately disclose that the information or services it is offering to the public are available without charge from the federal government, assuming that is in fact the case.

This disclosure requirement is violated where (1) a tax-exempt organization offers to sell (or solicits money for) specific information or a routine service for an individual that could be readily obtained by that individual without charge (or for a nominal charge) from an agency of the federal government; (2) the exempt organization, when making the offer (or solicitation), fails to make an express statement in a "conspicuous and easily recognizable format" that the information or service can be so obtained; and (3) the failure is due to intentional disregard of these requirements.

This requirement applies only if the information to be provided involves the specific individual solicited. Thus, for example, the requirement applies with respect to obtaining the social security earnings record or the social security identification number of an individual solicited, while the requirement is inapplicable in connection with the furnishing of copies of newsletters issued by federal agencies or providing copies of or descriptive material concerning pending legislation.

This requirement is also inapplicable to the provision of professional services (such as tax-return preparation, assistance with respect to the submission of an application for a grant, or medical services), as opposed to routine information retrieval services, to an individual even if they may be available from the federal government without charge (or at a nominal charge).

There is a penalty for failure to comply with this rule, which is applicable for each day on which the failure occurred. It is the greater of $1,000 or 50 percent of the aggregate cost of the offers and solicitations that occurred on any day on which the failure occurred and with respect to which there was this type of failure.

TAX SHELTERS

There is considerable interest in tax shelters, by promoters and users of them, by the media, and by federal and state regulators. Much attention is being given to inversions, conversions, improper use of trusts, inflated business expense deductions, off-sheet financing schemes, unfounded constitutional law or other legal arguments, frivolous refund claims, and the like. This matter of tax shelters is not confined to for-profit businesses and the for-profit sector in general; tax shelter activity is also taking place in the nonprofit sector.

There is no single, and certainly no simple, definition of the term *tax shelter*. Basically, however, a tax shelter has two elements. One, it can be an entity (such as a partnership or trust) or a plan, transaction, or other arrangement (investment or otherwise).

Two, the sole or principal purpose of the entity or arrangement is avoidance or evasion of taxes. An abusive tax shelter is a scheme created and used to obtain, or to try to obtain, tax benefits that are not allowable by law.

There are disclosure obligations imposed on taxpayers that participate in reportable transactions. There are several types of these transactions, including listed transactions. These are transactions that the IRS has identified as having a tax avoidance purpose and whose tax benefits are subject to disallowance under existing law. The IRS, from time to time, identifies these transactions, some of which involve or are used by (sometimes as accommodation parties) tax-exempt organizations.

Examples of tax shelters in the exempt organizations context include the accelerated charitable remainder trust (see Chapter 5), overvaluation of property contributed to charity, certain trust arrangements that purport to qualify as multiple-employer welfare benefit funds in order to deduct what would otherwise be nondeductible life insurance premiums, and misuse of the tax exemption afforded small insurance companies (see Chapter 2). A tax-exempt organization may be an accommodation party in a tax shelter (e.g., a type of abusive tax-avoidance transaction) structured to improperly shift taxation away from taxable S corporation shareholders to an exempt entity (e.g., a charitable organization) for the purpose of deferring or avoiding taxes.

Indeed, depending on the definition of the term that is applied, tax shelters may embrace certain supporting organizations (see Chapter 3), certain donor-advised fund arrangements (see Chapter 3), charitable split-dollar insurance plans (largely outlawed), and charitable family limited partnerships. The IRS observed that it is being "confronted" with a number of "aggressive tax avoidance schemes," citing these four subjects as examples.

Bodies of law that may be brought to bear in connection with these transactions (particularly where the tax-exempt organization is a charitable entity) include the private inurement or private benefit doctrines (see Chapter 10), the intermediate sanctions rules (see Chapter 10), denial of a charitable deduction because of lack of a completed gift (see Chapter 5), or denial of the deduction because of an absence of donative intent (see Chapter 5).

There are various statutory provisions limiting tax benefits in certain transactions. Also, there are various penalties and sanctions applicable to tax shelters: the accuracy-related penalty, a fraud penalty, a penalty for understatement of a taxpayer's liability by an income tax return preparer, penalties with respect to the preparation of income tax returns for others, a penalty for promoting abusive tax shelters, a penalty for aiding and abetting an understatement of tax liability, a penalty for failure to register tax shelters, and a penalty for failure to maintain lists of investors in potentially abusive tax shelters.

The IRS also has the authority to pursue litigation to enjoin income tax return preparers from engaging in inappropriate conduct and to enjoin promoters of abusive tax shelters. There are still other laws used by the agency to combat unwarranted tax practices in the tax-exempt area, such as the property appraisal requirements and various anti-abuse rules in the tax regulations.

SUMMARY

One of the phenomena of contemporary nonprofit law is the emphasis on disclosure (or what some term *transparency*). The chapter summarized the disclosure requirements concerning applications for recognition of exemption and annual information returns. Other disclosure rules pertain to the charitable gift substantiation requirements, the quid pro quo contribution rules, giving to noncharitable organizations, gifts of certain property, disposition of certain contributed property, and the property appraisal requirements. The chapter also summarized special disclosure rules applicable to nonprofit organizations offering certain information or services to the public. A recent development is the involvement of tax-exempt organizations in tax shelters; the chapter summarized disclosure rules in that setting.

CHAPTER 7

Unrelated Business Activities

The purpose of this chapter is to summarize the federal tax law concerning the conduct of unrelated businesses by tax-exempt organizations. This field is one of the major components of the law of tax-exempt organizations. Inasmuch as nearly every undertaking of a nonprofit organization is a business, as that term is defined for tax purposes, it is critical for these organizations to know if their activities are related or unrelated businesses. Specifically, this chapter will:

- Analyze the rules for determining whether an activity is a business
- Review the rules for ascertaining whether a business is regularly carried on
- Explore the difference between related and unrelated businesses
- Enumerate the various exceptions to the unrelated business rules
- Identify the exceptions to these exceptions
- Interrelate the doctrine of commerciality with the unrelated business rules

STATUTORY FRAMEWORK

For more than 50 years, the federal tax law has categorized the activities of tax-exempt organizations as those that are related to the performance of exempt functions and those that are not. The net revenue occasioned by the latter type of activities, *unrelated activities,* is subject to tax. Gross revenues gained from unrelated activities are potentially taxable; however, in computing unrelated business taxable income, the organization is only entitled to deduct expenses incurred that are directly related to the conduct of the unrelated business.

For organizations that are incorporated, the net revenue from unrelated activities is subject to the regular federal corporate income tax. The federal tax on individuals applies to the unrelated activities of organizations that are not corporations (usually, trusts). Unlike the intermediate sanctions rules (see Chapter 10) and the private foundation rules (see Chapter 3), the law as to related and unrelated activities does not impose any taxes on the directors and officers of tax-exempt entities.

To decide whether any of its activities are taxable, an otherwise tax-exempt organization must first ascertain whether a particular activity is a business, then determine whether it is regularly carried on, then whether activities are related or unrelated, and then (if necessary) whether one or more exceptions are available. The judgments that go into assigning activities into these two categories are at the heart of one of the greatest controversies facing nonprofit organizations. Somewhat similar issues are brewing in relation to eligibility for exempt status, by virtue of the commerciality doctrine (see "Commerciality Doctrine" section later in this chapter).

The objective of the unrelated business income tax is to prevent unfair competition between tax-exempt organizations and for-profit, commercial enterprises. The rules are intended to place the unrelated business activities of an exempt organization on the same tax basis as those of a nonexempt business with which it competes.

To be tax exempt, a nonprofit organization must be organized and operated primarily for exempt purposes (see Chapter 1). The federal tax law thus allows a tax-exempt organization to engage in a certain amount of income-producing activity that is unrelated to its exempt purposes. Where the organization derives net income from one or more unrelated business activities, known as unrelated business taxable income, a tax is imposed on that income. A nonprofit organization's tax exemption will be denied or revoked if an appropriate portion of its activities is not promoting one or more of its exempt purposes.

Business activities may preclude the initial qualification of an otherwise tax-exempt organization. If the organization is not being operated principally for exempt purposes, it will fail the operational test. If its articles of organization empower it to carry on substantial activities that are not in furtherance of its exempt purpose, it will not meet the organizational test.

A nonprofit organization may still satisfy the operational test, even when it operates a business as a substantial part of its activities, as long as the business promotes the organization's exempt purpose. If the organization's primary purpose is carrying on a business for profit, it is denied exempt status, perhaps on the ground that it is a feeder organization.

Occasionally, the IRS will assume a different stance toward the tax consequences of one or more unrelated businesses when it comes to qualification for tax exemption. That is, the IRS may conclude that a business is unrelated to an organization's exempt purpose and thus is subject to the unrelated business income tax. Yet, the IRS may also agree that the purpose of the unrelated business is such that the activity helps further the organization's exempt function (by generating funds for exempt purposes), even if the business activity is more than one-half of total operations. In this circumstance, then, the exempt organization can be in the anomalous position of having a considerable amount of taxable business activity—and still be tax exempt.

AFFECTED TAX-EXEMPT ORGANIZATIONS

Nearly all types of tax-exempt organizations are subject to the unrelated business rules. They include religious organizations (including churches), educational organizations (including universities, colleges, and schools), health care organizations (including hospitals), scientific organizations (including major research institutions), and similar organizations. Beyond the realm of charitable entities, the rules are applicable to social welfare organizations (including advocacy groups), labor organizations (including unions), trade and professional associations, fraternal organizations, employee benefit funds, and veterans' organizations.

Special rules tax all income not related to exempt functions (including investment income) of social clubs, homeowners' associations, and political organizations.

Some exempt organizations are not generally subject to the unrelated income rules, simply because they are not allowed to engage in any active business endeavors. The best example of this is private foundations, where the operation of an active unrelated business (internally or externally) would trigger application of the excess business holdings restrictions (see Chapter 4). Generally, an exempt title-holding company cannot have unrelated business taxable income; an exception permits such income in an amount up to 10 percent of its gross income for the tax year, where the income is incidentally derived from the holding of real property.

Instrumentalities of the United States, like governmental agencies generally, are exempt from the unrelated business rules. These rules are, however, applicable to colleges and universities that are agencies or instrumentalities of a government, as well as to corporations owned by such institutions of higher education.

CONDUCT OF BUSINESS

For purposes of the federal tax rules, the term *trade or business* includes any activity that is carried on for the production of income from the sale of goods or the performance of services. Most activities that would constitute a trade or business under basic tax law principles are considered a trade or business for the purpose of the unrelated business rules. That definition is a statutory one; a court may ignore that definition and compose its own, such as by holding that the activity simply does not rise to the level of business functions.

This definition of the term *trade or business*—often referred to simply as *business*—embraces nearly every activity of a tax-exempt organization; only passive investment activities and the provision of administrative services among related organizations generally escape this classification. In this sense, a nonprofit organization is viewed as a bundle of activities, each of which is a business. (It must be emphasized that this term has nothing to do with whether a particular business is related or unrelated; there are related businesses and unrelated businesses.)

The IRS is empowered to examine each of a nonprofit organization's activities in search of unrelated business. Each activity can be examined as though it existed wholly independently of the others; an unrelated activity cannot, as a matter of law, be hidden from scrutiny by tucking it in among a host of related activities. As Congress chose to state the precept, an "activity does not lose identity as a trade or business merely because it is carried on within a larger aggregate of similar activities or within a larger complex of other endeavors which may, or may not, be related to the exempt purposes of the organization." This is known as the *fragmentation rule,* by which—as a matter of legal fiction—a non-profit organization's disparate activities may be fragmented and each discrete fragment reviewed in isolation. For example, the activity of advertising in a nonprofit organization's exempt publication is severed from the publication activity and regarded as an unrelated activity, even though otherwise the publication activity is a related business.

The federal law also provides that, where an activity "carried on for profit constitutes an unrelated trade or business, no part of such trade or business shall be excluded from such classification merely because it does not result in profit." In other words, just because an activity results in a loss in a particular year, that is insufficient basis for failing to treat the activity as an unrelated one. Conversely, the mere fact that an activity generates a profit is not alone supposed to lead to the conclusion that the activity is unrelated (although on occasion that is the conclusion).

An activity that consistently results in annual losses likely will not be regarded as a business. If that is the only unrelated activity, then it cannot be an unrelated business. Some nonprofit organizations, however, have more than one unrelated business. They can offset the losses generated by one business against the gains enjoyed by another business in calculating unrelated business taxable income. But, if the loss activity is not a business, its losses cannot be credited against unrelated gain.

It is common for a tax-exempt organization to provide management or other administrative services to another exempt organization. These services, where they are not inherently exempt functions, are known as corporate services. The general rule is that the provision of these types of services, even where the exempt organizations involved have the same exempt status, is a business. (Indeed, the providing of corporate services is generally considered by the IRS to be an unrelated business.) Nonetheless, where the relationship between the exempt organizations is that of parent and subsidiary, or is analogous to that of parent and subsidiary, the financial dealings will be regarded as a matter of accounting, which means they will be disregarded for federal income tax purposes.

Just as the element of profits is not built into the statutory definition of the term *trade or business,* so, too, is the factor of unfair competition missing from that definition. Yet, unfair competition was the force that animated enactment of the unrelated business rules; the IRS and the courts sometimes take the matter of competition into consideration in assessing whether an activity is related or unrelated to exempt purposes.

Another term absent from the statutory definition of business is *commerciality.* Nothing in that definition authorizes the IRS and the courts to conclude that an activity is an unrelated one solely because it is conducted in a commercial manner, which basically means it is undertaken the way a comparable activity is carried on by for-profit businesses (see the discussion of commerciality at the end of the chapter). Yet, they engage in the practice anyway.

REGULARLY CARRIED-ON BUSINESSES

To be considered an unrelated business, an activity must be *regularly carried on* by a nonprofit organization. That is, income from an activity is considered taxable only when (assuming the other criteria are satisfied) the activity is conducted more often than sporadically or infrequently. The factors that determine whether an activity is regularly carried on are the frequency and continuity of the activities, and the manner in which the activities are pursued. (In this context, the statutory law comes the closest to employing a doctrine of *commerciality.*)

These factors are to be evaluated in light of the purpose of the unrelated business rules, which is to place nonprofit organizations' business activities on the same tax law basis (what some are wont to call a level playing field) as those of their nonexempt competitors. Specific business activities of a tax-exempt organization will generally be deemed to be regularly carried on if they are, as noted, frequent and continuous, and pursued in a manner that is generally similar to comparable commercial activities of for-profit organizations.

Where a nonprofit organization duplicates income-producing activities performed by commercial organizations year-round, but conducts these activities for a period of only a few weeks a year, they do not constitute the regular carrying on of a business. Similarly, occasional or annual income-producing activities, such as fundraising events, do not amount to a business that is regularly carried on. The conduct of year-round business activities, such as the operation of a parking lot one day every week, however, constitutes the regular carrying on of a business. Where commercial entities normally undertake income-producing activities on a seasonal basis, the conduct of the activities by an exempt organization during a significant portion of the season is deemed the regular conduct of the activity. For this purpose, a season may be a portion of the year (such as the summer) or a holiday period.

Generally, the law, in ascertaining regularity, looks only at the time consumed in the actual conduct of the activity. The IRS, however, is of the view that time expended preparing for the event (preparatory time) should also be taken into account. This can convert what appears to be an exempted activity into a taxable business.

Outsourcing has become a popular management technique for nonprofit organizations. They often attempt to outsource unrelated activities (and try to bring the profits in as nontaxable income, usually royalties (see "Exempted Income" section later in this chapter)). This arrangement entails a contract that sometimes casts the party with whom the nonprofit organization is contracting as the organization's agent. While this is meritorious from a management perspective (such as to ensure quality), it is a bad idea from the tax law viewpoint. Pursuant to the law of principal and agent, the activities of the agent are attributable to the principal. In this setting, the nonprofit organization is the principal. Attribution of the agent's activities to the exempt organization obliterates what would otherwise be the tax law outcome from the outsourcing, by treating the exempt organization as if it directly is conducting the outsourced activity.

RELATED OR UNRELATED?

The term *unrelated trade or business* is defined to mean "any trade or business the conduct of which [by a tax-exempt organization] is not substantially related (aside from the need of such organization for income or funds or the use it makes of the profits derived) to the exercise or performance by such organization of its charitable, educational, or other purpose or function constituting the basis for its exemption." The parenthetical clause means that an activity is not related, for these purposes, simply because the organization uses the net revenue from the activity in furtherance of exempt purposes.

The revenue from a regularly conducted trade or business is subject to tax, unless the activity is substantially related to the accomplishment of the organization's exempt purposes. The key to taxation or nontaxation in this area is the meaning of the words *substantially related*. Yet the law provides merely that, to be substantially related, the activity must have a substantial causal relationship to the accomplishment of an exempt purpose.

The fact that an asset is essential to the conduct of an organization's exempt activities does not shield from taxation the unrelated income produced by that asset. The income-producing activities must still meet the causal relationship test if the income is not to be subject to tax. This issue arises when a tax-exempt organization owns a facility or other assets that are put to a dual use. For example, the operation of an auditorium as a motion picture theater for public entertainment in the evenings is regarded as an unrelated activity even though the theater is used exclusively for exempt functions during the daytime hours. The fragmentation rule (see previous discussion) allows this type of use of a single asset or facility to be split into two businesses.

Activities should not be conducted on a scale larger than is reasonably necessary for the performance of exempt functions. Activities in excess of what is needed for the achievement of exempt purposes may be seen as unrelated businesses.

There is a host of court opinions and IRS rulings providing illustrations of related and unrelated activities. Colleges and universities operate dormitories and bookstores as related businesses but can be taxed on travel tours and the conduct of sports camps. Hospitals may operate gift shops, snack bars, and parking lots as related businesses but may be taxable on sales of pharmaceuticals to the general public and on performance of routine laboratory tests for physicians. Museums may, without taxation, sell items reflective of their collections but are taxable on the sale of souvenirs and furniture. Trade associations may find themselves taxable on sales of items (such as uniforms, tools, and manuals) and particular services to members, of which dues and subscription revenue are nontaxable. Fundraising events may be characterized as unrelated activities, particularly where the activity is regularly carries on or compensation is paid.

UNRELATED BUSINESS TAXABLE INCOME

As previously noted, to be subject to the unrelated business income tax, the revenue involved must be derived from an activity that satisfies (or, depending on one's point of view, fails) three tests. Thus, unrelated *business taxable income* is gross income derived by a tax-exempt organization from an unrelated trade or business that is regularly carried on by it, less any allowable deductions that are directly connected with the carrying of the trade or business. (This definition does not incorporate the application of certain *modifications.*)

Some tax-exempt organizations are members of partnerships (see Chapter 9). In computing its unrelated business taxable income, it must (subject to the modifications) include its share (whether or not distributed) of the partnership's gross income from the unrelated business and its share of the partnership deductions directly connected with the gross income. (This is an application of what the tax law terms the look-through rule.) A tax-exempt organization's share (whether or not distributed) of the gross income of a publicly traded partnership must be treated as gross income derived from an unrelated business, and its share of the partnership deductions is allowed in computing unrelated business taxable income (again, subject to the modifications).

EXEMPTED ACTIVITIES

The foregoing general rules notwithstanding, certain businesses conducted by tax-exempt organizations are exempted from unrelated business income taxation. One of the frequently used exemptions from this taxation is for a business in which substantially all the work is performed for the organization without compensation. Thus, if an exempt organization conducts an unrelated business using services provided substantially by volunteers, the net revenue from that business is spared taxation. This exemption protects from taxation many ongoing fundraising activities for charitable organizations. Caution must be exercised, however, because *compensation* is not confined to a salary, wage, or fee; the slightest amount of remuneration (such as gratuities) can nullify an individual's status as a *volunteer.*

Also exempted is a business carried on by the organization primarily for the convenience of its members, students, patients, officers, or employees. This exception is available, however, only to organizations that are charitable, educational, and the like, or are governmental colleges and universities.

Exemption is accorded a business that consists of the selling of merchandise, substantially all of which has been received by the exempt organization as contributions. This exemption shelters the revenue of exempt thrift stores from unrelated income taxation. Its use, though, is not confined to thrift shops. For example, it can protect auction revenue from taxation—even if auctions are regularly carried on. Likewise, this exemption applies in the case of used vehicle donation programs; the charity involved is not taxed as though it is in the used car business.

Unrelated trade or business does not include qualified public entertainment activities. A public entertainment activity is any entertainment or recreational activity traditionally conducted at fairs or expositions promoting agricultural and educational purposes. Typically, these activities attract the public to fairs or expositions or promote the breeding of animals or the development of products or equipment.

To be qualified, a public entertainment activity must be conducted in (1) conjunction with an international, national, regional, state, or local fair or exposition; (2) accordance with the provisions of state law which permit the activity to be operated or conducted solely by a qualifying organization or by a governmental agency; or (3) accordance with the provisions of state law which permit a qualifying organization to be granted a license to conduct no more than 20 days of the activity, on payment to the state of a lower percentage of the revenue from the licensed activity than the state requires from nonqualifying organizations.

To warrant application of the public entertainment activities exception, a qualifying organization must be a tax-exempt charitable, social welfare, or labor organization that regularly conducts, as one of its substantial exempt purposes, an agricultural or educational fair or exposition.

The term *unrelated trade or business* also does not include qualified convention and trade show activities. Activities of this nature, traditionally conducted at conventions, annual meetings, or trade shows, are designed to attract attention from persons in an industry. There is no requirement for these persons to be members of the sponsoring organization. The purposes of these shows are to display industry products; to stimulate interest in, and demand for, industry products or services; or to educate persons within the industry in the development of new products and services or new rules and regulations affecting industry practices.

To be qualified, a convention and trade show activity must be carried out by a qualifying organization in conjunction with an international, national, regional, state, or local convention, annual meeting, or show that the organization is conducting. One of the purposes of the organization in sponsoring the activity must be the promotion and stimulation of interest in, and demand for, the products and services of that industry in general, or the education of attendees regarding new developments or products and services related to the exempt activities of the organization. The show must be designed to achieve its purpose through the character of the exhibits and the extent of the industry products displayed. A qualifying organization is a charitable, social welfare, or labor organization, or a trade association, which regularly conducts such a show as one of its substantial exempt purposes.

The concept of unrelated business does not include situations where cooperative hospital service organizations furnish services to one or more tax-exempt hospitals. The services, however, (1) must be furnished solely to hospitals that have facilities for no more than 100 inpatients; (2) if performed on its own behalf by the recipient hospital, must constitute exempt activities of that institution; and (3) must be provided for a fee or cost that does not exceed the actual cost of providing the services. The cost must include straight-line depreciation and a reasonable amount for return on capital goods used to provide the services.

Unrelated business also does not include bingo games conducted by tax-exempt organizations. The game must be (1) of a type in which usually the wagers are placed, the winners are determined, and the prizes or other property are distributed in the presence of all persons placing wagers in the game; (2) not an activity ordinarily carried out on a commercial basis; and (3) not in violation of any state or local law.

For a charitable, veterans', or other organization, as to which contributions are deductible, the term *unrelated business* does not include activities relating to a distribution of low-cost articles that is incidental to the solicitation of charitable contributions. A low-cost article is an item that has a maximum cost of $5.00 (indexed for inflation) to the organization that distributes the article (directly or indirectly). A distribution qualifies under this rule if it is not made at the request of the recipients, if it is made without their express consent, and if the articles that are distributed are accompanied by a request for a charitable contribution to the organization and a statement that the recipients may retain the article whether or not a contribution is made.

For a charitable, veterans', or other organization to which deductible contributions may be made, the term *business* does not include exchanging with another like organization the names and addresses of donors to or members of the organization, or the renting of these lists to another like organization.

Still other exceptions apply with respect to certain local organizations of employees, the conduct of certain games of chance, and the rental of poles by mutual or cooperative telephone or electric companies.

EXEMPTED INCOME

Certain types of passive and other income (principally research revenue) are exempt from the unrelated business income tax.

Because the unrelated income tax applies to businesses actively conducted by tax-exempt organizations, most types of passive income are exempt from taxation. This exemption generally embraces dividends, interest, securities loans payments, annuities, royalties, rent, capital gains, and gains on the lapse or termination of options written by exempt organizations. Income in the form of rent, royalties, and the like from an active business undertaking is taxable; that is, merely labeling an item of income as rent, royalties, and so forth does not make it tax-free.

The following exemptions apply to the conduct of research: income derived from research (1) for the United States or any of its agencies or instrumentalities, or any state or political subdivision of a state; (2) performed for any person at a college, university, or hospital; and (3) performed for any person at an organization operated primarily for purposes of carrying on fundamental research, the results of which are freely available to the general public.

Some organizations do not engage in research; rather, they merely test products for public use just prior to marketing or undertake certification tasks. Other organizations, principally universities and scientific research institutions, are engaging in research, but their discoveries are licensed or otherwise transferred to for-profit organizations for exploitation in the public marketplace. This closeness between businesses and nonprofit organizations—known as *technology transfer*—can raise questions as to how much commercial activity is being sheltered from tax by the research exception.

For the most part, the tax law is clear regarding what constitutes dividends, interest, annuities, rent, and capital gain. There can, however, be considerable controversy concerning what constitutes a royalty. The term, not defined by statute or regulation, is being defined by the courts.

Generally, a *royalty* is a payment for the use of one or more valuable intangible property rights. In the tax-exempt organizations setting, this is likely to mean payment for the use of an organization's name and logo. The core issue usually is the extent to which the exempt organization receiving the (ostensible) royalty can provide services in an attempt to increase the amount of royalty income paid to it. This issue was the subject of extensive litigation spanning many years, principally involving revenue from the rental of mailing lists and revenue derived from affinity card programs. The resulting rule is that these services are permissible as long as they are insubstantial. Beyond that, the IRS may contend that the exempt organization is in a joint venture (see Chapter 9), which is an active business undertaking that defeats the exclusion.

There is a specific deduction of $1,000. This means that the first $1,000 of unrelated business income is spared taxation.

EXCEPTIONS TO EXCEPTIONS

There are two exceptions to the foregoing exceptions, one involving unrelated debt-financed income, the other concerning income from subsidiaries.

A tax-exempt organization may own debt-financed property; the use of the property may be unrelated to the organization's exempt purposes. In a situation where both facts are present, when the exempt organization computes its unrelated business taxable income, income from the debt-financed property must be included as gross income derived from an unrelated business. The income is subject to tax in the same proportion that the property is financed by debt. The debt involved must be what the federal tax law terms *acquisition indebtedness.* This body of law applies even where the income is paid to an exempt organization in one of the otherwise protected forms, such as interest or rent.

Some tax-exempt organizations elect to spin off their unrelated activities to taxable subsidiaries. The tax on the net income of the unrelated business is then not borne directly by the exempt organization. The managers of an exempt organization may be averse to reporting any unrelated business income or the unrelated activity may be too large in relation to related activity.

If funds are transferred from a taxable subsidiary to an exempt parent, that income will be taxable as unrelated business income to the parent, if it is interest, rent, royalties, or capital gains. This is the outcome where the parent has, directly or indirectly, more than 50 percent control of the subsidiary. As an exception to an exception to an exception, if the subsidiary pays dividends to the tax-exempt parent, the dividends are not taxable to the parent because they are not deductible by the subsidiary.

CORPORATE SPONSORSHIPS

A subject of some controversy surrounds the provision of substantial financial support by a for-profit corporation to a tax-exempt (almost always charitable) entity, as sponsorship of a program, event, or other function of the entity. The business corporation receives considerable favorable publicity in exchange for its largesse. The law struggles to differentiate between treatment of the payment as a gift, with the publicity merely an acknowledgment of the contribution, and treatment of it as a payment for advertising services, in which case it would likely be unrelated business income. Unique statutory rules address the tax law aspects of *corporate sponsorships.*

In general, the receipt of a qualified sponsorship payment by a tax-exempt organization is not the receipt of income that is considered unrelated business income. These rules hinge, in considerable part, on two concepts: the qualified sponsorship payment and the substantial return benefit.

A qualified sponsorship payment is any payment of money, transfer of property, or performance of services, by a person engaged in a trade or business to an exempt organization, with respect to which there is no arrangement or expectation that the person will receive any substantial return benefit. For this purpose, it is irrelevant whether the sponsored activity is related or unrelated to the recipient organization's exempt purposes. It is also irrelevant whether the sponsored activity or other function is temporary or permanent.

A substantial return benefit is any benefit, other than goods, services, or other benefits of substantial value that are disregarded, or certain uses and acknowledgments. A substantial return benefit includes advertising; the provision of facilities, services, or other privileges to the payor or persons designated by the payor (collectively, the payor) (with exceptions, discussed later in the chapter); and granting the payor an exclusive or nonexclusive right to use an intangible asset (such as a trademark, patent, logo, or designation) of the exempt organization.

A substantial return benefit does not include the use or acknowledgment of the name or logo (or product lines) of the payor's trade or business in connection with the activities of the exempt organization. Use or acknowledgment does not include advertising but may include logos and slogans that do not contain qualitative or comparative descriptions of the payor's products, services, facilities, or company; a list of the payor's locations, telephone numbers, or Internet address; value-neutral descriptions, including displays or visual depictions, of the payor's product line or services; and the payor's brand or trade names and product or service listings.

Logos or slogans that are an established part of a payor's identity are not considered to contain qualitative or comparative descriptions. Mere display or distribution, whether without charge or for remuneration, of a payor's product by the payor or the exempt organization to the general public at the sponsored activity is not considered an inducement to purchase, sell, or use the payor's product and thus will not affect the determination of whether a payment is a qualified sponsorship payment.

An arrangement that acknowledges the payor as the exclusive sponsor of an exempt organization's activity, or the exclusive sponsor representing a particular trade, business, or industry, generally does not, alone, result in a substantial return benefit. For example, if in exchange for a payment, an organization announces that its event is sponsored exclusively by the payor (and does not provide any advertising or other substantial return benefit to the payor), the payor has not receive a substantial return benefit.

By contrast, an arrangement that limits the sale, distribution, availability, or use of competing products, services, or facilities in connection with an exempt organization's activity generally results in a substantial return benefit. For example, if in exchange for a payment, an exempt organization agrees to allow only the payor's products to be sold in connection with an activity, the payor has received a substantial return benefit.

Thus, the tax law distinguishes between an exclusive sponsor and an exclusive provider.

For these purposes, the term *advertising* means a message or other programming material that is broadcast or otherwise transmitted, published, displayed, or distributed, and that promotes or markets any trade or business, or any service, facility, or product. Advertising includes messages containing qualitative or comparative language, price information or other indications of savings or value, an endorsement, or an inducement to purchase, sell, or use any company, service, facility, or product. A single message that contains both advertising and an acknowledgment is nonetheless considered advertising.

Goods, services, or other benefits are disregarded under two sets of circumstances. One is where the benefits provided to the payor have an aggregate fair market value that is not more than 2 percent of the amount of the payment or $75 (adjusted for inflation), whichever is less.

The other situation where benefits are disregarded is where the only benefits provided to the payor are token items (such as bookmarks, calendars, key chains, mugs, posters, and t-shirts) bearing the exempt organization's name or logo that have an aggregate cost within the limit established for low-cost articles. Token items provided to employees of a payor, or to partners of a partnership that is the payor, are disregarded if the combined total cost of the token items provided to each employee or partner does not exceed the low-cost article limit.

If the fair market value of the benefits (or, in the case of token items, the cost) exceeds the above amount or limit, then (unless they constitute a use or acknowledgment) the entire fair market value of the benefits, not merely the excess amount, is a substantial return benefit.

If there is an arrangement or expectation that the payor will receive a substantial return benefit with respect to a payment, then only the portion of the payment (if any) that exceeds the fair market value of the substantial return benefit is a qualified sponsorship payment. The fair market value is determined on the date on which the sponsorship arrangement was created. If, however, the exempt organization does not establish that the payment exceeds the fair market value of any substantial return benefit, then no portion of the payment constitutes a qualified sponsorship payment.

The unrelated business income tax treatment of any payment (or portion of one) that is not a qualified sponsorship payment is determined by application of the general unrelated business rules. For example, payments related to the exempt organization's provision of facilities, services, or other privileges to the payor, advertising, exclusive provider arrangements, a license to use intangible assets of the exempt organization, or other substantial return benefits are evaluated separately in determining whether the exempt organization realizes unrelated business income.

To the extent necessary to prevent avoidance of this allocation rule, where the exempt organization fails to make a reasonable and good-faith valuation of any substantial return benefit, the IRS is empowered to determine the portion of a payment allocable to the substantial return benefit. The IRS can treat two or more related payments as a single payment.

Qualified sponsorship payments in the form of money or property (but not services) are treated as contributions received by the exempt organization for purposes of determining public support. This is the case irrespective of whether the donative organization or the service provider organization rules are applicable (see Chapter 3).

The fact that a payment is a qualified sponsorship payment that is treated as a contribution to the payee organization is not determinative of whether the payment is a business expense or a charitable contribution from the standpoint of the payor.

The existence of a written corporate sponsorship agreement does not, in itself, cause a payment to fail to be a qualified sponsorship payment. The terms of the agreement—not the fact of its existence or degree of detail—are relevant to the determination of whether a payment is a qualified sponsorship payment. Likewise, the terms of the agreement and not the title or responsibilities of the individuals negotiating the agreement determine whether a payment (or a portion of one) made pursuant to the agreement is a qualified sponsorship payment.

The term *qualified sponsorship payment* does not include any payment of which the amount is contingent, by contract or otherwise, on the level of attendance at one or more events, broadcast ratings, or other factors indicating the degree of public exposure to the sponsored activity. The fact that a payment is contingent on sponsored events or activities actually being conducted does not, alone, cause the payment to fail to be a qualified sponsorship payment.

These rules do not apply with respect to payments made in connection with qualified convention and trade show activities. These rules also do not apply to income derived from the sale of advertising or acknowledgments in exempt organization periodicals. For this purpose, the term *periodical* means regularly scheduled and printed material published by, or on behalf of, the exempt organization. A periodical is not related to, or primarily distributed in connection with, a specific event conducted by the exempt organization.

INTERNET ACTIVITIES

The IRS observed that the "use of the Internet [by tax-exempt organizations] to accomplish a particular task does not change the way the tax laws apply to that task. Advertising is still advertising and fundraising is still fundraising." In general, unrelated business is still unrelated business.

Regarding marketing, merchandising, advertising, and the like via the Internet, the IRS has yet to provide much guidance as to application of the unrelated business rules. The agency has stated that it is "reasonable to assume that as the Service position develops it will remain consistent with our position with respect to advertising and merchandising and publishing in the off-line world."

The IRS has gingerly broached the subject of charity Web site hyperlinks to related or recommended sites. Link exchanges may be treated as mailing list exchanges. Compensation for a linkage may be unrelated business income. The purpose of the link will be determinative: is its purpose furtherance of exempt purposes (such as referral of the site visitor to additional educational information) or is it part of an unrelated activity (such as advertising)?

Also involved are corporate sponsorships, inasmuch as exempt organizations sometimes seek corporate support to underwrite the production of all or a portion of the organization's Web site. These relationships may be short-term or continue on a long-term basis. The financial support may be acknowledged by means of display of a corporate logo, notation of the sponsor's Web address and/or 800 number, a moving banner (a graphic advertisement, usually a moving image, measured in pixels), or a link. The issue is this: Is the support a qualified sponsorship payment, in which case the revenue is not taxable, is it advertising income, which generally is taxable as unrelated business income, or is it something else?

A tax-exempt organization may provide a link to a corporate sponsor and still preserve treatment of the revenue as a nontaxable corporate sponsorship. Even with a link, the organization's public statement of appreciation for the payment can retain its character as a mere acknowledgment. That is, without more, the presence of a link is not considered a substantial return benefit. A statement on a sponsor's Web site, whereby an exempt organization endorses the sponsor's products or services, by contrast, will be attributed to the exempt organization, considered a substantial return benefit, and the safe harbor protection for qualified corporate sponsorships will be forfeited.

Other issues involving use of the Internet by tax-exempt organizations for unrelated purposes include application of special rules by which an online publication may be considered a periodical, tax treatment of virtual trade shows, online storefronts, online auctions, and affiliate and other co-venture programs with merchants.

COMMERCIALITY DOCTRINE

The courts are fashioning a body of jurisprudence known as the *commerciality doctrine*. This doctrine is rested on the presumption that, if an activity is conducted in the for-profit sector, it ought not be undertaken in the nonprofit sector. That is, charitable organizations should not, pursuant to this view, be operating in a *commercial* manner. The commerciality doctrine is usually applied in determining eligibility for tax-exempt status, although the IRS occasionally uses it to detect unrelated business.

Courts employ a variety of criteria when inquiring as to commerciality. The principal elements are competition with for-profit entities, the extent and degree of low-cost services provided, pricing policies, and the reasonableness of financial services. Other factors include, as one court stated, "commercial promotional methods," namely, advertising; a court was disturbed that an organization had a "jingle." Other facts that can lead to a finding of commercial behavior are the use of employees rather than volunteers, training of employees, and the lack of charitable contributions.

The commerciality doctrine appears only briefly in the Internal Revenue Code, where Congress has legislated as to prohibitions on charitable and social welfare organizations issuance of commercial-type insurance. Congress is beginning, however, to review other situations involving alleged commerciality (and competition). A primary area is that of hospitals, where comparisons with the operations of for-profit hospitals are causing some to call for more charity care by nonprofit health care institutions. Another area is tax exemption for nonprofit credit unions, with the commercial banking community demanding an end to credit unions' tax exemption. Still another field engendering this type of controversy is the insurance activities of exempt fraternal beneficiary societies in relation to those of taxable commercial insurers.

SUMMARY

One of the major components of the law regulating nonprofit organizations is the federal tax law concerning the conduct of unrelated business; this chapter summarized that body of law. The analytical process in this setting, as described in the chapter, is ascertainment as to whether an activity is a business, whether that activity is regularly carried on, whether the business is related or unrelated to the purposes of the nonprofit organization, and whether various exceptions for types of income or activities are available. A frequent use of these exceptions is the structuring of a transaction or arrangement so that the resulting income constitutes royalties. The chapter also summarized the exceptions to the exception: revenue in the form of unrelated debt-financed income and income from a subsidiary. The chapter further summarized the relatively new unrelated business law concerning a popular form of fundraising: corporate sponsorships.

CHAPTER 8

Fundraising Regulation

The purpose of this chapter is to summarize the federal and state laws that regulate the process of fundraising for charitable purposes. State regulation of charitable gift solicitation is sweeping; its magnitude is often underestimated. Recent years have witnessed the entry of the federal government into this field of law enforcement. Overall, government regulation of charitable fundraising is pervasive. Specifically, this chapter will:

- Survey the scope of state regulation of fundraising
- Review the components of a typical state charitable solicitation act
- Provide a constitutional law perspective on state regulation
- Summarize the federal law regulating charitable fundraising
- Examine issues raised by fundraising by means of the Internet

STATE REGULATION OF FUNDRAISING

Government regulation of fundraising for charitable objectives has traditionally been at the state level. Forty-six states have some form of a *charitable solicitation act*—a statute regulating the charitable fundraising process (see next section). Many counties, cities, and towns compound the regulatory requirements with comparable ordinances. Recently, the federal government has also become heavily involved in the regulation of fundraising for charitable purposes.

Most fundraising charitable organizations realize that they must comply with the charitable solicitation act (if any) of the state in which they are principally located. These laws also frequently mandate compliance by professional fundraisers, commercial co-venturers, and others who assist in fundraising endeavors, or that they are expected to adhere to the law in *each state* in which they are soliciting funds. A charitable organization that is fundraising nationwide should be in annual compliance with these 46 laws. Enforcers of county and city ordinances on fundraising often expect the national charities to comply with their rules as well.

Compliance in this setting varies from state to state, but essentially the term means that a charity must obtain permission from the appropriate regulatory authorities before a fundraising effort can begin. This permission is usually termed a permit or license, acquired as the result of filing a registration statement. Most states also require a filing fee, a bond, and/or the registration of professional fundraisers and others who will assist in the effort. The registration is usually updated by annually filing a report on the fundraising program, including financial information.

This process would be amply difficult if the registration and annual reporting requirements were uniform. The staff time and expense required to obtain, maintain, and disseminate the information throughout the states can be enormous. Historically, there has not been uniformity; recent years have brought limited progress toward use of a uniform registration form by several states (often accompanied nonetheless with schedules requiring varying information). Charities must constantly face differing registration and reporting forms, accounting methods, due dates, enforcement attitudes, and other substantial twists in the states' statutes, regulations, and forms. All of this becomes much more complex when fundraising by means of the Internet is contemplated, because then the charity is (presumably) soliciting funds in every state, county, township, city, and town.

STATE CHARITABLE SOLICITATION ACTS

What follows is an analysis of this type of law, based on the principal features of these acts as found in the majority of these statutes.

Definitions

The typical state charitable solicitation act opens with a series of definitions. A fundraising professional is often termed a *professional fundraiser* or a *fundraising counsel*, frequently defined as a person who, for compensation, "plans, manages, advises, consults, or prepares material for" the solicitation in the state of contributions for a charitable organization; this type of person does not "employ, procure, or engage" any compensated person to solicit contributions. A volunteer or salaried employee of a charitable organization is not a fundraising counsel, nor are lawyers, investment counselors, or bankers.

A paid solicitor is often defined as a person who, for compensation, performs for a charitable organization any service in connection with which contributions are or will be solicited in the state by that person or by any other compensated person the solicitor employs, procures, or engages, directly or indirectly, to solicit. There is often an exclusion from this definition for officers, employees, and volunteers of charitable organizations.

Other terms often defined in these laws are *charitable organization*, *professional fundraisers*, *solicitors*, *solicitation*, *charitable purpose*, *contribution*, *commercial co-venturer*, and *charitable sales promotion*.

Regulation of Charitable Organizations

Generally, every *charitable organization* desiring to solicit contributions in the state must, in advance, file a registration statement with the appropriate state agency. This requirement applies whether the charity is to solicit on its own behalf or have funds solicited for it by another organization, or be the recipient of gifts generated through the services of a commercial co-venturer or paid solicitor.

If the organization is in compliance, the state issues a certificate of registration, and the solicitation can then proceed. The statement must be filed in every year in which the charitable organization is soliciting in the state. A registration fee is levied.

A charitable organization usually is also required to file an annual financial report with the state. An organization with gross support and revenue not exceeding a certain amount (which will vary from state to state) is, however, often excused from filing an annual financial report. The financial information may sometimes be provided by submitting a copy of the annual information return filed with the IRS (see Chapter 4). Where the gross support and revenue of a charitable organization exceeds a certain amount (again, it will vary), the organization must submit audited financial statements.

Churches, other religious organization, and charitable organizations closely affiliated with them usually are exempt from the registration requirements. Also often exempt are organizations that engage in small annual solicitations—that is, they do not receive gifts in excess of a certain amount or do not receive gifts from more than a few persons—but sometimes only if all of their functions (including fundraising) are carried on by persons who are not paid for their services.

Under some of these laws, every charitable organization engaged in a solicitation in the state must disclose, at the point of solicitation, its name, address, telephone number, a "full and fair" description of the charitable program that is the subject of the fundraising campaign, and the fact that a financial statement is available on request. Where the services of a paid solicitor are utilized, additional disclosures at the point of solicitation are required (see "Regulation of Paid Solitors" section later in this chapter).

Regulation of Professional Fundraisers

Many state charitable solicitation acts go beyond the regulation of fundraising charities and impose obligations on *professional fundraisers*. The definition of this term varies considerably—an additional source of confusion generated by these laws.

Conceptually, a professional fundraiser is a person (an individual consultant or a company) retained by a charity who does not solicit contributions but, rather, designs and oversees implementation of a fundraising program. (As noted, employees of charitable organizations are usually excluded from professional fundraiser status for purposes of these laws.) Normally, they do not take custody of charitable gifts. They are usually paid a fixed fee for their advice and services in structuring a fundraising program.

Thus, under this conceptualization, the actual asking for and receipt of charitable gifts is left to others. In the contemporary era, however, this distinction has collapsed and the functions overlap. Those who plan may also solicit. Thus, the confusion in the law mirrors reality.

The registration of professional fundraisers is annual, for a fee. The application contains such requests for information as the state deems appropriate. The bond requirement and amount varies from state to state. Within a stated period (such as 90 days) following the completion of a solicitation, and on the anniversary of the commencement of a fundraising campaign longer than one year, the professional fundraiser must account in writing to the charitable organization for all income received and expenses paid.

Often, every contract between a charitable organization and a professional fundraiser must be in writing. The professional fundraiser must file it with the state prior to performing any material services. From the contract, the state regulator must be able to identify the nature of the services the professional fundraiser is to provide.

Regulation of Paid Solicitors

Confusion as to the regulation of solicitors also reigns throughout the states. A paid solicitor is often required to register annually with the state prior to any activity—using an application containing the information the state may require—and to pay a fee. At that time, the solicitor almost certainly will have to post a bond.

A *paid solicitor* conceptually is an (perhaps the) active participant in the gift solicitation process. He or she literally asks for gifts. This can be done by any form of communication, most likely in person (as in door-to-door or on a street corner) or by telephone. Other modes are letters, other publication (such as a newsletter or journal), fax, or Internet (see "Fundraising by Means of the Internet" section later in this chapter). Again, however, this fine distinction is often obliterated in modern charitable fundraising.

In many instances, prior to a solicitation campaign, the paid solicitor must file with the state a copy of his, her, or its contract with the charitable organization. In addition, the paid solicitor will likely have to file a solicitation notice with the state. In a typical requirement, the notice must include a copy of the contract, the projected dates when soliciting will commence and terminate, the location and telephone number from where the solicitation will be conducted, the name and residence address of each person responsible for directing and supervising the conduct of the campaign, a statement as to whether the paid solicitor will at any time have custody of contributions, and a full and fair description of the charitable program for which the solicitation campaign is being carried out.

Often, every contract between a paid solicitor and a charitable organization must be in writing. More than one state patronizingly requires that this document "clearly state the respective obligations" of the parties. The contract may have to provide for a fixed percentage of the gross revenue (or a reasonable estimate of it) from the solicitation effort, which is the amount the charitable organization will (or is expected to) receive. The stated minimum percentage may not include the expenses of the solicitation paid by the charity.

Many of these laws impose a point-of-solicitation requirement, for which paid solicitors are responsible. Under versions of this rule, before a verbal request or within a written request for a contribution, the potential donor must be advised that the solicitor is a paid solicitor and that the charitable organization will receive a percentage of gross receipts as stipulated in the contract. The disclosure must be "clear" and "conspicuous." In an oral solicitation, a written receipt must be sent to the contributor within a short period (such as five days), and it must include a clear and conspicuous disclosure of the point-of-solicitation items.

Following completion of a solicitation campaign (such as within 90 days), and on the anniversary of the start of a solicitation campaign longer than one year, the paid solicitor may be required to file with the state a financial report for the fundraising campaign.

A paid solicitor may be required to maintain certain information during each solicitation campaign and for a significant period of time (such as three years) afterward. This information is likely to include the name and address of each contributor, the date and amount of each contribution, the name and residence address of each employee or other person involved in the solicitation, and all expenses incurred during the course of the solicitation campaign.

Monies collected by a paid solicitor may have to be deposited in a bank account in a timely manner; the account almost certainly will have to be in the name of the charitable organization involved. The charity may have to have sole control over withdrawals from the account.

Special rules may be applicable in situations where paid solicitors represent that tickets to an event will be donated for use by other persons. These rules include limitations on solicitations for donated tickets and record-keeping requirements.

Regulation of Commercial Co-Venturers

Under the laws of some states, every charitable sales promotion must be the subject of a written contract, when a charitable organization enters into an arrangement with a commercial co-venturer. A copy of the contract must be filed with the state prior to the start of the promotion.

The law defines a *commercial co-venturer* as a person who for profit is regularly and primarily engaged in trade or commerce (other than in connection with charitable fundraising) and who conducts a charitable sales promotion. A *charitable sales promotion* is an advertising or sales campaign, conducted by a commercial co-venturer, where there is a representation that the purchase or use of goods or services offered by the commercial co-venturer will benefit, in whole or in part, a charitable organization or purpose. Example: Fast-food company franchise A, located in city B, advertises (by television, radio, and newspapers) that, during weekend C, every time there is a purchase of sandwich D, 5 cents of the sales amount will be paid to charity E. The promotion is undertaken both to encourage sales and to benefit a charity— hence the term *co-venture*.

The charitable sales promotion contract must include a statement of the goods or services to be offered to the public, the geographic area where the promotion will occur, the starting and ending dates of the promotion, the manner in which the name of the charitable organization will be used (including the representation to be made to the public as to the amount or percent per unit of goods and services purchased or used that will benefit the charitable organization), a provision for a final accounting on a per-unit basis by the commercial co-venturer to the charitable organization, and the date by when and the manner in which the benefit will be conferred on the charitable organization.

The commercial co-venturer is required to disclose in each

advertisement for the charitable sales promotion the amount per unit of goods or services purchased or used that will benefit the charitable organization or purpose. This amount may be expressed as a dollar amount or percentage.

The final accounting will probably have to be retained by the commercial co-venturer for a period of time (such as three years) and must be made available to the state authorities on request.

Prohibited Acts

Nearly all of the state charitable solicitation acts contain a list of one or more types of conduct—often termed *prohibited acts*—that may not be lawfully engaged in by a charitable organization (and perhaps not by a professional fundraiser, paid solicitor, and/or commercial co-venturer).

For example, state law may provide that a person may not, for the purpose of soliciting charitable contributions, use the name of another person without consent. Or, a person may not, for gift solicitation purposes, use a name, symbol, or statement so closely related to that used by a charitable organization or government agency that it would tend to confuse or mislead the public.

Other examples of a prohibited act is to lead the public to believe that registration with the state constitutes an endorsement of the fundraising organization by the state or to represent that a solicitation is for a charitable organization without proper authorization from the organization.

Other Provisions

These laws may provide that all documents required to be filed with the state (principally applications, registration statements, reports, and contracts) are matters of public record.

True records may have to be maintained by every charitable organization, fundraising counsel, professional fundraiser, paid solicitor, and/or commercial co-venturer required to register. These records, which must be retained for a stated period (as noted, usually three years), must be available to state officials for inspection.

The law may authorize the state to enter into reciprocal

agreements with other states or the federal government for the purpose of exchanging or receiving information filed by a charitable organization in another state, instead of requiring the organization to file under the particular state's law.

The state agency (probably the attorney general's or secretary of state's office) will undoubtedly be authorized to conduct investigations and enjoin solicitations. Under various circumstances, a registration can be revoked, canceled, or suspended. Civil penalties can be imposed for failure to adhere to the law. Willful violations of portions of these laws may even amount to criminal behavior, occasioning imprisonment.

STATES' POLICE POWER

The authority underlying the enactment and enforcement of these charitable solicitations acts lies in the *police power* inherently possessed by each of the states (and municipalities). Its police power enables a state to regulate—within the bounds of constitutional law principles—the conduct of its citizens and others to the end of protecting the safety, health, and welfare of its people. Consequently, in requiring a charitable organization planning on fundraising in the jurisdiction to register with the appropriate regulatory authority, to periodically render reports on the results of the solicitation, and to impose fees and bonding requirements, the state is exercising its police power.

The rationale is that charitable solicitations may reasonably be regulated by the states in order to protect the public from deceit, fraud, unreasonable annoyance, or the unscrupulous obtaining of money or property under a pretense that the money or property is being collected for a charitable purpose. The laws that regulate charitable solicitations are thus by no means constitutionally deficient; they are, instead, manifestations of the states' police power. At the same time, these laws, like all legislation, must conform to certain basic constitutional law standards.

It is highly unlikely that a court will void a charitable solicitation act in its entirety because of constitutional law violations. Rather, when a court acts in this area, it does so with precision, striking out only the discrete provision or provisions that are overbroad, that is—go beyond the ambit of narrowest-of-means regulation. For example, a state charitable solicitation act was found to be unconstitutional because of the burden imposed by the requirement that a professional fundraiser obtain a bond or post a letter of credit and because of too much "unbridled discretion" conferred on state officials.

The principal legal issue in this context has been the attempts over the years by many states to preclude charities from fundraising in their jurisdictions if their fundraising costs are "excessive," as computed as a percentage of gifts received (see the following section). The Supreme Court has, to the dismay of state regulators, repeatedly struck down laws of this nature as being unconstitutional. Nonetheless, a group of states recently tried to convince the Court that high fundraising costs evidence per se fraud, so that certain charities and their fundraiser could be prosecuted. The Court sidestepped the issue, however, holding only that fraudulent charitable fundraising cannot be protected by free speech principles—which was the state of the law before the litigation (consuming nearly 12 years) was initiated.

CONSTITUTIONAL LAW CONSIDERATIONS

Fundraising regulation of charitable organizations is more than the states' charitable solicitation acts (see preceding section) and the rules governing the deductibility of charitable gifts. This aspect of the law also involves fundamental principles of constitutional law (see Chapter 11).

The principal constitutional law precept is the doctrine of free speech, protected at the federal level by the First Amendment to the U.S. Constitution and at the state level by the Fourteenth Amendment. There are two forms of free speech: pure free speech, which may be regulated by the states by only the narrowest of means, and commercial free speech, which may be regulated by the states by means that are reasonable. Fundraising by charitable organizations is one of the highest forms of free speech—it is pure free speech.

The courts have held that, although government has legitimate interests in regulating this field—such as in exercise of the states' police power—it may not do so by broad and arbitrary classifications. As the Supreme Court has written, government can regulate charitable fundraising but "must do so by narrowly drawn regulations designed to serve those interests without unnecessarily interfering with First Amendment freedoms." The Court has also observed: "Broad prophylactic rules in the area of free expression are suspect. Precision of regulation must be the touchstone."

One of the most significant clashes between governmental police power to regulate for the protection of a citizenry and rights of free speech involves the application of percentage limitations on fundraising costs as a basis for determining whether a charity may lawfully solicit funds in a jurisdiction. Many aspects of this head-on conflict were resolved in 1980, when the Supreme Court held that a municipal ordinance was unconstitutionally overbroad and in violation of free speech. The ordinance had prohibited solicitation by charitable organizations that expend more than 25 percent of their receipts for fundraising and administrative expenses (known as an absolute percentage limitation). Subsequently, the Court addressed a law stating that fundraising expenses in excess of a certain percentage are presumed to be unreasonable, with charities given the opportunity to demonstrate that the expenses are in fact reasonable (the rebuttable percentage limitation); the Court found that this type of law also is contrary to charities' rights of free speech. Thereafter, these principles of free speech rights were extended to apply in situations where charities obtain outside fundraising assistance (such as that provided by paid solicitors).

Both the absolute percentage limitation and the rebuttable percentage limitation can entail another constitutional law violation: denial of due process. Laws regulating the fundraising activities of charitable organizations must afford due process rights to persons subject to the laws, as prescribed in the Fifth and Fourteenth Amendments.

A state charitable solicitation act must be in conformance with the guarantee of equal protection of the laws provided by the Fourteenth Amendment. This means that such an act may not discriminate in its classification of organizations. An equal protection argument can be raised because of exceptions from the coverage provided in a charitable fundraising regulation law. Indeed, some state laws exclude from compliance charitable organizations by name.

A cardinal doctrine of administrative law is that a governmental agency may issue rules and regulations. The agency must do so, however, in the context of a policy established by the legislative body involved that has fixed standards for the guidance of the agency in the performance of its functions. A charitable solicitation act may run afoul of this doctrine (born of the separation-of-powers principle) where the executive regulatory agency is granted such a wide range of discretionary authority that it is impermissibly exercising legislative power.

FEDERAL REGULATION OF FUNDRAISING

Although the regulation of charitable fundraising was once the sole province of the states, it is now also being vigorously undertaken at the federal level, largely by application of the tax law. Agencies such as the U.S Postal Service, the Federal Trade Commission, and the Federal Election Commission may also be involved.

Fundraising Disclosure

Congress brought the IRS into the realm of fundraising regulation when it legislated three forms of fundraising disclosure rules. One package of these rules requires that most charitable gifts be *substantiated* in writing. Another set of rules mandates certain disclosures where there is a *quid pro quo contribution* (see Chapter 6). The third area of disclosure is that occasioned by the requirement that copies of a tax-exempt organization's application for recognition of tax exemption and annual information returns be made available to the public on request (see Chapter 4).

Exemption Recognition Process

To be tax-exempt as charitable entities and to be charitable donees, organizations are required to secure a letter to that effect from the IRS. The application process requires the organization to reveal much information about itself (see Chapter 2). The application for recognition of tax exemption requires the submission of details on the applicant's fundraising program and on its fundraising expenditures (in the financial statements or the proposed budgets submitted with the application).

Reporting Requirements

The annual information return (see Chapter 4) requires charitable organizations to use the functional method of accounting to report their expenses. This accounting method requires not only the identification, line by line, of discrete categories of expenses but also an allocation of expenses by function—program services, management and general, and fundraising.

To properly comply with the requirements of the functional method of accounting, organizations need to maintain detailed records on their fundraising (and other) expenses; the fundraising component of each line-item expenditure must be separately identified and reported. Because of this separate identification, some indirect fundraising costs may be revealed, which—when combined with direct fundraising expenses—result in considerably higher total outlays for fundraising. This result could have adverse repercussions for the organization's status in relation to state charitable solicitation acts (discussed previously), particularly those that force disclosure of total fundraising expenses. The IRS may make inquiry of an organization that reports substantial amounts of charitable contributions and little or no fundraising expenses.

The instructions accompanying the annual information return define the term *fundraising expense* as "all expenses, including allocable overhead costs, incurred in: (a) publicizing and conducting fundraising campaigns; (b) soliciting bequests, grants from foundations or other organizations, or government grants . . .; (c) participating in federated fundraising campaigns; (d) preparing and distributing fundraising manuals, instructions, and other materials; and (e) conducting special fundraising events that generate contributions." The IRS does not differentiate, when using the term *professional fundraising*, between fundraising counsel and paid solicitors. The agency defines the phrase professional fundraising fees to mean the organization's fees paid to "outside fundraisers for solicitation campaigns they conducted or for consultation services connected with a solicitation of contributions by the organization itself."

Three other areas of disclosure pertaining to fundraising are mandated by the annual information return:

1. Organizations must separately identify their sources of *program service revenue.*
2. Organizations must report their receipts from and expenses of "[s]pecial fund-raising events and activities," separating the information for each type of event. Typi-

cally, these events include dinners, dances, carnivals, raffles, bingo games, and door-to-door sales of merchandise.

3. Organization must adhere to the federal tax law requirements as to unrelated business income (see following discussion and Chapter 7).

Regarding special fundraising events, the IRS observes in the return's instructions that "[t]hese activities only incidentally accomplish an exempt purpose" (thus being differentiated from program) and that "[t]heir sole or primary purpose is to raise funds that are other than contributions to finance the organization's exempt activities. . . . This is done by offering goods or services that have more than a nominal value (compared to the price charged) for a payment that is more than the direct cost of those goods or services." An activity that generates only contributions, such as a direct-mail campaign, is not a *special fundraising event*. That description applies to events that generate both contributions and income, such as when a purchaser pays more than the value of the goods or services furnished.

The contents of the annual information return pertain to how the federal government and state regulatory agencies share the regulation of fundraising for charity. These levels of government are coordinating their respective roles. The IRS has taken a significant step toward implementation of this process by noting in the return's instructions that some states and local governments accept a copy of the annual return in place of all or part of their own financial report forms. Some states may require additional information, requiring attachments; this additional information need not be filed with the IRS.

If the annual information return is amended, a copy of the revised return is to be sent to each state with which the original return was filed. More states than ever before use the Form 990 for compliance with the states' charitable solicitation acts. The IRS expects reporting organizations to identify the states in which copies of the return are filed.

The instructions accompanying the annual information return suggest that fundraising is a form of doing business in the states and therefore may require separate registration pursuant to the states' nonprofit corporation acts.

Unrelated Business Rules

One of the ways in which the IRS is regulating the charitable fundraising process is by means of the unrelated business rules (see Chapter 7). These rules may cause the receipts from fundraising activities to be characterized as unrelated business income.

Many fundraising practices possess all of the technical characteristics of an unrelated business: they are trades or businesses, are regularly carried on, and are not efforts that are substantially related to the performance of tax-exempt functions (even though the resulting income is used to support exempt functions). Applying the tests often used by the IRS and the courts, there is no question that some fundraising endeavors have a commercial counterpart and are being undertaken in competition with for-profit businesses, and with the objective of realizing a profit.

Some fundraising activities, however, are sheltered by law from consideration as taxable businesses. Three examples are an activity in which substantially all of the work is performed for the organization by volunteers; one that is carried on primarily for the convenience of the organization's members, students, patients, officers, or employees; and one that consists of the sale of merchandise, substantially all of which has been received by the organization as gifts.

As the functional accounting method's rules (see preceding section, "Reporting Requirements") indicate, the law regards program activities and fundraising activities as separate types of undertakings. Even a simple fundraising activity such as a car wash or bake sale technically is an unrelated business. These businesses, nonetheless, are usually immune from taxation because they are not regularly carried on or are protected from taxation by an exception. Yet occasionally, when considering a special fundraising event, the IRS takes into account not only the time consumed by the event but also the time expended by the organization in preparing for it (known as preparatory time) in concluding that the fundraising event is a business that is regularly carried on—and thus is taxable.

Lobbying Restrictions

Tax regulations define the term *fundraising costs* and spell out rules by which these costs are distinguished from (often allocated across) the categories of program and administration expenses. These regulations were crafted as part of the effort to state the rules governing elective lobbying restrictions for eligible public charities (see Chapter 10).

Under these lobbying rules, certain percentages are applied to the organization's outlays for program expenditures but not most fundraising expenditures. An organization endeavoring to comply with these rules must, therefore, differentiate between its fundraising expenses and its other costs. The amounts against which these percentages are applied are termed exempt purpose expenditures. These expenditures do not include amounts paid or incurred to or for (1) a separate fundraising unit of the organization or an affiliated organization's fundraising unit, or (2) one or more other organizations, if the amounts are paid or incurred primarily for fundraising.

To adhere to these rules, an electing public charity must determine its direct and indirect fundraising costs, utilizing the scope of the term fundraising in this context.

Public Charity Classifications

A charitable organization is classified as either a *public charity* or a *private* one—the latter being a private foundation (see Chapter 3). One of the ways to avoid private foundation status is to be a publicly supported charitable organization; one of the ways to accomplish that is to qualify as a *donative type* publicly supported charity. An organization can achieve that classification by satisfying a *facts-and-circumstances test*, where the amount of public support normally received by the organization may be as low as 10 percent of its total support.

A variety of criteria may be used to demonstrate compliance with this test. One criterion is the extent to which the charitable organization is attracting public support. Thus, an element of this test is whether the organization is able to show that it has an active and ongoing fundraising program. The tax regulations state that an entity may satisfy this aspect of the test "if it maintains a continuous and bona fide program for solicitation of funds from the general public, community, or membership group involved, or if it carries on activities designed to attract support from governmental units or other [publicly supported] organizations."

Substantiation Rules

Another way that the federal tax law regulates the charitable fundraising process is by means of the gift substantiation rules. Under this body of law, a donor who makes a separate charitable contribution of at least $250 in a year, for which a charitable contribution deduction is claimed, must obtain written substantiation of the contribution from the donee charitable organization. This document must contain certain information. If these rules are not followed, the donor is deprived of the charitable deduction (see Chapter 5).

Quid Pro Quo Contribution Rules

The federal tax law likewise regulates in the field of charitable fundraising by means of the quid pro quo contribution rules. A quid pro quo contribution is a payment made partly as a charitable contribution and partly in consideration for goods or services provided to the payor by the donee organization. These rules require the charitable donee to provide the donor with certain information in writing. Penalties are imposed for failure to comply with these rules (see Chapter 6).

Other Aspects of Federal Regulation

Federal tax law prohibits a private educational institution from qualifying as a tax-exempt entity if it has racially discriminatory policies. Under IRS guidelines, schools must follow an assortment of record-keeping requirements. Every private school must maintain, for at least three years, copies of all materials used by or on behalf of it to solicit charitable contributions. Failure to maintain or to produce the required reports and information creates a presumption that the school has failed to comply with the guidelines and thus has a racially discriminatory policy toward its students. Loss or denial of tax-exempt status could result.

Charitable and other organizations solicit gifts via the mail; consequently, the rules imposed by the U.S. Postal Service are a component of federal regulation of fundraising. Other federal agencies are involved in fundraising regulation, such as the Federal Trade Commission and its rules concerning telemarketing, and the Federal Election Commission and its rules pertaining to fundraising for political purposes (see Chapter 12).

FUNDRAISING BY MEANS OF THE INTERNET

The Internet has greatly expanded the number of charitable organizations capable of carrying out, and actually engaged in the practice of, multistate gift solicitation activities. Essentially, to reach potential donors in all of the states, an organization needs nothing more than a computer and an account with an Internet service provider. Once established, the organization's charitable appeal can instantly be sent or made available to the entire Internet community. The large national and international charities with the resources necessary to assure compliance with the various state regulatory regimes are thus no longer the only ones affected by the state charitable solicitation laws. Instead, even the smallest organizations are beginning to tap the national contribution market. Thus, the new technology indeed is altering the nature of communication in the charitable solicitations context—it renders these communications inexpensive.

General Precepts

One of the most difficult of contemporary issues in the nonprofit law setting is whether fundraising by charitable organizations by means of the Internet constitutes fundraising in every state and locality. Current thinking is that, technically, it does. If states asserting jurisdiction over Internet fundraising are justified in doing so, the result will be that even the smallest organizations—those too small to afford multistate solicitation efforts using any other medium—will be required to register and report under tens, maybe hundreds, of state and local charitable solicitation laws simply by virtue of utilizing the new communications technology to seek contributions. If they do not or cannot assure state-law compliance, they will be forced to decide between risking adverse legal action in several states or refrain from engaging in this form of speech altogether. The question thus is whether, under this unfolding mix of facts, state laws enforced in this fashion would impermissibly restrict speech protected by free speech principles.

There is another question that needs to be addressed. From a legal perspective, should Internet fundraising appeals be treated any differently simply because they take place via the Internet? That is, should communication over this newest medium be treated as anything other than communication, for which there already is a rich regulatory regime? For federal tax purposes, the answer to this question from the IRS is no.

To determine whether the various state charitable solicitation schemes unduly intrude on the protected speech interest in this type of solicitation, the existing regulatory framework must be applied to the new set of facts. The first step in this analysis is to ascertain whether the act of an organization in placing an appeal for funds in a document on a computer in one state subjects the organization to the jurisdiction of one or more other states. There is as yet no law directly on this subject. Nonetheless, while not directly on point, a court opinion sheds some light on the matter.

A federal court of appeals had the opportunity to discuss the legal status of computer-borne communications in the First Amendment context. Two individuals operated an adult-oriented bulletin board service from their home. This site was accessible to others around the nation via modems and telephone lines.

Working with a U.S. Attorney's office in another state, a postal inspector purchased a membership in this bulletin board service and succeeded in downloading allegedly obscene images from the bulletin board. The U.S. Attorney's office filed criminal charges against these individuals for, among other reasons, transmitting obscenity over interstate telephone lines from their computer. The images involved were found by a jury to constitute obscene materials; the couple was convicted.

On appeal, this federal appellate court affirmed the convictions, holding that the crime of "knowingly us[ing] a facility or means of interstate commerce for the purpose of distributing obscene materials" did not require proof that the defendants had specific knowledge of the destination of each transmittal at the time it occurred. Of interest in the Internet setting, in determining that the crime occurred in the second state, the court placed considerable weight on its finding that "substantial evidence introduced at trial demonstrated that the . . . [bulletin board service] was set up so members located in other jurisdictions could access and order [obscene] files which would then be instantaneously transmitted in interstate commerce."

If the reasoning of this appellate court is followed by state courts, it appears that communication via computer constitutes sufficient contact with foreign states to subject the communicator to local law requirements. Applied in the charitable solicitation regulation context, then, the import of this court decision is clear: Soliciting funds by means of the Internet, where users residing in foreign jurisdictions download Web pages, in all likelihood will constitute sufficient contact to subject the organization to the jurisdiction of the foreign state or states and therefore to the foreign charitable solicitation regulatory regime or regimes.

It must next be determined whether interstate communication of this nature constitutes solicitation encompassed by the fundraising regulation laws of the states. Although a definite answer cannot be divined from the language of any one statute, a brief survey of some state laws strongly indicates that Internet solicitation will be held in many jurisdictions to be subject to regulation.

For example, in one state, solicitation embraced by the charitable solicitation act is defined as the making of a fundraising request "through any medium," regardless of whether any contribution is actually received. In another state, the charitable solicitation law applies to all "request[s] of any kind for a contribution." In another state, the law encompasses "each request for a contribution." The statutory scheme in another state applies to "any request, plea, entreaty, demand or invitation, or attempt thereof, to give money or property, in connection with which . . . any appeal is made for charitable purposes." In still another state, the law applies to organizations "soliciting or collecting by agents or solicitors, upon ways or in any other public places within the [state] to which the public have a right of access."

Certainly it is difficult to see how Internet fundraising is not caught by any of these strikingly broad provisions. As currently written, then, the statutes of at least five states can easily be construed to reach Internet charitable fundraising.

Indeed, it is likely that most, if not all, of the state charitable fundraising regulation regimes may be so construed and that these statutes that fail as currently written can be appropriately amended without much trouble.

Charleston Principles

If the assumption is that the solicitation of funds (and perhaps other property) by charitable and other nonprofit organizations by means of the Internet constitutes, as a matter of law, fundraising in every state (and municipality), then, as suggested, the charitable community is facing an enormous burden. Many in the regulatory sector realize that, if this technically is the law, some form of relief for charities that solicit gifts by means of the Internet is warranted.

To this end, the National Association of State Charity Officials (NASCO) developed guidelines to assist state regulators, charitable organizations that solicit contributions, and their fundraisers, in deciding whether it is necessary to register fundraising efforts in one or more states when the solicitations are made by e-mail or on the organizations' websites. These guidelines are a product of discussion initiated at a NASCO conference in Charleston, South Carolina; hence the guidelines are termed the "Charleston Principles" ("Principles"). The Principles are not law but, rather, nonbinding guidance to NASCO members.

The Principles rest on this proposition: "Existing registration statutes generally, of their own terms, encompass and apply to Internet solicitations." An unstated assumption is that it is untenable to require registration and reporting of all charities soliciting gifts solely by means of the Internet, and their fundraisers, in all of the states with reporting requirements. Thus, the scope of potential registration must be narrowed or, as the Principles put it, state charity officials should "address the issue of who has to register where."

The Principles differentiate between entities that are domiciled in a state and those that are domiciled outside the state. (An entity is domiciled in a state if its principal place of business is in that state.)

An entity that is domiciled in a state and uses the Internet to conduct charitable solicitations in that state must, according to the Principles, register in that state. This position reflects the prevailing view that the Internet is a form of communication and the law does not make a distinction between that type of communication and another (such as use of regular mail). The rule applies "without regard to whether the Internet solicitation methods it uses are passive or interactive, maintained by itself or another entity with which it contracts, or whether it conducts solicitations in any other manner."

Matters become more complex in situations where an entity is fundraising, using the Internet, in a state in which it is not domiciled. Registration in the state is nonetheless required if:

- The organization's non-Internet activities alone are sufficient to require registration;
- It solicits contributions through an interactive Web site; and
- The entity
  - Specifically targets persons physically located in the state for solicitation, or
  - Receives contributions from donors in the state on a repeated and ongoing basis or a substantial basis through its Web site, or
  - The entity solicits contributions through a site that is not interactive but either specifically invites further offline activity to complete a contribution or establishes other contacts with that state, such as sending e-mail messages or other communications that promote the Web site, and the entity engages in one of the foregoing two activities.

Often considerable line drawing will be required in the application of these guidelines. The matter becomes more intricate when some definitions are factored in.

An interactive Web site is a site that "permits a contributor to make a contribution, or purchase a product in connection with a charitable solicitation, by electronically completing the transaction, such as by submitting credit card information or authorizing an electronic funds transfer." These sites include those through which a donor "may complete a transaction online through any online mechanism processing a financial transaction even if completion requires the use of linked or redirected sites." A Web site is considered interactive if it has this capacity, irrespective of whether donors actually use it.

The phrase *specifically target persons physically located in the state for solicitation* means to engage in one of two practices:

1. Include on the Web site an express or implied reference to soliciting contributions from persons in that state.
2. Otherwise affirmatively appeal to residents of the state, such as by advertising or sending messages to persons located in the state (electronically or otherwise) when the entity knows, or reasonably should know, that the recipient is physically located in the state.

Charities operating on a "purely local basis," or within a "limited geographic area," do not target states outside their operating area if their Web site makes clear in context that their fundraising focus is limited to that area, even if they receive contributions from outside that area on less than a repeated and ongoing basis or on a substantial basis.

To receive contributions from a state on a repeated and ongoing basis or a substantial basis means "receiving contributions within the entity's fiscal year, or relevant portion of a fiscal year, that are of sufficient volume to establish the regular or significant (as opposed to rare, isolated, or insubstantial) nature of these contributions."

States are encouraged to set, and communicate to the regulated entities, "numerical [sic] levels at which it [sic] will regard this criterion as satisfied." These levels should, the Principles provide, define *repeated and ongoing* in terms of a number of contributions and substantial in terms of a total dollar amount of contributions or percentage of total contributions received by or on behalf of the charity. The meeting of one of these thresholds would give rise to a registration requirement but would not limit an enforcement action for deceptive solicitations.

Another Principle is that an entity that solicits via e-mail in a particular state is to be treated the same as one that solicits by means of telephone or direct mail, if the soliciting party knew or reasonably should have known that the recipient was a resident of or was physically located in that state.

The Principles address the circumstance as to whether a charity is required to register in a particular state when the operator of a website, through which contributions for that charity are solicited or received, is required to register but the charity does not independently satisfy the registration criteria. If the law of the state does not universally require the registration of all charities on whose behalf contributions are solicited or received through a commercial fundraiser, commercial co-venturer, or fundraising counsel who is required to register, then the state should independently apply the criteria to each charity and only require registration by charities that independently meet the tests. If, however, the law of the state universally requires registration of all charities under these circumstances, the state should consider whether, as a matter of "prosecutorial discretion, public policy, and the prioritized use of limited resources," it would take action to enforce registration requirements as to charities that do not independently meet the criteria.

Still another Principle is that solicitations for the sale of a product or service that include a representation that some portion of the price shall be devoted to a charitable organization or charitable purpose (commercial co-venturing, charitable sales promotion, or cause-related marketing) shall be governed by the same standards as otherwise set out in the Principles governing charitable solicitations.

There are two exclusions from the registration requirements. One is that maintaining or operating a Web site that does not contain a solicitation of contributions but merely provides program services by means of the Internet does not, by itself, invoke a requirement to register. This is the case even if unsolicited contributions are received.

The other exclusion is for entities that solely provide administrative, supportive, or technical services to charities without providing substantive content or advice concerning substantive content; they are not required to register. These entities include Internet service providers and organizations that do no more than process online transactions for a separate firm that operates a website or provide similar services. This exclusion does not encompass professional fundraisers, fundraising counsel, or commercial co-venturers.

The Principles provide that state charity officials "recognize that the burden of compliance by charitable organizations and their agents, professional fundraisers, commercial co-venturers and/or professional fundraising counsel should be kept reasonable in relation to the benefits to the public achieved by registration." Projects to create "common forms," such as the unified registration statement, are "strongly encouraged."

State charity offices are also "strongly encouraged" to publish their registration and reporting forms, their laws and regulations, and other related information on the Internet to facilitate registration and reporting by charitable organizations and their agents.

The Principles encourage development of information technology infrastructure to facilitate electronic registration and reporting. Also encouraged is Internet posting by charitable organizations of their application for recognition of tax-exempt status, their IRS determination letter, their most recent annual information returns, and their state registration statement(s). (This posting practice is also encouraged by the federal tax law, which obviates the need to provide hard copies of these federal documents to requestors when they are made available on the Internet (see Chapter 4).)

SUMMARY

One of the most frustrating bodies of law pestering charitable organizations is fundraising regulation by the federal and state governments. This chapter summarized the components of a typical state charitable solicitation act, and provides an analysis of the clash between constitutional law principles and the states' police power. This chapter also summarized the law regulating professional fundraisers, paid solicitors, and commercial co-venturers. The chapter further summarized the many ways the federal tax law regulates the charitable fundraising process. The chapter concluded by analyzing fundraising by means of the Internet—and the host of new legal issues that are being raised.

CHAPTER 9

Building on the Basics

The purpose of this chapter is to build on the law summarized in the previous chapters by addressing the principal ways in which tax-exempt organizations can bring more structure, protection, and sophistication to their operations. Certainly for the larger exempt organizations, one entity often is insufficient. Tax-exempt entities today are finding creative and productive uses of subsidiaries, partnerships, limited liability companies, and other joint ventures. Specifically, this chapter will:

- Summarize the fundamentals of bifurcation
- Review the rules concerning tax-exempt and taxable subsidiaries
- Summarize the law pertaining to public charities in partnerships
- Focus on the use by exempt organizations of limited liability companies
- Address the legal consequences of exempt organizations' involvement in other joint ventures
- Summarize the rules concerning the tax treatment of revenue from controlled entities
- Review the rules as to liquidation of for-profit subsidiaries

FUNDAMENTALS OF BIFURCATION

The word *bifurcation* essentially means the separation of something into two parts. Many tax-exempt organizations find that their operations are enhanced (although not necessarily simplified) by the use of two organizations instead of one. Indeed, this phenomenon is not confined to a division of functions but may extend to utilization of three or four, or perhaps tens, of organizations. As to the former, there may be an association with a related foundation and political action committee. The latter is illustrated by a health care or university system.

From a law standpoint, the creation and maintenance of a fruitful parent–subsidiary relationship require a variety of elements. One is that the new entities must have real and substantial business functions. This means that there must be some substance as to their operations. Also, success of a venture necessitates a certain degree of separation of the entities, in terms of both governance and operational structure, and form. Overall, from the federal tax law viewpoint, it is essential that the substance and independence of the entities are respected. This outcome is critical when the parent is a nonprofit, tax-exempt entity and the subsidiary is a for-profit, taxable one; it is usually desirable when the subsidiary is also a tax-exempt organization, particularly where the exemptions of the two entities are based on different tax law provisions.

If the extent of control and management is inordinate, in that the parent organization's control of the affairs of the subsidiary is so pervasive that the latter is merely an extension of the former, the subsidiary may not be respected—by the IRS or a court—as a separate entity. In extreme situations, the parent–subsidiary relationship is regarded as a sham and consequently ignored for tax purposes. With this outcome, the tax consequences (undesirable from a planning standpoint) are that the two entities are deemed to be one.

All of this pivots on the element of day-to-day management: If the parent organization is involved in the day-to-day management of the subsidiary organization, the two are likely to be treated as one entity. The factors that determine these conclusions are the identity and overlap of officers and employees, location(s) of operations, office sharing, and co-investing. Also important is record keeping (as to expenses and time allocations) and contracts between the organizations (such as for cost reimbursement and/or rental arrangements). Nonetheless, IRS rulings illustrate the fact that close and intertwined operations do not necessarily defeat tax planning in connection with a parent–subsidiary structure.

In one instance, a tax-exempt organization established a for-profit subsidiary to serve as the sole general partner in a limited partnership (as to both topics, see discussions later in this chapter), to limit legal liability for claims to the assets of the two organizations, and to isolate exempt functions from unrelated business activities (see Chapter 7). The exempt organization elected all of the directors of the subsidiary; no more than three of the seven members of the subsidiary's board of directors were also members of the board of the exempt organization. The subsidiary rented office space and purchased professional services from the parent; the two organizations shared employees. The two entities shared investment leads and made joint investments, and the subsidiary generally had, in the words of the IRS, a "close working relationship" with the parent organization. Both organizations maintained separate accounting and corporate records. The IRS ruled that this subsidiary had a "separate corporate existence and business purpose" and that the tax-exempt parent did not "actively participate" in the day-to-day management of the subsidiary, so that the subsidiary was not regarded as a mere instrumentality of the parent and the "corporate existence" of the subsidiary would not be disregarded for federal tax purposes.

This ruling takes the two organizations to the edge of permissibility in this context. To reiterate: (1) the two organizations share office space, (2) the subsidiary purchases administrative and professional services from the parent, (3) the subsidiary reimburses the parent for the services of some of the parent's employees, (4) the two organizations share "investment leads" and co-invest, and (5) the parent and subsidiary "maintain a close working relationship." This ruling reflects a most munificent view of the facts by the IRS and illustrate how closely a tax-exempt organization and its subsidiary (in this instance, a for-profit one) can operate in tandem without crossing the line into attribution and causing the exempt entity to become entangled in what the IRS termed the *daily operations* of the subsidiary.

The tax consequences of a finding that a parent–subsidiary relationship will not be respected for federal tax purposes can be enormous. A large unrelated business in the subsidiary could cause the parent to lose its tax-exempt status if the subsidiary is treated as a mere instrumentality of the parent (i.e., the relationship is regarded as a sham). The same adverse outcome could result if the parent is a charitable entity and lobbying activities (see Chapter 4) in the subsidiary are attributed to it. By contrast, if both the parent and the subsidiary are charitable organizations, the collapsing of operations presumably would not trigger any adverse tax consequences—and thus there is little likelihood that attribution would be imposed.

DEFINITION OF SUBSIDIARY

A *subsidiary organization* is an entity that is controlled by another organization, with that other entity often termed the *parent organization*. Thus, the element of *control* is built into the definition of the term—the subsidiary organization is subordinate or supplementary to the parent entity. By contrast, organizations can be *related* or *affiliated* without the presence of a control relationship.

The control relationship can be manifested in several ways. There are, however, essentially three choices:

1. *Interlocking directorate.* One way for an organization to control another one is by means of the origin and composition of the subsidiary's governing board. That is, an organization can be the parent of another organization by having the power to determine who constitutes at least a majority of the other organization's board of directors or trustees. There are many mechanisms for achieving this; here are the common ones:
   - The board of the parent organization appoints at least a majority of the board of the subsidiary organization.
   - Individuals holding certain positions with the parent organization (such as officers) are members of the board of the subsidiary organization by virtue of those positions (termed *ex officio* positions), with those positions representing at least a majority of the subsidiary's board.
   - There may be a blend of the foregoing options.
   - The members of the board of the parent organization are also members of the board of the subsidiary organization (complete overlap).
2. *Membership.* The subsidiary organization can be organized as a membership organization, with the parent entity serving as the sole member of the subsidiary. The member is responsible for selecting the board of the subsidiary.
3. *Stock.* The subsidiary organization can be organized as a

stock-based corporation, with the parent organization owning a majority or all of the stock of the subsidiary entity. The stockholder is responsible for selecting the board of the subsidiary.

The federal tax law generally is silent on this subject. Tax-exempt organizations are generally free to structure parent–subsidiary relationships as they wish, subject to the particulars of state law. For example, it is rare for a state to allow the formation of a nonprofit organization as a stock-based corporation. At the federal level, one of the few pronouncements of the law on this point is that disqualified persons may not control supporting organizations.

DETERMINING NEED FOR SUBSIDIARY

Conceptually, the principal reasons a tax-exempt organization may desire to utilize one or more subsidiaries is that a facet of the law and/or a management consideration suggests or requires it.

A nontax law reason (although one with legal overtones) for using a subsidiary is to avoid or minimize legal liability on the part of the parent organization. That is, the parent–subsidiary relationship will (or is intended to) insulate assets in the two entities from liability that may be incurred by the parent.

The chief tax law reasons for the creation of a subsidiary are (1) to house in the subsidiary organization an activity in which the parent organization may not or should not engage, and (2) to enhance the parent's operations by use of a subsidiary. Thus, for example, deployment of a subsidiary may be used to preserve the tax-exempt status of the parent. The types of activities that are commonly spun off to or incubated in a subsidiary (particularly by a charitable organization) are unrelated business, attempts to influence legislation, and political campaign efforts.

Another tax law use for a subsidiary is its function as a partner in a limited partnership or limited liability company (discussed later). A for-profit entity may be used to attract capital and/or create assets (stock).

Management considerations (as contrasted with law ones) often lead to a decision to place the fundraising function of a tax-exempt organization and/or one or more program activities of an exempt organization in a subsidiary organization. The latter approach may lead to deductibility of contributions and/or access to grant funding that would not otherwise be available.

Where the parent tax-exempt organization is not a charitable entity, placement of the fundraising function in a separate foundation is nearly essential. In this fashion, as noted, contributions and grants can be attracted to support the charitable programs within the entity; without the separate charitable organization, this type of gift support would not be available because of the absence of eligibility for the charitable contribution deduction. Once the two entities are operational, one of two models (or, perhaps, a blend of the two) can be selected. Pursuant to one approach, all of the charitable activities are placed in the charitable organization and the fundraising supports these activities. Under the other approach, the charitable activities remain in the parent organization; the fundraising entity makes restricted grants to the parent organization in support of these programs.

Bifurcation involving fundraising, where both entities are tax-exempt charitable organizations, is a classic example of the use of a subsidiary primarily for nonlaw reasons. (Where the two organizations are charitable, contributions to either of them are deductible.) This type of bifurcation is predicated on two factors: fundraising usually is not program and the fundraising function often is best separated from the overall governance function. With a related fundraising foundation, there can be a board of directors (or trustees) that has fundraising as it sole concern and function. Board members of the parent organization may be averse to fundraising; others relish the opportunity. By means of bifurcation, the fundraising function is placed in an entity where those who direct it know that fundraising (not the organization's governance) is their responsibility.

Allocation of programs between two exempt charitable programs may be appropriate, depending on the facts and circumstances of the particular case. Generalizations as to which of these types of bifurcation is suitable are not possible; much depends on the personalities and politics involved.

A subsidiary may be essential to maximizing an income flow or creating a more favorable (from a tax law standpoint) type of income. Thus, for example, a tax-exempt educational organization was ruled to be able to, without adversely affecting its exempt status, create and wholly own (and receive tax-free licensing income from) a for-profit subsidiary formed to maximize for membership and business purposes what would otherwise be the organization's Web site. Likewise, a medical research organization formed a supporting organization that, in turn, created a for-profit subsidiary to facilitate the transfer of technology incubated in the research organization. Following commercialization of the technology, the for-profit subsidiary will provide tax-free royalty income to the research organization.

The spin-off approach, as opposed to the incubation approach, may not be appropriate. For example, this election is not available in the case of an association that must utilize a political action committee to avoid tax (see Chapter 10). In other situations, an activity can begin as a function of the exempt organization and be transferred to a subsidiary when and if the activity expands to the point where the spin-off is desirable or necessary. Thus, the lobbying activity of a public charity may be appropriately transferred to a controlled social welfare organization if that activity increases beyond the bounds of insubstantiality. Similarly, an unrelated business of a tax-exempt may have to be moved to a subsidiary if it becomes too extensive to be conducted within the exempt organization.

LEGAL FORM OF SUBSIDIARY

Once the decision is made to create and use a subsidiary, the question as to its form may arise. If the subsidiary entity is to be a tax-exempt organization, the choices as to form generally are nonprofit corporation, trust, or unincorporated association. If the subsidiary organization is to be a taxable entity, the choices as to form generally are a regular (C) corporation, small business (S) corporation, or limited liability company.

The factors that dictate the nature of the subsidiary include the following:

- The value of or need for tax exemption for the subsidiary
- The motives of those involved in the enterprise (such as a profit motive)
- The desirability of creating an asset (such as stock that may appreciate in value and/or serve as the means for transfer of ownership) for equity owners of the enterprise
- The compensation arrangements contemplated for employees (including deferred and retirement compensation)

TAX-EXEMPT SUBSIDIARIES

It is common, in a parent–subsidiary relationship, for the parent entity and the subsidiary entity to both be tax-exempt organizations. An illustration of this type of in-tandem arrangement is the supporting organization (see Chapter 3).

Choice of Form

The form of the tax-exempt subsidiary is essentially the same as that selected by its parent: nonprofit corporation, trust, or unincorporated association (see Chapter 1). For the most part, the form of both organizations is likely to be a nonprofit corporation.

Bifurcation Revisited

The elements as to successful bifurcation usually apply when both organizations are tax-exempt. For example, the exempt charitable organization does not want the activities of its exempt lobbying subsidiary to be attributed to it for tax purposes, nor does the exempt business league want the functions of its exempt political action committee attributed to it. Where both organizations are exempt charitable entities, the adverse tax consequences of attribution are minimized, although in most instances attribution should be avoided (if only for management purposes).

Common Relationships

Following are the most common forms of these relationships when an exempt charitable organization is the parent (see Chapter 2 for an inventory of types of exempt organizations):

- *A charitable organization with an exempt social welfare organization as the (or a) subsidiary.* The function of this subsidiary probably is lobbying (see Chapter 10).
- *A charitable organization with an exempt business league as its subsidiary.* The function of the subsidiary may be a certification program.

Following are the most common forms of these relationships when an exempt charitable organization is the subsidiary:

- *An exempt business league with a charitable foundation.* This subsidiary, which is likely to be a supporting organization, conducts charitable, educational, and/or scientific programs; may engage in fundraising activities and/or maintain an endowment; and/or own real property.
- *An exempt social welfare organization with a charitable foundation.* This entity is structured and functions much like the charitable foundation associated with a business league.
- *Another type of noncharitable tax-exempt organization with a charitable foundation.* These exempt parent organizations include labor organizations, agricultural organizations, social clubs, fraternal organizations, and veterans' organizations. Again, the functions of this type of subsidiary are likely to be the same as previously described. The subsidiary is likely to be, in cases involving labor and agricultural organizations, a supporting organization.
- *A foreign charitable organization with an exempt U.S.-based charitable entity.* This subsidiary, usually a fundraising organization (to facilitate deductibility of contributions), is also likely to be a supporting organization.
- *An exempt charitable organization (parent) with an exempt charitable organization (subsidiary).* The function of this type of charitable organization subsidiary will probably be fundraising, holding and growing one or more endowment funds, and/or operating one or more programs. As before, this type of subsidiary is likely to be a supporting organization.

As to supporting organizations, it is important to reiterate that there are different types of these entities. Only one of these types is the parent-subsidiary model. The brother–sister model can, however, look much like the parent–subsidiary structure. With the operated in connection with approach, a supporting organization can function without being formally controlled by one or more supported organizations.

The following tax-exempt organizations are subsidiary organizations, with the parent exempt organization potentially one of a wide variety of tax-exempt organizations:

- Political organizations
- Title-holding companies
- Employee benefit funds

FOR-PROFIT SUBSIDIARIES

Nearly all types of tax-exempt organizations may utilize a for-profit, taxable subsidiary. This is, however, less common than use of a tax-exempt subsidiary, with the issues in play nonetheless often more complex.

Choice of Form

The taxable subsidiary of a tax-exempt organization is likely to be a corporation. Here, some of the interests of the exempt parent organization and those of the subsidiary may diverge. The exempt organization presumably would want the subsidiary to be a regular (C) corporation, so that the resulting income would be in the form of tax-free dividends. Those involved with the subsidiary may want it to be a small business (S) corporation or a limited liability company so as to avoid double taxation. The exempt organization (here, only a charitable one), however, should avoid use of an S corporation, if only because all resulting income and gain are automatically considered unrelated business income (see Chapter 7). It should be cautious when contemplating use of a limited liability company (discussed under "Partnerships and Joint Venture Basics"), because the exempt organization's share of income (whatever its nature) is automatically passed along to it (either in actuality or for tax purposes).

Another choice is the taxable nonprofit corporation. These entities are taxed the same as the for-profit corporation, yet it may prove advantageous for the parent exempt entity to have its subsidiary cast as a nonprofit organization.

In nearly all instances, the function of this type of subsidiary is to house one or more businesses that are, in relation to the exempt organization involved, unrelated businesses.

Capitalization

Although there is no specific law on the point, a tax-exempt organization should give serious consideration as to the amount of capital contributed to a taxable subsidiary. This is particularly the case where the parent is a charitable entity; charitable dollars are thus being applied for noncharitable purposes (albeit it in a controlled organization). The best guiding standard in this regard is that of the prudent investor.

Accumulations

A nonprofit organization may find that its subsidiary has accumulated a substantial amount of assets, due to successful business activity and/or investment performance. At some point, the IRS may contend that these accumulations are evidence of a substantial nonexempt purpose.

It is the view of the agency that, in situations involving tax-exempt organizations, the entities "bear a very heavy burden" to demonstrate, by "contemporaneous and clear evidence," that they have plans for the use of substantial assets for exempt purposes. "This growth [of assets in a subsidiary] presents a continuing obligation," the IRS has said, on the organization to "translate this valuable asset into funds, and use these funds for the expansion" of its exempt activities. The IRS suggests that some of the subsidiary's assets be sold or a portion of the subsidiary's stock be sold, with the proceeds used to fund programs. The "highest priority" should be given to repayment by the subsidiary of any loans made by the exempt organization; these funds too can be devoted to exempt ends. The IRS's lawyers said that the organization "cannot be allowed to focus its energies on expanding its subsidiary's commercial business and assets, and neglect to translate that financial success into specific, definite and feasible plans for the expansion" of its exempt activities.

An IRS pronouncement concluded that the "fact that the assets are being accumulated in a for-profit company under the formal legal control of [a tax-exempt organization] does not excuse [the exempt organization] from using such assets" for exempt purposes. This analysis ended with this sweeping pronouncement: "Excess accumulations maintained in a subsidiary entity under legal control of the exempt organization, but under the de facto control of the founder, are deemed to be for the founder's personal purposes if no exempt purpose is documented or implemented."

Bifurcation Revisited

The elements as to successful bifurcation certainly apply when the parent organization is tax-exempt and the subsidiary is a taxable entity. In this setting, it is almost always critical that the activities of the subsidiary are not attributed to the parent. Even in the best of circumstances, treatment of this type of subsidiary as an instrumentality of the parent is likely to result in unrelated business income to the parent.

Thus, the properly managed tax-exempt organization is cautious when organizing and operating a taxable subsidiary, so as not to be placed in a position where it is cast (or perceived) as being involved in the day-to-day management of the subsidiary, so that the subsidiary is disregarded for tax purposes. Following are the principal elements to be taken into account in assessing these situations:

- Overlap of board directors (This element is of lesser concern because control is assumed; at the same time, control is manifested by means of stock, so there is no need to have a complete or majority interlock of directors.)
- Overlap of officers
- Overlap of employees
- Sharing of office space, furniture, and/or equipment
- Co-investment arrangements
- Other circumstances that indicate undue involvement by the parent in the daily operations of the subsidiary

Liquidations

If a taxable subsidiary liquidates and distributes its assets to its tax-exempt parent, the general rule is that the distribution is treated for tax purposes as though the assets are being sold to the parent organization. This means that, to the extent these assets are capital assets, there is potential for exposure to the tax on capital gains.

There are other noteworthy elements of these rules:

- If a capital asset transferred in this fashion is used by the parent in an unrelated business, capital gains taxation is not triggered (as long as the asset is used in that manner).
- The rules as to liquidation are basically the same, irrespective of whether the liquidating entity is a subsidiary of the transferee.
- These rules generally apply when a taxable entity *converts* (assuming that is permissible under state law) to a tax-exempt organization.
- In a situation where the transferee is *not* the parent of the liquidating entity, there are exceptions that may need to be considered.

- Where these exceptions are applicable, the IRS is requiring the organization to file an application for recognition of tax-exempt status, even though the tax regulations expressly provide that the application does not have to be filed if it is not otherwise required (see Chapter 2).

TAX TREATMENT OF REVENUE FROM SUBSIDIARY

Most tax-exempt organizations develop an unrelated business with the anticipation that it will serve as a source of revenue. If the unrelated business is conducted in and by means of a subsidiary, presumably a revenue flow to the parent is likewise desired.

Generally, passive income received by tax-exempt organizations is not taxable as unrelated business income (see Chapter 7). A major exception to this rule pertains to the receipt of certain income by an exempt parent organization from a subsidiary. That is, interest, rent, annuity, or royalty payments made by a controlled entity to an exempt organization are includable in the exempt organization's unrelated business income (other than in the rare instance where the revenue is from an exempt function) and are subject to the unrelated business income tax to the extent the payment reduces the net unrelated income (or increases any net unrelated loss) of the controlled entity (determined as if the entity were tax-exempt).

A controlled entity is a taxable or tax-exempt subsidiary that is at least 50 percent controlled by the parent tax-exempt organization. In the case of a stock-based subsidiary, control means ownership by vote or value of 50 percent or more of the stock. In the case of a partnership or other entity, control means ownership of 50 percent or more of the profits, capital, or beneficial interests. Moreover, there are constructive ownership rules by which a parent exempt organization is deemed to control an entity indirectly, such as in the case of a second-tier subsidiary.

PARTNERSHIPS AND JOINT VENTURE BASICS

A partnership is a form of business entity, recognized in the law as a separate legal organization, as is a corporation or trust. It is usually evidenced by a document (partnership agreement). The term *joint venture* is broader than, and subsumes, the concept of a partnership. There can be a joint venture without establishment of an entity and without a document signifying it; indeed, the joint venture form can be imposed on parties in particular factual circumstances, even contrary to their intent and wish. A joint venture can, however, be a formal legal entity other than a partnership; the best example of this is the *limited liability company*.

The parties to a partnership are *partners*. Parties to another type of joint venture, including a limited liability company, are *members*.

Partnerships

Partnerships basically are of two types. This delineation largely turns on the nature of the partners, who can be *general* or *limited*. Generally, liability for the consequences of a partnership's operations rests with the general partner or partners, while the exposure to liability (if any) for the functions of the partnership for the limited partners is confined to the amount of the limited partner's or partners' contribution(s) to the partnership.

The partnership that has only general partners is the general partnership. In this type of partnership, the interests of the general partners may or may not be equal. These partners are generally equally liable for satisfaction of the obligations of the partnership and can be called on to make additional capital contributions to the entity.

Capital in a partnership can be derived from investors, namely, limited partners. A limited partner is in the venture not to control and administer the underlying business but to obtain a return on investment and perhaps to procure some income tax advantages. A partnership with both general and limited partners is termed a limited partnership.

A tax-exempt organization may be a general partner or limited partner in a partnership. Nearly all of the federal tax law on this point pertains to public charities functioning as a general partner in a limited partnership.

Joint Ventures

A *joint venture* is an association of two or more persons with intent to carry out a business enterprise for joint profit, for which purpose they combine their efforts, property, money, skill, and knowledge. Often, as noted, this arrangement is something less than a formal legal entity such as a partnership.

There are three types of joint ventures:

1. One or more of the venturers places itself, in its entirety, in the venture.
2. One or more of the venturers places a primary portion of its operations in the venture.
3. One or more of the venturers places a small portion of its operations in the venture.

From the standpoint of the law of tax-exempt organizations, the first type of these joint ventures is the whole entity joint venture. This arrangement started in the health care context and is thus known in that setting as the whole hospital joint venture. The second and third of these joint ventures is the ancillary joint venture. Thus, a tax-exempt organization can be a participant in a joint venture.

Limited Liability Companies

A limited liability company is a legal entity that has some of the attributes of a corporation (e.g., limitations as to legal liability for persons other than the entity) and (as the consequence of an election) some of the characteristics of a partnership (principally, taxation as a partnership).

A limited liability company may have two or more members. If state law permits, a limited liability company may have only one member. A single-member liability company generally is disregarded for federal income tax purposes. A tax-exempt organization may be a member of either type of limited liability company.

FLOW-THROUGH ENTITIES

Partnerships and other joint venture entities are, for federal income tax purposes, *flow-through entities*. This means that these entities are not taxpaying organizations—rather, they are conduits of net revenue (and perhaps other items) to the partners or members, who bear the responsibility for the payment of tax on their net income.

For tax-exempt organizations, the receipt of income from a joint venture raises issues as to unrelated business income taxation (and, in some instances, ongoing eligibility for exempt status). In resolving these issues, a look-through rule is used. Pursuant to that rule, if a business regularly carried on by a partnership or other joint venture, of which an exempt organization is a member, is an unrelated business with respect to the organization, in computing its unrelated business income the organization must include its share of the gross income of the venture. Likewise, if the business in the venture is a related one as to the organization, the resulting income is treated as exempt function revenue. Thus, in application of the look-through rule, the business conducted by the joint venture is evaluated to determine what the outcome would be if the exempt organization directly conducted the business.

The IRS and the courts apply an aggregate approach rule in this context. This means that, when the eligibility for tax-exempt status of the nonprofit organization is being evaluated (anew or on an ongoing basis) because of its involvement in a joint venture, the activities of the organization and the activities of the venture in which the organization is a partner or member are taken into consideration.

PUBLIC CHARITIES AS GENERAL PARTNERS

The concern of the IRS with the matter of public charities as general partners in limited partnerships has been and continues to be that the resources of a charitable organization are being used to provide substantial benefits to the for-profit participants in the partnership (usually the limited partners). The issue, then, is eligibility for tax-exempt status when a public charity is engaged in this endeavor.

A three-step analysis is used in this context; where they are satisfied, exemption is allowed or is preserved:

1. Does the public charity's involvement in the partnership further a charitable purpose?
2. Does the partnership agreement reflect an arrangement that permits the exempt organization to act primarily in furtherance of its exempt (charitable) purposes? That is, does the organization's role as general partner preclude or deter it from advancing its exempt ends?
3. Does the arrangement cause the exempt organization to

provide an impermissible private benefit to the limited partners?

Involvement in a limited partnership by a public charity as a general partner is almost always in furtherance of charitable ends. The principal rationales for such a participation in a partnership are the raising of needed capital, the creation of new programs, the sharing of a risk inherent in a new exempt activity, and/or the pooling of diverse areas of expertise.

The second criterion looks to means by which the exempt organization may, under the particular facts and circumstances, be insulated from the day-to-day responsibilities as general partner. This element of the equation is conceptually difficult: once an entity is a general partner in a partnership, it cannot escape the responsibility and potential liability of that position.

The third criterion is met where the economic benefits to the limited partners are reasonable. Elements to avoid in this regard include disproportionate allocation of profits and/or losses in favor of the limited partners, commercially unreasonable loans by the exempt organization to the partnership, insufficient capital contributions by the limited partners, and guarantees to the limited partners (such as in connection with return on investment or projected tax credits) by the exempt organization.

SUBSIDIARIES IN PARTNERSHIPS

One use of a subsidiary by a tax-exempt organization is its participation as a partner in a partnership, in lieu of participation in the partnership by the parent exempt organization. One reason to do this is to avoid endangering the exempt status of the parent entity. (A single-member limited liability company may also be used for this purpose.)

This can be an effective stratagem as long as all of the requirements of the law as to the bona fides of the subsidiary are satisfied, including the requirement that the subsidiary organization be an authentic business entity. As discussed, however, if the tax-exempt organization parent is intimately involved in the day-to-day management of the subsidiary, the IRS or a court may impute the activities of the subsidiary to the parent, thereby possibly jeopardizing the exempt status of the parent by treating it as if it were directly involved as a partner in the partnership.

WHOLE ENTITY JOINT VENTURES

As noted, an exempt organization is a participant in a whole entity joint venture when it places itself, in its entirety, in the venture. The law to date concerns only public charities in this type of arrangement; the participation in the venture becomes the charitable organization's sole activity. A for-profit entity usually is the other venturer. The joint venture vehicle is likely to be a limited liability company.

The key issue in this context is the element of control. That is, the IRS and the courts will look to see whether the charity, by involving itself in this type of venture, lost control of its resources to the for-profit co-venturer. The phraseology often used is determination as to whether the exempt organization "ceded its authority" over its operations to the other venturer. Elements to be considered are the composition of the board of the limited liability company and whether the arrangement is managed by a for-profit management company that is affiliated with the for-profit co-venturer. Tax-exempt status is forgone where this control is forfeited by the charitable organization.

As noted, the law on this subject has unfolded to date in the health care setting. In one case where tax exemption was lost, the court termed the public charity's involvement "passive participation in a for-profit health-service enterprise." The for-profit participant was portrayed as having an "independent economic interest in the same activity," that is, the activity previously conducted solely by the charitable organization. Further, the venture itself had "no obligation to put charitable purposes ahead of profit-making objectives." Exemption was lost because the exempt organization conferred "significant private benefits" on the for-profit party (see Chapter 10).

Consequently, a public charity contemplating involvement in a whole entity joint venture should, to retain tax-exempt status, strive to not lose control over program activities. The composition of the board of the venture and the nature of any management company are, as noted, critical elements. Another factor is documentation: the agreements and other documents involved should stress the powers and functions of the nonprofit organization. Contracts should be negotiated at arm's length. Contracts for services should not have unduly long terms. The partnership documentation should be clear that, should the venturers' interests clash, charitable purposes would trump commercial ends.

ANCILLARY JOINT VENTURES

It is the view of the IRS that the principles involved in the jurisprudence concerning whole entity joint ventures apply fully when an exempt organization is involved in an ancillary joint venture. Thus, the element of control and application of the private benefit doctrine is seen by the agency as likewise applicable in this context. A difference, however, is that, in an instance of an ancillary joint venture, an outcome may be unrelated business income taxation rather than extinguishment of tax exemption.

In one instance, a tax-exempt university entered into a joint venture (a limited liability company) with a for-profit company that specialized in the conduct of interactive video training programs. The sole purpose of the venture was to offer teacher-training seminars at locations off the university's campus using interactive video technology. The university and the for-profit company each held a 50 percent interest in the venture, which was proportionate to the value of their respective capital contributions. All returns of capital, allocations, and distributions were to be made in proportion to the members' respective ownership interests. The company was managed by a governing board composed of three directors selected by the university and three selected by the company. The university retained the exclusive right to approve the curriculum, training materials, and instructors, and to determine the standards for successful completion of the seminars. The company had the exclusive right to select the locations where participants could receive a video link to the seminars and to approve other personnel (such as camera operators).

Under these facts, the IRS concluded that the university retained control over the venture. This guidance is marred, however, because the agency concluded that the (1) business of the venture was related to the exercise of the university's exempt functions and (2) the activities the university conducted through the limited liability company are merely an insubstantial part of its total activities. The private benefit doctrine does not apply where the inappropriate benefit conferred is incidental (see Chapter 10).

It is not clear, therefore, what the outcome is in a situation

such as this, where the business of the venture is unrelated to the
public charity's exempt purposes and/or its involvement is more
than insubstantial. The IRS seemed to indicate that, if the public
charity loses control over its resources in an ancillary joint venture, the business of the venture would be transformed from a related one to an unrelated one—a novel theory. Also, even if the
activities in the ancillary venture are related, if the public charity
cedes authority over the resources to the for-profit venturer and
the exempt organization's participation in the venture is more
than incidental, it would seem that the organization's tax exemption would be jeopardized, by application of the private inurement or private benefit doctrine.

LIMITED LIABILITY COMPANIES

As noted, limited liability companies are of two varieties: the multimember company and the single-member company. The former
is emerging as the joint venture vehicle of choice in the tax-
exempt organizations context.

Multimember LLC

A limited liability company can have two or more members. One
or more of the members may be tax-exempt organizations; there
may be for-profit co-venturers as well. For that matter, all of the
members of a limited liability company may be exempt organizations.

In assessing whether the participation by a charitable organization as a member of a multimember limited liability company,
also consisting of one or more nonexempt persons, will have an
adverse impact of the charitable organization's tax-exempt status,
the criteria previously summarized must be applied. To reiterate,
the tax law outcome will turn on the element of control.

Following are examples of tax-exempt organizations' involvement in a multimember limited liability company involving for-
profit entities:

- An exempt health care system and a group of physicians
  formed a limited liability company for the purpose of owning and operating an ambulatory surgery center.
- An exempt hospital owned and operated six cardiac cathe-

terization laboratories; these facilities were in the hospital's building. The hospital wanted to develop a seventh cardiac catheterization laboratory as an outpatient facility and wanted to involve the physicians who had staff privileges at the institution. The hospital created a limited liability company, consisting of its supporting organization and the physicians, for this purpose.

Following are examples of tax-exempt organizations' involvement in a multimember limited liability company involving only exempt entities:

- An exempt institution of higher education operated two neonatal intensive care units in its capacity as a component of an academic medical center. An exempt hospital also operated a neonatal intensive care unit. The two organizations formed a limited liability company for the purpose of administering the hospital's existing facility, and a new and expanded neonatal intensive care unit.
- Private colleges and universities can maintain their own qualified prepaid tuition plans (see Chapter 2). A single plan was established, structured for use by these colleges and universities throughout the nation; this program was stitched together by means of a consortium agreement. The vehicle for this plan is a limited liability company, with the colleges and universities its members.
- Three trade associations having comparable exempt purposes and members with congruent interests for years operated their own trade shows. To reduce the administrative costs of the shows, the associations created a limited liability company for the purpose of conducting a single trade show.

Single-Member LLC

A limited liability company may be formed with only one member (assuming state law permits); the member may be a tax-exempt organization. This type of entity is disregarded for federal tax purposes. This means that, while the company has the feature as to limitation on liability afforded pursuant to state law, the federal tax law regards the economic activity in the exempt organization and in the limited liability company as conducted in one entity (the exempt organization). Consequently, the exempt organization in this circumstance must report on its annual information return (see Chapter 4) the economic activity, assets, and/or liabilities of the company.

A disregarded limited liability company is treated as a branch or division of its member owner. Thus, although the single-member limited liability company is a separate legal entity for nontax purposes, it is regarded as a component of its owner for federal income tax purposes. The IRS observed that, when the sole member of a limited liability company is a tax-exempt organization, the function of the company is seen as an activity of the exempt organization.

Tax-exempt organizations are making creative use of the single-member limited liability company. Some examples:

- A public charity was working with a city government to transform the older, downtown sections of the city into a center of industry, commerce, housing, transportation, government services, and cultural and educational opportunities. These sections lacked adequate parking due to the completion of several major development projects. The charity organized a single-member limited liability company to address the need for affordable downtown parking; it acquired a parking garage and two parking lots by means of a bond issue. The IRS that the company was a disregarded entity for tax purposes and that its operations would not jeopardize the charity's exempt status because it, by means of the company, was lessening the burdens of the city government (see Chapter 2).

- A charitable organization may accept a gift of property that carries with it exposure of the donee to legal liability (such as environmental or premises tort liability). Before the advent of the single-member limited liability company, a charitable organization could attempt to shield its other assets from liability by placing the gift property in a separate exempt entity, such as a supporting organization (see Chapter 3) or a title-holding company (see Chapter 2). Among the difficulties with this approach is the need or desire to file an application for recognition of tax exemption (see Chapter 2) for the new entity and/or file annual information returns (see Chapter 4) on its behalf. As an alternative, however, a charitable organization can utilize a single-member limited liability company as the vehicle to receive and hold a contribution of this nature. Each of these contributed properties can be placed in a separate single-member limited liability company, thereby offering protection in relation to each of the other gift properties and providing the charity overall liability protection.

- A public charity, with the objective of constructing, owning, and leasing student housing for the benefit of a tax-exempt college, developed and operated the project through a single-member limited liability company. In this fashion it issued taxable and tax-exempt bonds, and provided temporary construction jobs and permanent employment opportunities in the community.
- A private operating foundation (see Chapter 3) took over the operation of a school within a tax-exempt university. The school was suffering financial difficulties; the foundation assumed management and financing of the school. It did so via a single-member limited liability company. (It is not an everyday occurrence for a private foundation to control and actively manage a program component of a public charity.)

SUMMARY

This chapter builds on the basics of the law concerning nonprofit organizations as summarized in the previous chapters. It addressed sophisticated aspects of nonprofit law, such as use of tax-exempt and taxable subsidiaries, involvement of nonprofit organizations in joint ventures, and the exciting emergence of nonprofit organizations' extensive and creative uses of multi-member and single-member limited liability companies. The chapter provided an overview of the controversial topics of whole entity joint ventures and ancillary joint ventures. The chapter also summarized the law concerning public charities as general partners in limited partnerships. It crystallized the rules pertaining to the tax treatment of revenue flowing from a subsidiary to a nonprofit organization. The chapter further reviewed the rules as to liquidation of subsidiaries.

CHAPTER 10

Nonprofit Law Traps

The purpose of this chapter is to inventory the significant traps that potentially await nonprofit organizations as they attempt to comport with federal tax law requirements. These areas of concern include bodies of law pertaining to impermissible private benefits provided by public charities to impermissible forms of advocacy. Specifically, this chapter will summarize the law underlying these significant elements of the tax-exempt organizations rules:

- Primary purpose rule
- Private inurement
- Private benefit
- Intermediate sanctions
- Legislative activities
- Political activities
- Other advocacy activities

PRIMARY PURPOSE RULE

The appropriate category of tax exemption (if any) for a nonprofit organization is dictated by application of the *primary purpose rule*. (Not all nonprofit entities are eligible for tax-exempt status.) Also, an organization's primary purpose can change; this development may cause the organization to evolve into a different type of exempt entity (or, in rare cases, to lose exempt status). The law, however, tolerates incidental nonexempt purposes.

The general rule, as stated by the Supreme Court, is that the "presence of a single . . . [nonexempt] purpose, if substantial in nature, will destroy the exemption regardless of the number or

importance of truly . . . [exempt] purposes." A federal court of
appeals held that nonexempt activity will not result in loss or denial of tax exemption where it is "only incidental and less than
substantial" and that a "slight and comparatively unimportant deviation from the narrow furrow of tax approved activity is not fatal." In the words of the IRS, the rules applicable to charitable organizations in general have been "construed as requiring all the
resources of the organization [other than an insubstantial part]
to be applied to the pursuit of one or more of the [allowable] exempt purposes."

There is no definition of the term *insubstantial* in this context. Thus, application of these rules is an issue of fact to be determined under the facts and circumstances of each case. In
some instances, this is a matter of weighing the relative importance of purposes. For example, an organization with some charitable and educational purposes will not qualify for exemption as a
charitable organization if its predominate purposes are social and
recreational; an organization in this situation will be classified as
a social club (see Chapter 2).

Nonprofit organizations should, therefore, frame their statement of purposes with care. Also, it is prudent to revisit the statement from time to time to be certain that it accurately reflects the
entity's contemporary activities and objectives.

PRIVATE INUREMENT

The doctrine of private inurement, which is the essential principle of law distinguishing nonprofit and for-profit organizations
(see Chapter 1), is applicable to nearly all types of tax-exempt organizations. It is most pronounced and developed, however, for
charitable organizations. By contrast, for a few types of nonprofit
organizations, forms of private benefit are the exempt function.

Charitable Organizations

The federal law of tax exemption for charitable organizations requires that each such entity be organized and operated so that
"no part of . . . [its] net earnings . . . inures to the benefit of any
private shareholder or individual." Literally, this means that the
profits of a charitable organization (and any other type of entity
subject to the doctrine) may not be passed along to individuals or

other persons in their private capacity, in the way that dividends are paid to shareholders. In actual fact, the private inurement rule, as expanded and amplified by the IRS and the courts, means much more.

The contemporary concept of private inurement is broad and wide-ranging. Lawyers for the IRS advised that inurement is "likely to arise where the beneficial benefit represents a transfer of the organization's financial resources to an individual solely by virtue of the individual's relationship with the organization, and without regard to accomplishing exempt purposes." That description is essentially correct for today's private inurement doctrine, but it is a substantial embellishment of the original (and antiquated) statutory rule.

The essence of the private inurement concept is to ensure that a charitable organization is serving public, not private, interests. To be tax-exempt, an organization must establish that it is not organized and operated for the benefit of private interests—designated individuals, the creator of the entity or his or her family, shareholders of the organization, persons controlled (directly or indirectly) by private interests, or any persons having a personal and private interest in the activities of the organization.

Insiders

The federal securities laws that govern for-profit business corporations target the notion of the *insider*—someone who has a special and close relationship with a corporation, frequently because he or she is a director, officer, and/or significant shareholder. Thus, for example, the securities laws prohibit insider trading. The private inurement rules, using the odd phrase *private shareholder or individual*, mirror the concept of the insider.

An insider for private inurement purposes includes an organization's directors, trustees, and officers. It also encompasses key employees, particularly where they have duties or responsibilities normally vested in officers. Further, the family members of insiders and entities controlled by insiders (such as corporations, partnerships, trusts, and estates) are covered. Indeed, the contemporary version of the term *insider* in the exempt organizations context is that it is any person who is in a position to exercise control over a significant portion of the affairs of an organization. It is not necessary that this control in fact be exercised.

The inurement doctrine prohibits a transaction between a tax-exempt organization subject to the rule and a person who is an insider, where the latter is able to cause the organization's net earnings to be turned to private purposes as the result of his, her, or its control or influence. The IRS once observed that, as a general rule, an organization's "trustees, officers, members, founders, or contributors may not, by reason of their position, acquire any of its funds." Stating its view another way, the IRS has rather starkly said that the "prohibition of inurement, in its simplest terms, means that a private shareholder or individual cannot pocket the organization's funds."

Standard of Reasonableness

Persons can receive private benefits in many ways; private inurement can take many forms. Still, a charitable organization may incur ordinary and necessary operating expenditures without losing its tax-exempt status. It may pay compensation, rent, interest, and maintenance costs without penalty, because these expenses, even if paid to insiders, further the organization's exempt purposes. The costs, however, must be justifiable and be for reasonable amounts.

The matter of *reasonableness* is one of *fact*, not *law*. The exercise in determining what is reasonable is closely akin to *valuation*. In complex instances, the services of an independent, competent consultant may be warranted. The law that is developing in the intermediate sanctions setting (see "Intermediate Sanctions" section later in this chapter) is helping to define the parameters of the term *reasonable*.

Compensation

The most common form of private inurement involving nonprofit organizations is excessive and unreasonable compensation. When a charitable organization pays an employee a salary, it is paying a portion of its earnings to an individual in his or her private capacity. Payment of reasonable compensation, however, is allowable; it is not private inurement. Payment of compensation becomes private inurement when the amount is excessive—and is made to an insider. In this context, *compensation* is not confined to payment of a salary or wage; it includes bonuses, commissions, royalties, expense accounts, insurance coverages, deferred compensation, and participation in retirement plans,

Whether compensation paid by a nonprofit organization is reasonable is, as noted, a question of fact, to be decided in the context of each case. Generally, allowable compensation is ascertained by comparing the compensation paid to individuals who have similar responsibilities and expertise, serving organizations of comparable type and size, in the same or similar communities. (Where similar entities are operating in the for-profit sector, compensation paid by them can be included in the evaluation.) Other factors are the need of the organization for a particular individual's services, the amount of time devoted to the job, and whether an independent or captive board approved the compensation.

Thus, individuals (and other persons) serving charitable (and other) tax-exempt organizations are allowed, by the law, fair compensation for their efforts. A federal court observed that the "law places no duty on individuals operating charitable organizations to donate their services; they are entitled to reasonable compensation for their services." Likewise, a congressional committee report contained the observation that "an individual need not necessarily accept reduced compensation merely because he or she renders services to a tax-exempt, as opposed to a taxable, organization."

Three aspects of compensation can make it unreasonable. One is the sheer amount of the compensation, in absolute terms. A federal court, in finding private inurement because of excessive compensation, characterized the salaries as being "substantial" amounts. Other courts, however, tolerate substantial amounts of compensation where the employees' services and skills warrant the level of payment.

The second aspect is extraordinary jumps—or spikes—in the level of compensation. An amount of compensation that might otherwise be reasonable can be suspect if there is a sudden significant increase in pay. A case in point: Two individuals who for years received annual compensation of $20,000 were each awarded a $700,000 bonus; the IRS and two courts found that level of compensation to be unreasonable. Another telling factor is whether the spike in compensation level causes the recipient to enjoy far more compensation than anyone else on the payroll.

The third aspect of compensation that can lead to private inurement is the manner in which the amount is calculated. The IRS may challenge, and courts may agree with the agency, compensation arrangements that are predicated on a percentage of the revenue flow of the tax-exempt organization employer. Caselaw on this point is inconsistent and unclear, but the prevailing view seems to be that private inurement will not be found simply because a commission system is used; the important fact is the reasonableness of the compensation. Private inurement has been found in a compensation arrangement based on a percentage of gross receipts, where an upper limit—a cap—was not placed on total compensation. In another instance, a court focused on the reasonableness of the percentage, not the reasonableness of the resulting compensation. The IRS has recently been rather tolerant of these forms of compensation, particularly in the health care area, where various forms of *gainsharing* have become prevalent.

Prompted by media reports of ostensible excess compensation paid by nonprofit organizations to insiders, the IRS in 2004 launched an enforcement effort to "identify and halt" the practice. The agency initiated contact with what is expected to ultimately be about 2,000 charitable organizations to seek information about the compensation they pay. The IRS terms this undertaking its *Tax Exempt Compensation Enforcement Project.*

Rents and Loans

A charitable organization generally may lease property and pay rent. The private inurement doctrine, however, requires that— where the landlord is an insider—the rental arrangement be beneficial to and suitable for the organization, and that the rental payments be reasonable in amount. Loans between charitable organizations and their insiders are subject to the same standard.

Rental arrangements and terms of a loan involving a charitable organization should be financially advantageous to the organization and in line with its exempt purposes. Where a charity is the borrower and an insider is the lender, the interest charges, amount of security, repayment period, terms of repayment, and other aspects of the loan must be reasonable. The scrutiny will heighten where an insider is borrowing from the charity (assuming state law permits the transaction). If a loan from a charity is not timely repaid, questions of private inurement may be raised.

A federal court observed that the "very existence of a private source of loan credit from [a charitable] organization's earnings may itself amount to inurement of benefit."

Some charitable organizations are called on to guarantee the debt of another entity, such as a related nonprofit or even a for-profit organization. The terms of such an arrangement should be carefully reviewed, particularly where an insider is involved. If the loan guarantee does not advance exempt purposes or cannot be characterized as part of a reasonable investment, private inurement may be occurring.

Joint Ventures

Charitable organizations are increasingly involved in partnerships with individuals and/or other joint ventures with individuals or for-profit entities (see Chapter 9). In a general partnership, all of the partners are subject to liability for the acts committed in the name of the partnership. In a limited partnership, which will have at least one general partner, the limited partners are essentially investors; their liability is confined to the extent of their investment. The general partner(s) in a limited partnership has the responsibility to operate the partnership in a successful manner; this includes efforts to enable the limited partners to achieve an economic return that is worth the commitment of their capital.

In this structure and set of expectations, there is the potential for private inurement. In its worst light, a limited partnership with a charitable organization at the helm can be construed as the running of a business for the benefit of private interests (the limited partners), particularly where the limited partners include or are insiders. This has rarely been the case in the nonprofit organizations context. A partnership (general or limited) basically is an entity formed to attract financing—it is a means to an end. In this fashion, a charitable organization is able to secure the funds of others for a legitimate purpose. As long as involvement in the partnership does not deter the charity from advancing its exempt ends and as long as the limited partners' return on their investment is reasonable, there will not be private inurement— notwithstanding the participation of any insiders.

The IRS is having some success in situations where a tax-exempt charitable organization is involved in a joint venture (usually where the venture vehicle is a limited liability company) to the extent that the entirety of the entity is in the venture. If the charitable organization loses control of its resources to (or, as one court put it, "cedes its authority" to) one or more for-profit companies, the charity will lose its tax-exempt status (see Chapter 9). This may, however, entail application of the private benefit doctrine (see next section) rather than the private inurement doctrine.

Sanction

The sanction for violation of the private inurement doctrine is loss or denial of the organization's tax-exempt status. There is no other penalty; there is no sanction imposed on the insider who received the unwarranted benefit.

The private inurement doctrine and the intermediate sanctions rules (discussed shortly) have much in common. The general expectation is that the IRS will first apply intermediate sanctions, and invoke private inurement principles (i.e., pursue revocation of tax exemption) only in egregious cases. Nonetheless, it is certainly possible for the IRS to simultaneously apply both bodies of law, thus penalizing both the insider or insiders who obtained the excess benefit and the tax-exempt organization that provided it.

PRIVATE BENEFIT

The body of law that concerns *private benefit* is somewhat different from the law encompassed by the doctrine of *private inurement*. The private benefit doctrine, created largely by the courts, is the more sweeping of the two; it covers a wider range of activities. Most significantly, the private benefit rule does not require involvement of an insider—this fact alone accounts for its breadth. The law tolerates incidental private benefit. The private benefit doctrine is applicable only to tax-exempt charitable organizations.

The private benefit rule was illustrated by a case involving a nonprofit school, which satisfied all of the federal tax statutory law for exempt status. Individuals were trained there to become political campaign consultants, but the graduates of the school seemed to always end up working for candidates and organizations of the same political party. The school's instructional activities did not constitute political campaign activity (see "Political Activities" section later in this chapter). The judge in the case, offended by the fact that all of the school's graduates gravitated to this party's candidates and campaigns, decided to deny tax-exempt status to the school. Thus, he ruled that the school could not be exempt because it provided private benefits in the form of assistance to political candidates by the school's alumni.

The private benefit doctrine has, in recent years, emerged as a potent force in the law concerning charitable organizations. The doctrine is not applied only where individuals are benefited. Private benefit can also occur where the beneficiary is a for-profit corporation, as joint venture law developments (see Chapter 9) attest. Indeed, it is in this context that the doctrine has grown to be so expansive; the very involvement of a for-profit entity in connection with the operations of a charitable organization can trigger application of the doctrine. A federal appellate court wrote: "The critical inquiry is not whether particular contractual payments to a related for-profit organization are reasonable or excessive, but instead whether the entire enterprise is carried on in such a manner that the for-profit organization benefits substantially from the operation of" the nonprofit organization.

In the case that is regarded as on the outer reaches of all this, several for-profit organizations were found to be exercising "considerable control" over the nonprofit entity in question. The for-profit entities set fees that the nonprofit organization charged the public for training sessions, required the nonprofit organization to carry on certain types of educational activities, and provided management personnel paid for by and responsible to one of the for-profit organizations. Because of these and other facts, a court concluded that the nonprofit organization was "part of a franchise system which is operated for private benefit and . . . its affiliation with this system taints it with a substantial commercial purpose." The "ultimate beneficiaries" of the nonprofit organization's activities were found to be the for-profit corporations; the nonprofit organization was portrayed as "simply the instrument to subsidize the for-profit corporations and not vice-versa." The nonprofit organization was held to not be operating primarily for charitable purposes.

Indeed, the IRS, supported to some degree by a court, has aggressively begun finding impermissible private benefit conferred by charitable entities on other types of tax-exempt organizations. The court held that an educational foundation affiliated with an exempt business league (see Chapter 2) could not be tax-exempt because its training activities conferred undue private benefit on the association and its members. It is the view of the IRS that foundations established to provide scholarships to participants in beauty pageants cannot qualify for tax exemption by reason of provision of impermissible private benefit to the exempt social welfare organizations that sponsor the pageants.

The private benefit doctrine posits a proverbial trap for the unwary. The private inurement doctrine (previously discussed) may not apply because of lack of involvement of an insider. The intermediate sanctions rules (see next section) may be inapplicable because there is no disqualified person in the transaction or an exception is available. Nonetheless, the private benefit doctrine may be applicable.

As is the case with the private inurement doctrine, the sole sanction for transgression of the private benefit doctrine is loss or denial of the organization's tax-exempt status.

INTERMEDIATE SANCTIONS

The intermediate sanctions rules are designed to curb and punish abuses in the arena of private inurement using an enforcement mechanism other than revocation of tax-exempt status. These rules are applicable with respect to all tax-exempt public charitable organizations (see Chapter 3) and all exempt social welfare organizations (see Chapter 2). Thus, for this purpose, these two categories of entities are termed *applicable tax-exempt organizations*.

The heart of this body of tax law is the *excess benefit transaction*. A transaction is considered an excess benefit transaction if an economic benefit is provided by an applicable tax-exempt organization directly or indirectly to, or for the use of, a disqualified person, if the value of the economic benefit provided exceeds the value of the consideration received by the exempt organization for providing the benefit.

The concept of the excess benefit transaction includes any transaction in which the amount of any economic benefit provided to, or for the use of, a disqualified person is determined in whole or in part by the revenues of one or more activities of the organization, where the transaction is reflected in tax regulations and its results in private inurement.

One of the principal aspects of intermediate sanctions is application of them to instances of unreasonable compensation—where a person's level or type of compensation is deemed to be in excess of the value of the economic benefit derived by the organization from the person's services. In that regard, an economic benefit may not be treated as compensation for the performance of services unless the exempt organization clearly indicated its intent to so treat the benefit. When that intent is not properly evidenced, the provision of the benefit is an *automatic excess benefit transaction.*

A *disqualified person* is any person, member of the family of such an individual, or a controlled entity who was, at any time during the five-year period ending on the date of the transaction, in a position to exercise substantial influence over the affairs of the organization.

A disqualified person who inappropriately benefited from an excess benefit transaction is subject to an initial tax equal to 25 percent of the amount of the excess benefit. (The intent or good faith of the parties is irrelevant to this determination.) Moreover, this person will be required to return the excess benefit amount (generally in cash) to the tax-exempt organization—this is known as *correction.* An *organization manager* (usually a trustee, director, or officer) who participated in an excess benefit transaction, knowing that it was such a transaction, is subject to a tax of 10 percent of the excess benefit. An additional tax may be imposed on a disqualified person where the initial tax was imposed and the appropriate correction of the excess benefit transaction did not occur. In this situation, the disqualified person is subject to a tax equal to 200 percent of the excess benefit involved.

A major exception to the intermediate sanctions rules is the *initial contract* exception. These rules do not apply to a fixed payment made by an applicable tax-exempt organization to a disqualified person pursuant to the first contract between the parties. A *fixed payment* is an amount of money or other property specified in the contract involved, or determined by a fixed formula specified in the contract, which is to be paid or transferred in exchange for the provision of specified services or property. An initial contract is a binding written contract between an applicable tax-exempt organization and a person who was not a disqualified person immediately prior to entering into the contract.

If a transaction creating a benefit was approved by an independent board of an applicable tax-exempt organization, or an independent committee of the board, a presumption arises that the terms of the transaction are reasonable. This presumption also requires a showing that the board or committee acted on the basis of appropriate data as to comparability and properly documented the transaction. When these three elements are met, the burden of proof shifts to the IRS, which has to overcome (rebut) the presumption to prevail.

In many respects, the concept of the excess benefit transaction will be based on existing law concerning private inurement. The statute, however, expressly states, as noted, that an excess benefit transaction also may include any transaction in which the amount of any economic benefit provided to a disqualified person is determined, at least in part, by the revenue flow of the organization. These transactions are referenced in the legislative history underlying the intermediate sanctions rules as *revenue-sharing transactions*.

The IRS and the courts have determined that a variety of revenue-sharing arrangements do not constitute private inurement. This includes arrangements where the compensation of a person is ascertained, in whole or in part, on the basis of the value of contributions generated, as well as other forms of incentive compensation. The legislative history of the intermediate sanctions rules states that the agency is not bound by these prior determinations when interpreting and applying intermediate sanctions.

As discussed, the sanctions in this context fall on disqualified persons; there is no penalty on applicable tax-exempt organizations. At the same time, the annual information return required to be filed by these organizations (see Chapter 4) poses this question: "Did the organization engage in any . . . excess benefit transaction during the year or did it become aware of an excess benefit transaction from a prior year?" If the answer to this question is yes, the filing organization is required to attach a statement to the return explaining the transaction or transactions. This disclosure requirement can place the exempt organization in an awkward position, particularly if the disqualified persons involved disagree as to the existence of an excess benefit transaction. Any such statement attached to the return is a public document.

The final tax regulations on this subject having been issued, IRS enforcement of the intermediate sanctions rules has begun.

Private letter rulings and technical advice memoranda are beginning to appear; litigation is underway. This body of law may be expected to be one of the most active components of the overall federal law of nonprofit organizations in the coming years.

LEGISLATIVE ACTIVITIES

Organizations that are tax-exempt because they are charitable must, to preserve the exemption, adhere to a variety of requirements (including those already summarized). One of these is that "no substantial part of the activities" of the organization may constitute "carrying on propaganda, or otherwise attempting, to influence legislation." This is known as the *substantial part test*. Another set of rules applicable to public charities is the *expenditure test* (discussed later in this section); this test, which applies in lieu of the substantial part test, must be elected.

A charitable organization that has lobbying as a substantial activity is an *action organization*. Excessive lobbying can cause a charitable organization to pay excise taxes. In some instances, too much lobbying results in revocation of tax-exempt status.

Lobbying

Legislative activities can take many forms. Some constitute *direct* lobbying, which occurs when one or more representatives of an organization make contact with a legislator and/or his or her staff, and/or the staff of a legislative committee. Direct lobbying includes office visits, presentation of testimony at hearings, correspondence, publication and dissemination of material, e-mail and other Internet communications, and entertainment,

Grassroots (indirect) lobbying is another form. This type of lobbying occurs when the organization urges the public, or a segment of the public, to contact members of a legislative body or their staffs for the purpose of proposing, supporting, or opposing legislation.

Generally, the federal tax rules concerning lobbying and political campaign activities are separate, discrete bodies of law. If, however, a nonprofit organization engages in lobbying, particularly grassroots lobbying, doing so in the context of a political campaign, so that the advocacy of the issue(s) involved can be tied to the political fortunes of a candidate (such as an incumbent legislator pursuing reelection), the lobbying activity can also be regarded as political campaign activity. Undertakings of this nature are known as *public policy advocacy communications*; they are said to have a *dual character.*

The federal tax law prohibition comprising the substantial part test does not differentiate between direct and indirect lobbying, nor does it distinguish between lobbying that is related to an organization's exempt purposes and lobbying that is not. The function remains lobbying; the various types of it are subject to the proscription. A charitable organization, however, that does not initiate any action with respect to pending legislation but merely responds to a request from a legislative committee to testify is not, solely because of that activity, considered an action organization. Also, a charitable organization can engage in nonpartisan analysis, study, and research, and publish the results. Even where some of the plans and policies formulated can only be carried out through legislative enactments, as long as the organization does not advocate the adoption of legislation or legislative action to implement its findings, it escapes classification as an action organization.

There can be a fine line between nonpartisan analysis, study, or research, and lobbying. A charitable organization may evaluate proposed or pending legislation and present an objective analysis of it to the public, as long as it does not participate in the presentation of suggested bills to a legislature and does not engage in any campaign to secure passage of the legislation. If the organization's primary objective can be attained only by legislative action, however, it is an action organization.

Legislation

Because these rules obviously apply to legislative activities—activities undertaken in connection with the championing or opposing of legislation—it is necessary to know what does and does not constitute *legislation*. The term *legislation* refers principally to action by the U.S. Congress, a state legislative body, a local council, or similar governing body, and by the general public in a referendum, initiative, constitutional amendment, or similar procedure.

Legislation generally does not include action by an executive branch of a government, such as the promulgation of rules and regulations, nor does it include action by independent regulatory agencies. Litigation activities, including the filing of amicus curiae briefs, also does not entail action with respect to legislation.

Substantiality

The most important concept under these rules is the meaning of the word *substantial*. As noted, the law offers no general formula for computing *substantial* or *insubstantial* legislative undertakings.

There are at least three ways to measure *substantiality* in this context:

1. Determine what percentage of an organization's annual *expenditures* are devoted to efforts to influence legislation.
2. Apply a percentage to legislative *activities*, in relation to total activities.
3. Ascertain whether an organization had a substantial *impact* on or *influence* over a legislative process simply by virtue of its prestige or because of significant information provided during consideration of legislation.

The true measure of substantiality in the lobbying setting remains elusive. In reports accompanying tax legislation over the years, the Senate Finance Committee characterized this state of affairs well. In 1969, the Committee wrote that the "standards as to the permissible level of [legislative] activities under the present law are so vague as to encourage subjective application of the sanction." In 1976, the Committee portrayed the dilemma this way: "Many believe that the standards as to the permissible level of [legislative] activities under present law are too vague and thereby tend to encourage subjective and selective enforcement."

Lobbying Taxes

To give the general restriction on lobbying by charities more strength, there is a system of excise taxes on excess lobbying outlays. If a charitable organization loses its tax exemption because of attempts to influence legislation, a tax of 5 percent of the *lobbying expenditures* is imposed on the organization. This tax, however, does not apply to an organization that is under the expenditure test or that is ineligible to make this election.

A separate 5 percent tax is applicable to each of the organization's managers (directors, officers, key employees) who agreed to the lobbying expenditures, knowing they were likely to result in revocation of exemption, unless the agreement was not willful and was due to reasonable cause. The burden of proof as to whether a manager knowingly participated in the lobbying expenditure is on the IRS.

The IRS has, in every instance involving a charitable organization's excessive lobbying, the discretion as to whether to revoke tax-exempt status, impose these taxes, or do both.

Expenditure Test

The *expenditure test* regarding permissible lobbying by charitable organizations arose from a desire to clarify the substantial part test. That is, the purpose of this test is to offer charitable entities some reasonable certainty concerning how much lobbying they can undertake without endangering their tax-exempt status. The test is a safe-harbor guideline.

The expenditure test rules provide definitions of terms such as *legislation, influencing legislation, direct lobbying,* and *grass-roots lobbying.* These terms are essentially the same as those used in connection with the substantial part test. In an attempt to define when the legislative process commences (and, therefore, when a lobbying process begins), however, the expenditure test offers a definition of legislative *action:* the "introduction, amendment, enactment, defeat, or repeal of Acts, bills, resolutions, or similar items."

The expenditure test measures permissible and impermissible legislative activities of charitable organizations in terms of sets of declining percentages of total exempt purpose expenditures. (These expenditures do not include fundraising expenses (see Chapter 8).) The basic permitted level of expenditures for legislative efforts (termed the *lobbying nontaxable amount*) is 20 percent of the first $500,000 of an organization's expenditures for an exempt purpose (including legislative activities), plus 15 percent of the next $500,000, 10 percent of the next $500,000, and 5 percent of any remaining expenditures. The total amount spent for legislative activities in any year by an electing charitable organization may not exceed $1 million. A separate limitation—amounting to 25 percent of the foregoing amounts—is imposed on grass-roots lobbying expenditures.

A charitable organization that has elected these limitations and exceeds either the general lobbying ceiling amount or the grass-roots lobbying ceiling amount becomes subject to an excise tax of 25 percent of the excess lobbying expenditures. The tax falls on the greater of the two excesses. If an electing organization's lobbying expenditures normally (an average over a four-year period) exceed 150 percent of either limitation, it will forfeit its tax-exempt status as a charitable organization.

The expenditure test rules contain exceptions for five categories of activities. Consequently, the term *influencing legislation* does not include these five categories:

1. Making available the results of nonpartisan analysis, study, or research
2. Providing technical advice or assistance in response to a written request by a governmental body
3. Appearances before, or communications to, any legislative body in connection with a possible decision of that body that might affect the existence of the organization, its powers and duties, its tax-exempt status, or the deductibility of contributions to it
4. Communications between the organization and its bona fide members regarding legislation or proposed legislation that is of direct interest to them, unless the communications directly encourage the members to influence legislation or to urge nonmembers to influence legislation
5. Routine communications with government officials or employees

The third of these exceptions is known as the *self-defense exception*. Sheltered by this exception is all lobbying by a public charity, as long as it can be reasonably rationalized as coming within one or more of the allowable forms of lobbying.

The expenditure test contains a method of aggregating the expenditures of affiliated organizations. The intent of these rules is to forestall the creation of numerous organizations for the purpose of avoiding the expenditure test.

Lobbying by Other Nonprofit Organizations

The federal tax law pertaining to tax-exempt status does not impose lobbying restrictions on nonprofit organizations other than

charitable ones. The only constraint is that the organization must
pursue its exempt functions as its primary purpose and that any
lobbying it may do (other than an insubstantial amount) must
further that principal requirement.

Basically, then, entities such as social welfare organizations,
labor organizations, business and professional associations, and
veterans' organizations may lobby without restriction. Special
rules can cause members' dues to not be fully deductible in an instance of lobbying by associations (business leagues). Legislative
activities are not normally exempt functions for political organizations (see Chapter 2).

POLITICAL ACTIVITIES

Congress has flatly decreed that charitable organizations may not
engage in political campaign activity. In fact, however, these organizations, frequently religious entities, often participate directly
and indirectly in political campaigns.

General Rules

The federal tax law states that charitable organizations must "not
participate in, or intervene in (including the publishing or distributing of statements), any political campaign on behalf of or in
opposition to any candidate for public office." Although this prohibition is framed as an absolute one, minor involvement in politics may not result in loss of tax exemption. As a court observed, a
"slight and comparatively unimportant deviation from the narrow
furrow of tax approved activity is not fatal."

The concept of an *action organization* is used in the political
campaign context. An action organization includes an entity that
participates or intervenes, directly or indirectly, in any political
campaign on behalf of or in opposition to a candidate for public
office; an action organization cannot qualify as a tax-exempt charitable one. Thus, an exempt charitable organization cannot make
a contribution to a political campaign, endorse or oppose a candidate, or otherwise support a political candidacy (also see Chapter 11).

Most of the law amplifying the political campaign proscription for charitable organizations is in IRS rulings. These determinations have, over the years, been uniformly rigid in their finding

that nearly any activity relating to a political process will prevent charitable organizations from being tax exempt. For example, the evaluation of candidates, the administration of a fair campaign practices code, and even assistance to individuals immediately after they have been elected to public office have been found to be prohibited activities.

In recent years, the IRS has relented somewhat, with the agency ruling that voter education activities are permissible for charitable organizations. As an illustration, a charitable organization can prepare and disseminate a compilation of the voting records of legislators on a variety of subjects, as long as there is no editorial comment and no approval or disapproval of the voting records is implied. A charitable organization may also conduct public forums where there is a fair and impartial treatment of political candidates.

Some charitable organizations have cautiously entered the political milieu, as part of the process of advancing education (see Chapter 2). For example, charitable organizations have been permitted to assemble and donate to libraries the campaign speeches, interviews, and other materials of a candidate for a historically important elective office, and to conduct public forums at which debates and lectures on social, political, and international questions are considered. In performing this type of educational activity, however, charitable organizations are expected to present a balanced view of the pertinent facts. Members of the public must be permitted to form their own opinions and conclusions independent of any presented by the organization.

Taxation of Political Expenditures

Federal law levies taxes in situations where a charitable organization makes a political expenditure. Generally, a *political expenditure* is any amount paid or incurred by a charitable organization in any participation or intervention (including the publication or distribution of statements) in any political campaign, on behalf of or in opposition to any candidate for public office.

In an effort to discourage ostensibly educational organizations from operating in tandem with political campaigns, the term *political expenditure* also applies with respect to an organization "which is formed primarily for purposes of promoting the candidacy (or prospective candidacy) of an individual for public office (or which is effectively controlled by a candidate or prospective candidate and which is availed of primarily for such purposes)."

A political expenditure can trigger an initial tax, payable by the organization, of 10 percent of the amount of the expenditure. An initial tax of 2½ percent of the expenditure can also be imposed on each of the organization's managers (such as directors and officers), where these individuals knew it was a political expenditure, unless the agreement to make the expenditure was not willful and was due to reasonable cause. The IRS has the authority to abate these initial taxes where the organization is able to establish that the violation was due to reasonable cause and not to willful neglect, and timely corrects the violation.

An additional tax can be levied on a charitable organization, at a rate of 100 percent of the political expenditure, where the initial tax was imposed and the expenditure was timely corrected. Such a tax can also be levied on an organization's manager, at a rate of 50 percent of the expenditure, where the additional tax was imposed on the organization and the manager refused to agree to part or all of the expenditure.

The IRS has, in every instance involving a charitable organization's involvement in political campaign activity, the discretion as to whether to revoke tax-exempt status, impose these taxes, or do both.

Under certain circumstances, the IRS is empowered to commence an action in federal district court to enjoin a charitable organization from making further political expenditures and for other relief to ensure that the assets of the organization are preserved for charitable purposes. If the IRS finds that a charitable organization has flagrantly violated the prohibition against political expenditures, the IRS is required to immediately determine and assess any income and/or excise tax(es) due, by terminating the organization's tax year.

Political Organization Taxes

The essential *exempt function* of a political organization is engagement in political activity (see Chapter 2). This exempt function involves actions of influencing or attempting to influence the selection, nomination, election, or appointment of an individual to a federal, state, or local public office. The wording of this definition makes the term *political activity* broader than *political campaign activity*. The term *political activity* includes the words *selection* and *appointment*, which means processes other than electioneering. For example, if a representative of a charitable or other tax-exempt organization testifies at a Senate Judiciary Committee hearing for or against an appointment by the president to a cabinet position or judgeship, the organization is not engaging in political campaign activity (inasmuch as there is no campaign and no election) but is engaging in political activity.

When an exempt organization engages in a political activity that is not a political campaign activity, it will presumably not forfeit its tax-exempt status (even if it is a charitable entity) but may be required to pay a tax. This tax is determined by computing an amount equal to the lesser of the organization's net investment income for the year involved or the amount expended for the political activity. This amount, characterized as *political organization taxable income*, is taxed at the highest corporate rates.

Political Activity by Other Exempt Organizations

Federal tax law does not address the subject of political campaign activities by tax-exempt organizations, other than charitable and political entities. (Federal and state campaign financing and regulation laws, however, limit the extent to which nonprofit organizations can participate in political campaigns (see Chapter 11).) Because of federal tax and other law restrictions, most nonprofit organizations do not directly engage in political campaign activities; instead, they use related political action committees. The nonprofit organizations that commonly use these committees are trade, business, and professional associations (business leagues), and unions and other labor organizations; some social welfare organizations also engage in this practice.

Noncharitable tax-exempt organizations make, as noted, *advocacy communications* pertaining to public policy issues. If this type of communication explicitly advocates the election or defeat of an individual in connection with a public office, the expenditure for the communication is, of course, a political expenditure. Otherwise, the IRS looks at the facts and circumstances in determining whether the expenditure is for a political exempt function. Two factors involved are whether the timing of the communication coincides with a political campaign and whether the communication identifies the position of a political candidate on a public policy issue. In some instances, what appears to be only an attempt to influence legislation also becomes political activity—and thus taxable.

SUMMARY

This chapter summarized the significant traps in the federal tax law awaiting unsuspecting nonprofit, tax-exempt organizations. It first addressed the primary purpose rule, which can either deprive a nonprofit organization of exempt status, cause it to lose such status, or force it into another category of exemption. The chapter summarized the fundamental (and increasingly controversial) private inurement doctrine and the swiftly emerging (and seemingly unlimited) private benefit doctrine. Related to these two doctrines is the relatively new intermediate sanctions regime, also summarized in the chapter. The chapter also analyzed the law in the realm of advocacy: attempts to influence legislation, political campaign activities, and public policy advocacy communications. The chapter further summarized the sanctions that are attached to these bodies of law. The chapter concluded with a look at one of today's hot issues in nonprofit law: the political organization.

CHAPTER 11

Still More Law

The purpose of this chapter is to summarize bodies of law applicable to nonprofit organizations, other than the federal tax and various state laws. While tax, corporation, trust, and fundraising regulation law predominate in the nonprofit, tax exemption context, this other jurisprudence can also be important. Indeed, these other elements of the law can constrain or be inconsistent with federal tax and state laws. Specifically, this chapter will summarize:

- Certain constitutional law principles
- Postal laws
- Campaign finance and election laws
- Securities laws
- Antitrust laws
- Investment laws

CONSTITUTIONAL LAW

Federal and state constitutional law constitutes the highest form of law in these jurisdictions, framing the bounds of statutes, regulations, rules, and court decisions. There are several elements of constitutional law that are applicable in the nonprofit organizations context.

Much of this applicable constitutional law is found in the First Amendment to the U.S. Constitution. There it is provided that "Congress shall make no law . . . abridging the freedom of speech" and that citizens have the right to petition government. That amendment also provides, in the *religion clauses*, that "Con-

231

gress shall make no law respecting an establishment of religion, or prohibiting the free exercise thereof." The Fifth Amendment provides for "due process of law." The protections afforded individuals from unconstitutional actions, such as denial of due process or equal protection of the laws, are made applicable in relation to state governments by operation of the Fourteenth Amendment.

Fundraising Regulation

The solicitation of contributions by charitable organizations is one of the highest forms of free speech. Thus, while governments can regulate charitable fundraising in the exercise of their police power, this aspect of law enforcement must be confined to the narrowest of means. There is, for example, inherent tension between the states' regulation of fundraising by application of their charitable solicitations acts and free speech principles (see Chapter 8).

Tax Exemption for Religious Organizations

Exemption from income and/or other taxes is an economic benefit that is accorded a wide variety of nonprofit organizations, including religious entities. This type of exemption is not unconstitutional, as a violation of the religion clauses, because the tax preference is *neutral* with respect to religion. Recognizing that either tax exemption or taxation of churches "occasions some degree of involvement with religion," the Supreme Court held that "[g]ranting tax exemption to churches [and other religious entities] necessarily operates to afford an indirect economic benefit and also gives rise to some, but yet a lesser, involvement than taxing them." The Court added that the provision of tax exemption for religious organizations "is not sponsorship since the government does not transfer part of its revenues to churches but simply abstains from demanding that the church support the state."

Nonetheless, a tax exemption solely for religious organizations violates the establishment clause. Thus, the Court held a state sales tax exemption "confined to religious organizations" to be a form of "state sponsorship of religion," and wrote that it should be struck down as "lacking a secular purpose and effect." The Court added that "[w]hat is crucial [to sustaining the validity of a tax exemption] is that any subsidy afforded religious organizations be warranted by some overarching secular purpose that justifies like benefits for nonreligious groups."

Regulation of Advocacy

Lobbying of legislators constitutes an exercise of the First Amendment right of petition. The Supreme Court has declared that the general advocacy of ideas is constitutionally protected as part of the country's "profound national commitment to the principle that debate on public issues should be uninhibited, robust, and wide-open." The federal tax law limitation on lobbying by charitable organizations (see Chapter 10) is not unconstitutional, however, because it does not on its face prohibit these organizations from engaging in efforts to influence legislation. This prohibition has also withstood challenges on equal protection grounds, even though no other category of nonprofit organization is barred from lobbying as a condition of tax exemption.

As to the free speech issue, the Court held that the federal tax law "does not deny . . . [a charitable organization] the right to receive deductible contributions to support its non-lobbying activity, nor does it deny . . . [a charity] any independent benefit on account of its intention to lobby"; rather, Congress "has merely refused to pay for the lobbying out of public moneys." As to the equal protection issue, noting that "[l]egislatures have especially broad latitude in creating classifications and distinctions in tax statutes," the Court concluded that the distinctions in the lobbying context made by Congress between charitable and other exempt organizations do not employ any "suspect classification," are not violative of equal protection principles, and are "within Congress' broad power in this area."

The principal federal election law is the Federal Election Campaign Act (FECA). The most sweeping and controversial revision of it occurred in 2002, when Congress enacted the Bipartisan Campaign Reform Act (BCRA). The Supreme Court, in 2003, upheld the constitutionality of nearly all of the 2002 amendments.

Freedom of Association

Tax exemption for nonprofit membership organizations may be viewed as a manifestation of the constitutionally protected right of association accorded the members of these entities. One type of this freedom—the *freedom of expressive association*—is a function of the right of free speech. By application of this doctrine, the formation and preservation of certain types of highly personal relationships are afforded a substantial measure of sanctuary from interference by government. This freedom to engage in group activity is viewed as a way of advancing political, social, economic, educational, religious, and cultural ends.

Government, however, can infringe on this right where compelling state interests, unrelated to the suppression of ideas and not achievable through means significantly less restrictive of associational freedoms, are served. This clash of principles is most frequent in instances of discrimination. For example, in ruling that a nonprofit organization lacked the constitutional right to exclude women from its membership, the Supreme Court—while conceding that the freedom of association "plainly presupposes a freedom not to associate"—held that the governmental interest in eradicating gender-based discrimination is superior to the associational rights of those who would confine the membership to men. By contrast, the Court ruled that a nonprofit youth organization has a constitutional right, under the First Amendment, to exclude gay individuals from its leadership positions because of their sexual orientation.

State Action Doctrine

Nonprofit organizations, being almost always private (that is, nongovernmental) entities, are not usually subject to constitutional law principles. This application of constitutional law can be made, however, by reason of the *state action doctrine*. The purpose of this doctrine is to treat otherwise private organizations as components of a state for the purpose of applying federal constitutional law standards in situations in which the state is responsible for the conduct at issue.

The Court has written that it can be difficult to "plot a line" between nonprofit organizations that are subject to the doctrine and those that are not. It explained why this dichotomy is not always apparent: "If the Fourteenth Amendment is not to be displaced, . . . its ambit cannot be a simple line between States and people operating outside formally governmental organizations, and the deed of an ostensibly private organization or individual is to be treated sometimes as if a State had caused it to be performed." The Court wrote that state action may be found if there is such a "close nexus between the State and the challenged action" that seemingly private behavior "may be fairly treated as that of the State itself." In one case, where a nonprofit association was bound by constitutional law principle as a part of a state, the Court observed that the "nominally private character of the [a]ssociation is overborne by the pervasive entwinement of public institutions and public officials in its composition and workings, and there is no substantial reason to claim unfairness in applying constitutional [law] standards to it."

The Fifth and Fourteenth Amendments prohibit racial discrimination by government and government-supported private institutions. In general, private organizations may lawfully discriminate, absent applicability of the state action doctrine by which government is deemed to have sufficiently supported or encouraged the private discrimination as to amount to a constitutional law violation. For example, tax exemption provided for fraternal organizations requires the absence of discriminatory practices, although this rationale does not extend to exempt social clubs because of the limited tax exemption provided to them (see Chapter 6).

POSTAL LAWS

Fundraising and other activities undertaken by tax-exempt organizations by means of the U.S. mail system is regulated to various extents by the federal postal laws. This regulation is largely accomplished by enforcement of the law concerning special mailing rates that are limited to use by qualified organizations when they are mailing eligible matter.

Only qualified organizations that have received specific authorization from the Postal Service may mail eligible matter at these specific rates of postage. These organizations cannot be organized for profit, and none of their net income may accrue to the benefit of persons in their private capacity.

Determination of Postal Rates

Rates for all classes of mail are determined in rate cases, which are public proceedings administered by the Postal Rate Commission. The congressional mandate for the Postal Service is recovery of all of its operating costs from the rates it charges. This rate making consists of assigning the Postal Service's projected costs in two categories of costs to each class of mail; combining the categories yields the rate. These categories are (1) *attributable costs*, which are costs that are directly measurable and traceable to a particular class of mail (such as nonprofit organization mailings) and (2) *institutional costs*, which are the overhead costs of the Postal Service, recovered by being assigned to each class in the form of a *markup*, stated as a percentage of the attributable cost.

The preferred rate for nonprofit, tax-exempt organizations has existed because Congress, in 1970, had undertaken to provide the Postal Service an annual appropriation (*revenue forgone*) in lieu of the markup that nonprofit organizations would otherwise pay. That is, nonprofit organizations paid the attributable cost portion only (which became the nonprofit rate) and the federal government absorbed the institutional costs.

Throughout the 1980s, a steady increase in the volume of mail sent by nonprofit organizations helped to increase the need for revenue forgone; this was true for all postal rate classes, which reached nearly $1 billion for the government's fiscal year 1995. Congress became reluctant to appropriate the funds necessary to support the revenue forgone subsidy. Absent full funding of revenue forgone, the Postal Service was authorized to raise the nonprofit organizations' postal rates.

In the intervening years, nonprofit organizations faced ongoing uncertainty as to the levels of the postal rates. There were increases from rate cases (at approximately three-year intervals) and struggles with Congress over appropriations to avoid annual increases in the nonprofit rates. Congress threatened changes in the eligibility rates; two were enacted after 1990.

By 1992, a solution was clearly necessary. Congress and the Postal Service did not want any more pressure from the nonprofit community as to the revenue forgone amounts. Commercial mailers using the third-class rates were fearful that they would bear the burden of rate increases. Nonprofit organizations were weary of these uncertainties and were concerned about the prospects of a severe increase in the applicable postal rates.

Compromise legislation was enacted in 1993. This measure—the Revenue Forgone Reform Act—eliminated the concept of revenue forgone and ensured continued preferred rates by establishing a favorable markup for nonprofit organizations. For the federal government's fiscal year 1994 and thereafter, the markup for each class of nonprofit rates was set at one-half of the comparable commercial markup amount. This legislation provided a phasing-in schedule to cushion nonprofit organizations from the effects of the new system. This schedule produces annual increases in the range of 2 to 3 percent (unless or until the intervention of a PRC rate case).

The special rate for nonprofit organizations is termed by the Postal Service the *nonprofit standard mail rate*. This rate provides authorized organizations an opportunity to realize significant savings in postage compared with that charged at the regular standard bulk mail rates.

Qualifying Organizations

The nonprofit standard mail rates are available to qualified nonprofit organizations. As noted, an organization may be authorized to mail at the nonprofit standard mail rates if it is not organized for profit and none of its net income accrues to the benefit of persons in their private capacity. A qualifying organization must have a primary purpose relating to at least one of the following categories: religious, educational, scientific, philanthropic (charitable), agricultural, labor, veterans, or fraternal ends. Also, certain political organizations can qualify for the nonprofit standard mail rates.

This purpose must be reflected in the manner in which the organization is organized and operated. Nonprofit organizations that occasionally or incidentally engage in qualifying activities are not eligible for the special mailing rates.

FEDERAL ELECTION LAWS

In addition to the considerable amount of federal tax law concerning political activities by tax-exempt organizations (see Chapter 10), the federal election laws restrict and regulate political election-related activities by exempt organizations.

The federal election laws operate largely independently of the federal tax laws. Consequently, the conduct by certain types of exempt organizations that may be prohibited under the federal election laws may be permissible under the federal tax laws; the

reverse may also be the case. Thus, an exempt organization engaging in advocacy that may be or is political campaign activity
should take the federal election law requirements and limitations
into consideration.

Federal Election Commission

The FEC is composed of six members appointed by the president,
by and with the advice of the Senate. No more than three of these
members may be affiliated with the same political party. Each
member of the FEC serves for a single term of six years. These
members are to be chosen on the basis of their experience, in-
tegrity, impartiality, and good judgment. They are to be fulltime
employees of the federal government.

The FEC has the responsibility for administering, enforcing,
and formulating policy with respect to the federal election laws. It
is charged with preparation of rules to implement these policies
and for the conduct of its activities. It is authorized to conduct investigations and participate in litigation.

Involvement of Corporations in the Election Process

In general, a corporation may not make a contribution or expenditure of corporate treasury funds in connection with a federal
election. This prohibition, which applies to nonprofit corporations, applies to contributions of money as well as to loans, advances, contributions of services, and gifts of anything of value.
There are special rules for applicable electioneering communications.

The federal election laws permit, subject to limitations, uses
of corporate facilities and assets. Shareholders and employees
may make incidental use of corporate facilities for individual volunteer activities. *Incidental* use means use that does not interfere
with the normal operations of the corporation. Activity that does
not exceed one hour a week or four hours a month is considered
incidental. Certain reimbursement requirements apply for more
than occasional, isolated, or incidental use. If a corporation regularly makes rooms available for civic or community groups, it may
offer rooms to political candidates on a nonpartisan basis on the
same terms.

A corporation may communicate with its executive or administrative personnel and their families on any subject, as well as to nonpartisan registration and get-out-the-vote campaigns aimed at these individuals. A corporation may establish, administer, and solicit contributions for an affiliated political committee. These exceptions also apply in connection with labor organizations and their members and their families.

Separate Segregated Funds

Despite the federal election law prohibitions on corporations from using corporate treasury money to make contributions or expenditures in connection with federal elections, a corporation may use treasury funds to establish and administer a political committee. These political committees may solicit and receive contributions from the restricted class and, in turn, make contributions and expenditures to influence federal elections. Committees of this nature are referred to as *separate segregated funds* (otherwise often known as *political action committees*). The funds of these committees, consisting of lawful contributions, are kept separate—segregated—from the sponsoring organization's treasury funds. Treasury funds include money obtained from commercial transactions, dues, and other membership fees.

Contributions by SSF

A contribution from a separate segregated fund usually entails the giving of money to one or more candidate committees, the purchase of goods or services on behalf of a candidate ("in-kind contributions"), or giving money to another political committee, such as a party committee, that in turn supports candidates. Contributions to and by these funds include gifts of money and property, in-kind contributions, and loans, endorsements and guarantees of loans; they also can receive sales proceeds.

Solicitation of Contributions to SSF

A corporation or its separate segregated fund may solicit only its *restricted class*, that is, its stockholders and executive and administrative personnel and their immediate families. An incorporated membership organization, including a trade association, cooperative, and corporation without capital stock and its separate segregated fund may solicit contributions from its noncorporate members and their families to a fund for political purposes. Noncorporate members include individuals and partnerships. With the exception of trade associations, a membership corporation may not solicit the employees of its members.

Definition of Member

An organization's *members* include all persons who currently satisfy the organization's requirements for membership. The courts and the FEC have attempted to clarify this vague definition.

Limitations on Contributions and Expenditures

There are limitations on the level of contributions that persons may make to candidates, political committees of candidates, and political committees of national political parties, with respect to elections for federal office. For example, a person may not make contributions to a candidate and his or her political committee, in connection with a federal election, in excess of $2,000. Likewise, contributions to a political committee maintained by a national political party may not, in a calendar year, exceed $25,000.

There are limitations and restrictions on the expenditures made, in connection with the general election campaigns of candidates for federal office, by the national committee of a political party and a state committee of a political party.

Generally, *expenditures* are any purchase, payment, distribution, loan, advance, deposit, or gift of money or anything of value, made by any person for the purpose of influencing any election for federal office, as well as any written agreement or promise to make an expenditure. The 2002 revisions of the FECA did not amend the definition of the term *expenditure* but categorized certain election-related activities into *federal election activity* and *electioneering communications*.

Soft Money Restrictions

Contributions for federal election purposes generally must be made with funds that are subject to the FECA's disclosure requirements, and source and amount limitations. These funds are known as *federal* or *hard* money. The term *contribution* is defined to include gifts, loans, advances, or like transfers of anything of value made by any person for the purpose of influencing any election for *federal* office. Contributions made solely for the purpose of influencing state or local elections are, therefore, unaffected by the FECA's requirements and prohibitions.

Prior to the enactment of the BCRA, federal law permitted corporations and unions, as well as individuals who had made the maximum permissible contributions to federal candidates, to contribute *nonfederal* or *soft* money to political parties for activities intended to influence state or local elections. In the case of contributions intended to influence both federal and state elections, the FEC ruled that political parties could fund mixed-purpose activities, including get-out-the-vote drives and generic party advertising, in part with soft money. This was done by means of establishment by these parties of federal and nonfederal accounts. Thereafter, the FEC concluded that the parties could also use soft money to defray the costs of *legislative advocacy media advertisements*, even if the advertisements mentioned the name of a federal candidate, as long as they did not expressly advocate the candidate's election or defeat. This solicitation, transfer, and other use of soft money—what the Supreme Court would later portray as the "FEC's allocation regime"—thus enabled parties and candidates to circumvent the FECA's limitations on the source and amount of contributions in connection with federal elections.

Congress, in 2002, made an "effort to plug the soft-money loophole." The FECA, as amended by the BCRA, prohibits national party committees and their agents from soliciting, receiving, directing, or spending soft money. State and local party committees are prohibited from using soft money for activities that affect federal elections. The Supreme Court observed that the "core [of this second rule] is a straightforward contribution regulation: It prevents donors from contributing nonfederal funds to state and local party committees to help finance 'federal election activity.'" The Court noted that this rule arose out of congressional recognition of the "close ties between federal candidates and state party committees."

Federal election activity encompasses four discrete categories of activities: (1) voter registration activity during the 120 days preceding a regularly scheduled federal election; (2) voter identification, get-out-the-vote, and generic campaign activity that is conducted in connection with an election in which a candidate for federal office appears on the ballot; (3) a public communication that refers to a clearly identified federal candidate and that promotes, supports, attacks, or opposes a candidate for that office; and (4) the services provided by certain political party committee employees. In finding these rules to be constitutional, the Supreme Court referred to these four types of activities collectively as *electioneering*.

These *federal election activities* are nearly identical to the mixed-purpose activities that were allowed by the FEC before enactment of the BCRA. Political parties are prohibited from soliciting and contributing funds to tax-exempt organizations that engage in electioneering activities. Federal candidates and officeholders are prohibited from receiving, spending, or soliciting soft money in connection with federal elections. This limits their ability to do so in connection with state and local elections. Circumvention of the restrictions on national, state, and local party committees is prevented by prohibiting state and local candidates from raising and spending soft money to fund advertisements and other public communications that promote or attack federal candidates.

Solicitations for, Contributions to, and Expenditures by Tax-Exempt Organizations

The FECA, as amended by the BCRA, prohibits national, state, and local party committees, and their agents or subsidiaries, from soliciting funds for, or making or directing any contributions to, any tax-exempt organization that makes expenditures in connection with an election for public office or to any exempt political organization "other than a political committee, a State, district, or local committee of a political party, or the authorized campaign committee of a candidate for State or local office."

The purpose of this law is to prevent circumvention of the FECA limits on contributions of soft money to national, state, and local party committees. The Supreme Court found it constitutional, by narrowly construing the prohibition to apply only to the donation of funds not raised in compliance with the FECA.

The FECA, as amended by the BCRA, also prohibits national, state, and local party committees from making or directing any contributions to tax-exempt political or other organizations.

The Supreme Court, to render this rule constitutional, narrowly construed the ban to apply only to donations of funds not raised in conformity to the FECA's prohibitions and limitations. Thus, the Court wrote that "political parties remain free to make or direct donations of money to any tax-exempt organization that has otherwise been raised in compliance with [the] FECA."

The FECA, as amended by the BCRA, regulates the raising and soliciting of soft money by federal candidates and officeholders. It prohibits federal candidates and officeholders from soliciting, receiving, directing, transferring, or spending any soft money in connection with federal elections. It also limits the ability of federal candidates and officeholders to solicit, receive, direct, transfer, or spend soft money in connection with state and local elections. Among the exceptions to these rules is that federal candidates and officeholders may make solicitations of soft money to tax-exempt organizations (1) the primary purpose of which is not to engage in *federal election activities* as long as the solicitation does not specify how the funds will be spent, (2) the primary purpose of which is to engage in federal election activities as long as the solicitations are limited to individuals and the amount solicited does not exceed $20,000 per year per individual, and (3) for the express purpose of carrying out federal election activities as long as the amount solicited does not exceed $20,000 per year per individual. The Supreme Court found these rules to be constitutional because, unlike an outright ban on solicitations to exempt organizations, this law permits "limited" solicitations of soft money, thereby "accomodat[ing] individuals who have long served as active members of nonprofit organizations in both their official and individual capacities."

The FECA, as amended by the BCRA, generally prohibits corporations and unions from using their general treasury funds to make election-related advertising expenditures, including the financing of electioneering communications. The Supreme Court found this ban constitutional, in that corporations and unions remain free to organize and administer separate segregated funds for that purpose.

Advocacy and Electioneering

The BCRA introduced the term *electioneering communication*, which encompasses any "broadcast, cable, or satellite communication" that refers to a clearly identified candidate for federal office; is made within 60 days before a general, special, or runoff election for the office sought by the candidate or 30 days before a primary or preference election, or a convention or caucus of a political party that has authority to nominate a candidate, for the office sought by the candidate; and in the case of a communication which refers to a candidate (other than one for president or vice president) that is targeted to the relevant electorate. The term is utilized in two contexts: there are disclosure requirements for persons who fund electioneering communications and there are restrictions on the ability of corporations and unions to fund electioneering communications. This term was created, the Supreme Court observed, "to replace the narrowing construction of [the] FECA's disclosure provisions adopted" by the Court previously. The Court wrote that "that construction limited the coverage of [the] FECA's disclosure requirement to communications expressly advocating the election or defeat of particular candidates."

This aspect of the law has been attended to by much confusion as to what the Court meant in its earlier pronouncement. The thinking in many quarters for years was that the Court drew a constitutionally mandated distinction between *express advocacy* and *issue advocacy*, with persons having an inviolable First Amendment right to engage in the latter category of speech. The challenge to this portion of the BCRA was predicated on the view that Congress cannot constitutionally require disclosure of, or regulate expenditures for, electioneering communications without making an exception for communications that do not involve express advocacy. "That position," the Court wrote, "misapprehends our prior decisions, for the express advocacy restriction was an endpoint of statutory interpretation, not a first principle of constitutional law."

In the earlier decision, the Court examined prior law restricting election-related expenditures and found some of the phraseology to be impermissibly vague. The Court cured the defect by interpreting the rule as being limited to communications that include explicit words of advocacy of election or defeat of a candidate. The express advocacy limitation, then, was the product of statutory interpretation; it "nowhere suggested that a statute that was neither vague nor overbroad would be required to toe the same express advocacy line." Thus, the "concept of express advocacy and the concomitant class of magic words were born of an effort to avoid constitutional infirmities." The Court's prior decisions "in no way drew a constitutional boundary that forever fixed the permissible scope of provisions regulating campaign-related speech."

Aside from the Court's prior holdings, it concluded that it was not persuaded that the First Amendment "erects a rigid barrier between express advocacy and so-called issue advocacy." The Court wrote of its "longstanding recognition that the presence or absence of magic words cannot meaningfully distinguish electioneering speech from a true issue ad." Proclaiming the "magic-words requirement" to be "functionally meaningless," the Court wrote that the "express advocacy line, in short, has not aided the legislative effort to combat real or apparent corruption, and Congress enacted [the] BCRA to correct the flaws it found in the existing system."

The term *electioneering communication* was found by the Court to not be vague, with its components "easily understood and objectively determinable." This portion of the FECA, then, is constitutional.

Political Organizations

Certain political organizations must file a statement of organization (register) with the FEC within certain time frames. These entities are authorized campaign committees, separate segregated funds, and certain other political committees.

An *authorized campaign committee* is the principal campaign committee or any other committee authorized by a candidate for federal office to receive contributions or make expenditures on behalf of the candidate. A *separate segregated fund* is a fund utilized for political purposes by entities such as corporations, labor organizations, and other membership organizations.

For federal election law purposes, a *political committee* includes any group of persons that receives contributions aggregating more than $1,000 in a calendar year or that makes expenditures aggregating more than $1,000 during a calendar year. The term also includes certain *separate segregated funds* and certain local committees of a political party.

The Supreme Court narrowed the definition of the term *political committee*, stating that the term "need only encompass organizations that are under the control of a candidate or the ma-

jor purpose of which is the nomination or election of a candidate," and that the term does not "reach groups engaged purely
in issue discussion." The FEC applies the *major purpose test* when
assessing whether an organization is a political committee.

The federal election law subjects political committees to
record-keeping and reporting requirements that are inapplicable
to organizations that are not political committees. It also imposes
limitations and prohibitions on the contributions they receive
and make,

Thus, some political organizations are recognized as such
for federal tax purposes but are not recognized as political entities by the FEC (and thus do not have to register with the FEC).
These *nonconnected 527 organizations* may nonetheless be required
to register with the IRS.

SECURITIES LAWS

At the federal level, the principal securities laws are the Securities
Act of 1933, the Securities Exchange Act of 1934, and the Investment Company Act of 1940. These laws are administered and enforced by the Securities Exchange Commission (SEC). Generally,
this body of law is designed to preserve a free market in the trading of securities, provide full and fair disclosure of the character
of securities sold in interstate commerce and through the mails,
and prevent fraud and other abuse in the marketing and sale of
securities. State securities laws have the same goal.

The federal securities law broadly defines the term *security* as
including not only stocks and bonds but also notes, debentures,
evidences of indebtedness, certificates of participation in a profit-
sharing agreement, investment contracts, and certificates of deposit for securities. It is rare for a charitable organization to offer
a financial benefit or package to the general public where that
benefit or package is considered a security, but some nonprofit
organizations offer *memberships* that, technically, constitute securities. There are, however, exceptions from the federal securities
laws for these types of securities.

Nonetheless, a charitable organization may find itself at least
within the potential applicability of the securities laws if it maintains one or more *charitable income funds*. The federal securities
laws include rules that are designed to shield charities against the
allegation that these funds are investment companies subject to

the registration and other requirements of the Investment Company Act. This legislation, introduced by the Philanthropy Protection Act of 1995, provides exemptions under the federal securities laws for charitable organizations that maintain these funds.

A charitable income fund is a fund maintained by a charitable organization exclusively for the collective investment and reinvestment of one or more assets of a charitable remainder trust or similar trust, a pooled income fund, an arrangement involving a contribution in exchange for the issuance of a charitable gift annuity, a charitable lead trust, the general endowment fund or other funds of one or more charitable organizations, or certain other trusts in which the remainder interests benefit or are revocably dedicated to one or more charitable organizations. The SEC has the authority to expand the scope of these exemption provisions to embrace funds that may include assets not expressly defined.

A fund that is excluded from the definition of an investment company must provide at the time of the contribution, to each donor to a charity by means of the fund, written information describing the material terms of operation of the fund. This disclosure requirement, however, is not a condition of exemption from the Investment Company Act. Thus, a charitable income fund that fails to provide the requisite information to donors is not subject to the securities laws, although the fund may be subject to an enforcement or other action by the SEC.

This exemption is also engrafted onto the Securities Act and the Securities Exchange Act. Thus, for example, the exemption in the Securities Act (from registration and other requirements) is available for "any security issued by a person organized and operated exclusively for religious, educational, benevolent, fraternal, charitable, or reformatory purposes and not for pecuniary profit, and no part of the net earnings of which inures to the benefit of any person, private stockholder, or individual."

The Securities Exchange Act provides that a charitable organization is not subject to the Act's broker-dealer regulation rules solely because the organization trades in securities on its behalf, or on behalf of a charitable income fund, or the settlors, potential settlors, or beneficiaries of either. This protection is also extended to trustees, directors, officers, employees, or volunteers of a charitable organization, acting within the scope of his or her employment or duties with the organization.

Exemptions similar to those available in the broker-dealer setting are provided for charitable organizations and certain persons associated with them, in connection with the provision of advice, analyses, or reports, from the reach of the Investment Advisors Act.

Interests in charitable income funds excluded from the definition of an investment company, and any offer or sale of these interests, are exempt from a state law that requires registration or qualification of securities. A charitable organization or trustee, director, officer, employee, or volunteer of a charity (acting within the scope of his or her employment or duties) is not subject to regulation as a dealer, broker, agent, or investment advisor under any state securities law because the organization or person trades in securities on behalf of a charity, charitable income fund, or the settlors, potential settlors, or beneficiaries of either.

ANTITRUST LAWS

The federal antitrust laws are, in certain respects, applicable to nonprofit organizations. The principal law in this regard, the Sherman Act, prohibits contracts, combinations, and conspiracies that unreasonably restrain trade. The Supreme Court wrote that "[t]here is no doubt that the sweeping language of section 1 [of the Sherman Act] applies to nonprofit entities." Civil actions under the antitrust laws may be brought by the Antitrust Division of the Department of Justice, the Federal Trade Commission (FTC), or private plaintiffs. The federal government can also bring criminal actions against entities and individuals for certain antitrust actions.

Basic Principles

Among the most common antitrust law violations are concerted or collusive activities involving two or more competitors. Thus, the nonprofit organizations usually involved in antitrust law matters are business or professional associations. These entities have the interesting feature—as mandated by federal tax law requirements (see Chapter 2)—of being composed of members that are competitors.

Consequently, an association constitutes what may be termed *a convenient vehicle* by means of which collusive activities may be undertaken. The law is clear that agreements relating in any way to prices or to fees, even agreements that affect prices or fees merely indirectly, are illegal *per se*. This standard means that there is no need to prove any actual injury to competition resulting from this type of an agreement. The simple existence of the anticompetitive agreement is sufficient to establish illegality. In one instance, an engineering society's ethical canon, that prohibited members from discussing prices with potential customers until there was an initial selection of an engineer, was held to be a *per se* violation of the Sherman Act.

Another context in which the antitrust laws can be applicable to nonprofit organizations is standard-setting. An example of this application of the antitrust laws is a court decision that an association that promoted harness racing did not violate these laws by standardizing the design of the two-wheeled vehicle (sulky) pulled by horses in this type of racing. In another case, the claim that an organization was attempting to monopolize the market of occupational therapy certification in violation of the Sherman Act was rejected. In still another instance, an Act violation claim was rejected in a dispute over the criteria used to determine whether to accredit certain clinical laboratories; the criterion that a laboratory must use reagent water produced on site for laboratory tests generated a lawsuit by a company that produced this type of water in bottled form.

Membership associations are vulnerable to antitrust allegations in still another context: member expulsion. If not undertaken for reasonable cause, an expulsion of this nature can be a *concerted refusal to deal* or a *group boycott*. For an association to engage in this type of illegal conduct, however, it must have the requisite *market power;* that is, membership in it has to be the exclusive access to some necessary element of the business involved. In one case, an expelled member failed to convince a court of antitrust wrongdoing by an association, inasmuch as the association lacked market power: of about 500 firms in the industry, only 85 were association members.

Restraints of trade that are not illegal *per se* are reviewed pursuant to a *rule of reason* standard. Application of this standard entails a full economic analysis of the practice(s) involved. This process can be time consuming and expensive,

A third approach has evolved: the *quick look*. Here, although the restraint in question is found to not be a *per se* violation, if there is anticompetitive effect, the practice is determined to be a sufficiently apparent transgression of the antitrust laws as to not warrant a rule-of-reason analysis. As the Supreme Court stated, the quick look is appropriate when an "observer with even a rudimentary understanding of economics could conclude that the arrangements in question would have an anticompetitive effect on customers and markets." If a quick look is inconclusive, a full economic analysis may follow.

The Court considered a case involving the code of ethics of an association of dentists; at issue were restrictions on price advertising. The FTC determined that these restrictions were a form of price-fixing and thus constituted a *per se* violation of the antitrust law. A court of appeals agreed but ruled that the practices were to be evaluated using the quick-look test. The Court was troubled with the standard of review, with the majority expressing the view that there may have to be a type of review that is more extensive than a quick look but less encompassing than a rule-of-reason analysis.

FTC Jurisdiction

The scope of the jurisdiction of the FTC over nonprofit organizations is not clear. The Federal Trade Commission Act prohibits "unfair methods of competition." This Act's phraseology encompasses not only all Sherman Act violations but also any other restraints of trade that are contrary to the policy or spirit of the antitrust laws.

The FTC has the authority to prevent "persons [that is, individuals], partnerships or corporations" from engaging in unfair competitive methods and unfair or deceptive acts or practices. The definition of the term *corporation* in this context includes any company or association, "incorporated or unincorporated, without shares of capital or capital stock, except partnerships." The law that authorizes the FTC to investigate and discipline organizations states that the agency may only investigate an "entity which is organized to carry on business for its own profit or that of its members."

Therefore, the FTC has jurisdiction over nonprofit trade, business, and professional associations—where they have for-profit members and where the economic benefits that are provided are substantial. Where the economic benefit is insubstantial, the agency lacks jurisdiction. The Supreme Court has observed that an organization "devoted solely to professional education may lie outside the FTC Act's jurisdictional reach, even though the quality of professional services ultimately affects the profits of those who deliver them." At any rate, *pure charity* is beyond the ambit of the antitrust laws.

MANAGEMENT OF INSTITUTIONAL FUNDS ACT

The board of a charitable organization may, pursuant to the Uniform Management of Institutional Funds Act (UMIFA), appropriate for expenditure for the purposes for which an endowment fund is established so much of the net appreciation, realized and unrealized, in the fair value of the assets of the fund over the historic dollar value of the fund as is prudent. This rule does not apply if the gift instrument involved indicates the donor's intention that net appreciation shall not be expended.

The board may invest and reinvest an institutional fund in any real or personal property deemed advisable by it, whether or not it produces a current return, including mortgages, stocks, bonds, and debentures. It may retain property contributed by a donor to an institutional fund for as long as it deems advisable. The board may include all or any part of an institutional fund in a pooled or common fund maintained by the institution.

Unless the law or the gift document provides otherwise, the board may delegate to its committees, officers, or employees of the institution or the fund, or agents, the authority to act in place of the board in investment and reinvestment of the organization's funds. It may contract with independent investment advisors, investment counsel or managers, banks, or trust companies for this purpose. It is authorized to pay compensation for investment advisory or management services.

In the administration of its powers in this regard, the members of the board are required to exercise ordinary business care and prudence under the facts and circumstances prevailing at the time of the action or decision. In so doing, they are to consider long- and short-term needs of the organization in carrying out its charitable purposes, its present and anticipated financial requirements, expected total return on its investments, price level trends, and general economic conditions.

OTHER LAWS

There are, of course, many other bodies of law applicable to non-profit organizations, some more directly than others and often with unique variances or special rules for nonprofit entities. Included are laws concerning banking, bankruptcy, bond financing, communications, consumer protection, criminal activities, education, employee benefits, employment, environmental matters, estate administration, federal contracts and grants, gambling, health, housing, insurance, international relations, labor, transportation, trust administration, and welfare.

SUMMARY

As the previous chapters attest, the law directly affecting the operations of nonprofit organizations largely consists of corporate and tax rules. But there is more significant law; that is the subject of this chapter. Here is a summary of applicable constitutional law principles: fundraising regulation (also Chapter 8), tax exemption for religious organizations, regulation of advocacy, freedom of association, and the state action doctrine. Still other bodies of law of pertinence to nonprofit organizations, and summarized in this chapter, are the postal, election, campaign finance, securities, antitrust, and investment laws.

CHAPTER 12

Governance Principles and Liability

The purpose of this chapter is to summarize the law—some of it just emerging—concerning corporate governance principles pertaining to nonprofit organizations and the matter of potential board member liability. Scandals embroiling for-profit corporations and accounting firms—involving fraud, tax avoidance, conflicts of interests, and questionable accounting practices—led to enactment of the Sarbanes–Oxley Act in 2002. The principles embodied in that legislation are quickly being imported into the nonprofit sector, as manifested by a range of initiatives at the federal and state levels. Specifically, this chapter will:

- Summarize the basics of corporate governance principles
- Inventory evolving governance precepts
- Summarize board member responsibilities and duties
- List protections against director and officer liability
- Address (revisit) the use of management companies
- Reference the watchdog agencies' guidelines

BASICS OF CORPORATE GOVERNANCE PRINCIPLES

Traditionally, the law as to governance of a nonprofit organization—corporation or otherwise—has been largely confined to state rules. These principles, however, are now quickly becoming part of the federal tax law. In late 2004, it is apparent that much new federal law on the subject is imminent: legislation, regulations, and IRS forms and instructions, for example.

The essence of the emerging corporate governance principles is that a charitable organization (and perhaps other types of tax-exempt entities) must be *managed* by its board of directors or board of trustees. It is becoming unacceptable for a board to meet infrequently and be merely the recipient of reports from an organization's officers and staff. The developing law is requiring the board of the nonprofit organization to become directly involved, to be knowledgeable about the organization's programs and finances, to understand the climate in which the entity operates, to avoid conflicts of interest, to place the objectives of the organization above personal desires—and to *govern*.

These emerging principles are also forcing structural changes in the operations of nonprofit organizations. No longer are the operative documents only articles of organization and by-laws. The law is beginning to demand organizational and management policies and procedures, conflicts of interest policies, codes of ethics for senior officers, investment policies, and written program objectives and performance measures. Independent audit committees are becoming common. Lawyers, accountants, and other consultants must be hired directly by the board, not the executive staff. Compensation arrangements for top positions have to be approved at the board level. Independent auditors may have to be rotated periodically, such as every five years. Corporate executives may have to certify financial statements and perhaps annual information returns.

Federal tax or other law may contain rules on topics that previously have been the sole province of state law, such as the composition of the board, the compensation of the board, a requirement of some independent board members, and prohibition on board service by certain individuals. The IRS may be accorded the authority to require the removal of board members, officers, or employees in instances of law violations. The agency may also be given the ability to prohibit certain types of individuals from sitting on the boards of nonprofit organizations, particularly charitable ones.

EMERGING CONCEPTS

The basics as to corporate governance principles are beginning to yield specific requirements. Much of what is inventoried next is not law, yet law (federal and state) on these points seems to be in the immediate offing. These concepts appear to be emerging:

- The governing board must establish basic organizational and management policies and procedures for the non-profit organization, and review any proposed deviations.
- The board must establish, review, and approve program objectives and performance measures.
- The board must review and approve the organization's budget and financial objectives.
- The board must review and approve significant transactions, investments, and joint ventures.
- The board must oversee the conduct of the organization's programs and evaluate whether the programs are being properly managed.
- The board must review and approve the auditing and accounting principles and practices used in preparing the organization's financial statements (and, as noted, must retain and replace the organization's independent auditor).
- The board must establish and oversee a compliance program to address regulatory and liability concerns.
- The board must establish procedures to address complaints and prevent retaliation against whistleblowers.
- The board may be required to adopt a policy forbidding loans by nonprofit organizations to their directors and/or officers.
- The board may be required to adopt a policy pursuant to which a nonprofit organization's lawyers are required to report breaches of fiduciary responsibility (see the next section) to the chief executive.

Many of these precepts will be reflected in the annual information return, in the form of questions as to whether the organization has prepared certain documents and developed certain policies and procedures. That is, the foregoing and/or other requirements may have to be confirmed on the organization's annual return. Penalties for breach of board member duties may be introduced into federal law.

Congress, the IRS, or other entities may establish *best practices* for nonprofit organizations. In determining the nonprofit organization recipients of federal grants and contracts, the government agency involved may be required to give favorable consideration to organizations that are accredited by IRS-designated entities that establish best practices for tax-exempt organizations. The IRS and the Office of Personnel Management may establish best practices for charitable organizations participating in the Combined Federal Campaign. There may be a federal law prudent investor standard.

BOARD MEMBER RESPONSIBILITIES

One of the principles that has been in the law for centuries is that trustees of charitable trusts are deemed to have the same obligation (duty of care) toward the assets of the trusts as they do toward their personal resources. Their responsibility is to act *prudently* in their handling of the nonprofit organization's income and assets. The trustees are *fiduciaries*; the law (for now, largely state law) imposes on them standards of conduct and management that, together, compose principles of *fiduciary responsibility*. Most state law, be it statute or court opinions, impose the standards of fiduciary responsibility on directors of nonprofit organizations, whether or not the organizations are trusts and whether or not they are charitable.

Contemporary Standards

The contemporaneous general standard is that a board member of a nonprofit organization is required to perform his or her duties in good faith, with the care an ordinarily prudent person in a like position would exercise under similar circumstances, and in a manner the director reasonably believes to be in the best interests of the mission, goals, and purposes of the organization.

Thus, one of the main responsibilities of nonprofit board members is to maintain financial accountability and effective oversight of the organization they serve. Fiduciary duty requires board members to remain objective, unselfish, responsible, honest, trustworthy, and efficient in relation to the organization. Board members are stewards of the entity, and are expected to act for the good of the organization rather than for their personal aggrandizement. They need to exercise reasonable care in all decision making, without placing the nonprofit organization at unnecessary risk.

The duties of board members of nonprofit organizations can be encapsulated in the *three Ds*: duty of care, duty of loyalty, and duty of obedience. These are the legal standards against which all director actions are tested. They are collective duties adhering to the entire board and require the active participation of all board members. Accountability can be demonstrated by a showing of the effective discharge of these duties.

Duty of Care

The duty of care requires that directors of a nonprofit organization be reasonably informed about the organization's activities, participate in the making of decisions, and do so in good faith and with the care of an ordinarily prudent person in similar circumstances. This duty, therefore, requires the individual board members to pay attention to the entity's activities and operations.

This duty is carried out by the following acts:

- Attendance at meetings of the board and committees to which assigned
- Preparation for board meetings, such as by reviewing the agenda and reports
- Obtaining information, before voting, to make appropriate decisions
- Use of independent judgment
- Periodic examination of the credentials and performance of those who serve the organization
- Frequent review of the organization's finances and financial policies
- Oversight of compliance with important filing requirements, such as annual information returns (see Chapter 4)

Duty of Loyalty

The duty of loyalty requires board members to exercise their power in the interest of the organization and not in their own interest or the interest of another entity, particularly one in which they have a formal relationship. When acting on behalf of the organization, board members must place the interests of the entity before their personal and professional interests.

This duty is carried out by the following acts:

- Disclosure of any conflicts of interest
- Adherence to the organization's conflict-of-interest policy
- Avoidance of the use of corporate opportunities for the individual's personal gain or benefit
- Nondisclosure of confidential information about the organization

Although conflicts of interest are not inherently illegal—in fact, can be common because board members are often affiliated with different entities in their communities—how the board reviews and evaluates them is important. Conflict-of-interest policies can help protect the organization and board members by establishing a process for disclosure and voting when situations arise in which board members may actually or potentially derive personal benefit as a consequence of the organization's activities.

Duty of Obedience

The duty of obedience requires that directors of a nonprofit organization comply with applicable federal, state, and local laws, adhere to the entity's articles of organization and bylaws, and remain guardians of the mission.

The duty of obedience is carried out by the following acts:

- Compliance with all regulatory and reporting requirements, such as overseeing filing of annual information returns and payment of employment taxes
- Examination and understanding of all documents governing the organization and its operation, such as the bylaws
- Making decisions that fall within the scope of the organization's mission and governing documents

Personal Liability

Generally, if a director carries out his or her duties faithfully, and in adherence to the three Ds, the director will not be found personally liable for a commission or omission. Personal liability can result when a trustee or director—and an officer or key employee—of a nonprofit organization breaches standards of fiduciary responsibility.

LAWSUITS AGAINST NONPROFIT ORGANIZATIONS

Nonprofit organization can be sued under federal, state, and/or local law. Although criminal prosecutions are rare, in the civil laws lurk many occasions for missteps leading to lawsuits. For the most part, nonprofit organizations can be sued for the same reasons as for-profit organizations.

Here are the usual bases on which a nonprofit organization can be sued:

- *Nonpayment of income or property taxes.* Governments seeking unpaid taxes bring these suits. The nonprofit organization may be generally tax-exempt, but the IRS may be after unrelated business income tax (see Chapter 7) or a state may be looking for real estate tax as to a parcel of real property that allegedly is not being used for exempt (usually charitable) purposes.

- *Violation of a state's charitable solicitation act.* A charitable (or similar) organization may be raising funds in a state without complying with the registration, reporting, or other requirements (see Chapter 8). A state will not proceed directly to litigation for a violation of this nature. If, however, after a few requests, the organization refuses to obey this law, an injunction or some other form of civil (or, infrequently, criminal) litigation may be initiated.

- *Defamation.* If an organization produces a libelous publication or one of its spokespersons uses terms or makes statements that another person finds offensive, it is not uncommon for a defamation suit to be filed in response.

- *Antitrust law violation.* Membership organizations are particularly susceptible to a charge of antitrust transgressions. For example, an association may wrongfully exclude or expel a person from its membership. (This can be a form of restraint of trade.) Or, an association may enforce a code of ethics and conclude that a member acted unethically; this finding could lead to a defamation charge or, if the person is expelled from membership, to an antitrust law violation complaint (see Chapter 11).

- *Employment discrimination, wrongful termination, breach of a lease or other contract, and personal injury.* These are increasingly common bases for lawsuits. As an example of a personal injury suit, recently a nonprofit swim club was sued by an individual and his spouse because of personal injuries he suffered when he fell, after swimming, in a stairway leading to the club's locker room; his spouse sued for loss of consortium.

In most of these lawsuits, the only party sued is the organization itself. There are exceptions, however, such as the liability that can be incurred by an organization as the result of something done (commission) or not done (omission) by another organization. For example, two or more nonprofit organizations may be involved in a partnership or other form of a joint venture. As a consequence of this arrangement, the conduct of one organization may bring liability to it and/or to another organization. Technically, the liability (if any) may be that of the venture, but this form of liability can quickly attach to the underlying parties.

Another illustration concerns national organizations and their chapters. It is possible for a chapter to incur liability and cause the national entity to be sued as well. (This is termed *ascending liability*.) The national organization may have done something or failed to do something in conjunction with the chapter. More commonly, however, the national entity is sued simply because it has the most resources. The outcome of this type of litigation often depends on whether the chapters are considered separate legal entities or whether they are integral parts of the national organization.

INDIVIDUALS AS DEFENDANTS

For the most part, as noted, the defendants in lawsuits involving nonprofit organizations are the organizations themselves. Seldom will the charges include other parties, such as individuals. It can happen though, and when it does, the individuals (including those acting as volunteers) that can be dragged into the fray are trustees, directors, officers, and/or key employees.

Conduct by employees in their role as such is generally considered conduct by the organization involved. If an employee's actions are outside the scope of his or her employment, however, they can be held responsible as individuals.

When an individual is personally sued because of something done or not done in the name of a nonprofit organization, the potential liability is termed *personal liability*. Its occurrence is rare, but when it happens it is usually for one or more of the following reasons:

- An individual had a responsibility to do something in connection with the operation of a nonprofit organization and failed to meet that responsibility.
- An individual had a responsibility to refrain from doing something in connection with a nonprofit organization and did it anyway.
- An individual failed to dissociate himself or herself from the wrongful conduct of others.
- An individual actively participated in a wrongful conduct.

For example, a nonprofit organization may have wrongfully terminated the employment of an individual on a discriminatory basis. If the termination was the result of discrimination by a manager who was an employee of the organization, the entity may be found to be the only wrongdoer. If, however, a member of the organization's board of directors actively conspired with the manager to cause the discriminatory firing, the director may be found personally liable. If another member of the board knew of the discriminatory action (and the conspiracy underlying it) and did nothing to thwart it, that board member may be found personally liable as well.

This example involves *commission*: One or more individuals committed a wrongful act and were found liable (along with the organization). But liability can also result from a failure to act. The members of a finance committee of a nonprofit organization may fail in their obligation to oversee the investment practices of the entity. Money may be lost or valuable resources may be squandered as a result. These individuals could be found personally liable for their *omissions*.

Thus, personal liability in the nonprofit (often charitable) context can flow out of a violation of fundamental principles of fiduciary responsibility (as discussed previously).

PROTECTION AGAINST PERSONAL LIABILITY

Self-protection, stemming from prudent behavior and fulfillment of fiduciary responsibility, can go a long way to ensuring that personal liability is avoided. There are, nonetheless, some *structural* and *formal* steps that can be taken to provide a greater shield against personal liability.

One is *incorporation* of the organization. The incorporated organization is clearly a separate legal entity (aside from shams); the corporate form generally protects against personal liability (see Chapter 1). That is, liability is generally confined to the organization and thus does not normally extend to those who set policy for or manage the organization. (This is one of the principal reasons a nonprofit organization should be incorporated.)

Another step is *indemnification*; if state law permits, an organization can indemnify its directors and officers (and perhaps others). This occurs when the organization agrees (usually provision in the bylaws) to pay the judgments and related expenses (including legal fees) incurred by those who are covered by the indemnity, when those expenses are the result of a misdeed (commission or omission) by those persons while acting in the service of the organization. This assumes that the indemnity is provided in cases of liability where the individuals acted in the interests of the organization and otherwise in good faith. The indemnification cannot extend to criminal acts; it may not cover certain willful acts that violate civil law. Because an indemnification involves the resources of the organization, its efficacy is dependent on the economic viability of the entity.

A nonprofit organization can purchase *insurance* to protect its directors and officers in similar circumstances. Instead of shifting the risk of liability from the individuals involved to the nonprofit organization (indemnification), however, the risk of payment for a liability is shifted to an independent third party—an insurance company. The responsibility for certain risks, such as criminal law liability, cannot be shifted by means of insurance (because it would be contrary to public policy). The insurance contract will likely exclude from coverage certain forms of civil law liability, such as defamation, employee discrimination, and/or antitrust matters. An organization can purchase insurance to fund one or more indemnities it has made of its directors and officers.

The fourth step is to determine what state law is on the subject of *immunity*. Immunity is available when the law provides that a class of individuals, under certain circumstances, is not liable for a particular act or set of acts or for failure to undertake a particular act or set of acts. Several states' laws provide for immunity from lawsuits, under certain circumstances, for nonprofit (usually charitable) organizations, and for their directors and officers, particularly where these individuals are serving as volunteers. (In the case of the swim club and the personal injury lawsuit discussed earlier, a court held that the nonprofit organization was immune from liability pursuant to the state's charitable immunity act.)

If a director or officer maximizes use of the *four Is*—incorporation, indemnification, insurance, and immunity—he or she can almost be guaranteed that personal liability for service for a nonprofit organization will be avoided, and in some instances, the organization itself will be protected. Directors of nonprofit organizations can follow additional guidelines to lessen the likelihood of personal involvement in litigation:

- *Board book.* Each board member should have, and keep up to date, a board book. In this book should be (at a minimum) the board address list, copies of important documents (such as articles of organization, bylaws, mission statement, and conflict-of-interest policy), copies of recent board meeting minutes, a copy of the ruling from the IRS recognizing the organization as a tax-exempt entity, a copy of the most recently filed state annual report, a copy of the most recent financial statements, and a copy of the most recently filed annual information return. Other documents that may be included are recent committee reports, a copy of the organization's application for recognition of tax exemption (see Chapter 2), and a copy of the entity's most recent unrelated business income tax return, if any (see Chapter 4).

- *Board address list.* Each member of the board should have, and keep in the board book, a current list of the organization's board members. This list should contain each individual's mailing address, telephone numbers (office, home, cell, car, pager), fax number, and e-mail address.

- *E-mail communications system.* There should be a system by which the board members can communicate by e-mail. Each member should have a group listing of all of the board members on his or her computer. (Board members should exercise some caution about what is said in e-mail messages; everything should be written from the perspective that it may someday become public.)

- *Minutes.* Careful consideration should be given to board meeting minutes. There should be minutes of every board meeting. These documents are summaries of important actions, perhaps accompanied by one or more resolutions; they are not transcripts of the proceedings. Some organizations have their legal counsel review drafts of board minutes before they are circulated to the directors for their consideration and review.
- *Meetings.* It is essential that directors attend board meetings (or, if by telephone, participate in them). If a board member cannot be involved in a meeting, the minutes should reflect that fact. A board member cannot exercise the requisite degree of fiduciary responsibility without attending meetings and interacting with the other directors. Directors should participate in the decision-making process; silence is deemed to be concurrence. If a director is opposed to an action to be undertaken by the organization at the behest of the board, the director should speak up and have his or her dissent noted in the minutes.
- *Understand the organization.* The directors should comprehend the legal form of the organization and its structure. For example, if the organization is a corporation, the directors should be intimately familiar with its articles of incorporation and bylaws. They should constantly compare the organization's actual operating methods with the structure and procedures that are reflected in these documents, and be certain that operations are not inconsistent with provisions in these documents.
- *Understand the organization's activities.* Board members should understand how the entity operates—the purposes of its programs, their rank order of priority (presumably as mirrored in the budgets), their number, possible overlap, and membership (if any) interest and support.
- *Understand the organization's other operations.* Committees, subsidiaries, directors' pet projects, members' personal interests or contacts, or community needs may have introduced activities (and expenditures) that were not properly authorized. Some may deserve more recognition and support, while others may be innocently jeopardizing the organization's tax-exempt status.
- *Ask questions.* Directors should never be afraid to ask about

any arrangement or information that is unclear to them. An individual with fiduciary responsibility has the obligation to ask these questions. This pertains to subjects such as the organization's form and structure, its finances, use of subsidiaries, involvement in joint ventures, and affiliations with other organizations.

- *Web site.* Directors should periodically visit the Web site (if any) of the organization they serve. They should understand everything that is posted there. Remember that officials of the IRS, attorney generals' offices, and other governmental agencies, as well as the media, other organizations, and prospective donors may visit these sites.
- *Conflict-of-interest policy.* Although for the most part it is not required as a matter of law, a nonprofit organization—particularly a charitable one—should give serious consideration to adoption of a conflict-of-interest policy. This policy enables an organization to identify its disqualified persons (see Chapters 3, 4) and to know about any potential conflict at the time it is entering into a transaction with such a person.
- *Intermediate sanctions compliance.* Board members of charitable and social welfare organizations need to be aware of the intermediate sanctions rules (see Chapter 10). This is the case if only because the penalties for violation of these rules are imposed on the disqualified persons with respect to the organization. These persons include the entity's directors and officers.
- *Use of the organization's lawyer.* Access to the lawyer or law firm representing the nonprofit organization by the board is a matter of great sensitivity. Some boards never interact with the organization's lawyer; this is left to the officers and executive employees. Other boards will not meet without a lawyer present for the entirety of the meeting. (In some instances, boards want to have some time with their lawyer without staff present.) Concern about legal fees is often a factor in this, of course, but nonprofit boards should be certain they are making the best use of their lawyers.
- *Materials and seminars.* Books, articles, and newsletters about the law of nonprofit organizations and the proper role of their directors and officers abound. These individ-

uals are well advised to continually update their knowledge of permissible and innovative practices and current developments in the law concerning nonprofit organizations. Seminars and conferences on these subjects are plentiful. Directors should take advantage of these resources (and document what they did).

MANAGEMENT COMPANIES REVISITED

It is becoming more common for a nonprofit organization to utilize the services of a management company (see Chapter 1). There are many variations on this theme. Some organizations rely on a management company to assume responsibility for all of their administrative needs, while others delegate only selected functions (such as meeting planning or fundraising). A management company may provide services in connection with the operations of programs. A popular term these days is *outsourcing*, the idea being that certain administrative (sometimes termed *back office*) functions should be handled by an outside company so as to make the operations of the nonprofit organization more economical and efficient. Still other tax-exempt nonprofit organizations elect to spin out functions that are unrelated businesses to such a company, to eliminate exposure to the unrelated business income tax (and to generate a revenue return that is exempt from that tax) (see Chapter 7).

There is nothing inappropriate about the use of a management company by a nonprofit organization. Indeed, use of a company of this nature may be one of the ways in which fiduciary responsibilities are met and legal liability avoided. The basic difficulty with this approach is that government officials—in particular, those with the IRS and offices of states' attorney general—are suspicious of the practice. Management companies are almost always for-profit corporations; these individuals are constantly on the lookout for instances where the resources of a nonprofit (particularly a charitable) organization are being improperly transferred to or used by persons in a private capacity.

The management company structure that inevitably attracts the highest scrutiny is the arrangement where there is director and/or officer overlap between the two organizations. The worst of these situations, from the standpoint of the regulators, is the management company that was established by the same individuals who started the nonprofit organization, and they simultaneously serve on both boards in a majority capacity. Government authorities almost always view this circumstance as a siphoning off of charitable resources for private gain.

This type of management company relationship can result in application of the private inurement, private benefit, and/or intermediate sanctions rules (see Chapter 10). At a minimum, it is essential to be able to show that the management services are necessary and in furtherance of exempt purposes, and that the management fees are reasonable. Even where those elements can be demonstrated, however, the IRS may conclude that the arrangement is inappropriate and violative of the private benefit rules. Even where the management company is not of suspicious origins, and where there is no overlap of directors and officers, it is nonetheless prudent to be able to demonstrate that the management company is necessary and that its fees are reasonable.

An illustration of the application of these principles is found in advice offered in 2004 by the IRS's lawyers as to the ability of certain credit counseling organizations, under investigation by the agency and the Federal Trade Commission, to qualify for tax exemption as charitable and educational entities. Relying on the private inurement doctrine, these lawyers recommended application of this body of law because of their findings of "extensive dealings of [these] exempt organizations with back-office service providers . . ., often owned by the principals." They also invoked application of the private benefit doctrine, writing that the credit agencies "appear to be operating to benefit these service providers rather than to serve any public purpose."

If the relationship between a nonprofit organization and a management company is too close, the IRS may contend that the arrangement is a joint venture. This argument is reflective of the fact that a joint venture relationship can be imposed as a matter of law on the operations of two affiliated entities.

WATCHDOG AGENCIES

From a compliance perspective, nonprofit organizations are principally concerned with operating in conformity with the law or rules of the accounting profession. There is, however, another consideration with which some organizations must also cope: the role and influence of the *watchdog agencies* that monitor and publicize the endeavors of nonprofit entities, principally those that solicit contributions from the public. These agencies have and enforce rules that sometimes are inconsistent with or attempt to supersede law requirements. For example, these standards may include requirements about board composition and frequency of board meetings.

A charity watchdog agency basically has three functions:

1. It writes standards to which charitable organizations are expected to adhere.
2. It enforces the standards, in part by rating organizations in relation to the standards and by making the ratings public.
3. It prepares and publicly circulates reports about charitable organizations.

The principal set of these standards is the *Standards for Charitable Accountability* issued by the Better Business Bureau Wise Giving Alliance. Included is a rule that the board of the organization should have a policy of assessing, at least every two years, the organization's "performance and effectiveness and of determining future actions required to achieve its mission." Solicitation and other information materials should be "accurate, truthful, and not misleading." There should be an annual report, including a summary of the past year's program service accomplishments, basic financial information, and a roster of directors and officers.

The organization's board of directors should provide "adequate oversight" of its operations and staff. This entails regularly scheduled appraisals of the chief executive officer and sufficient accounting procedures. There should be a board-approved budget. The charity's expenses should be "accurately" reported in its financial statements.

Audited financial statements should be obtained for organizations with annual gross income in excess of $250,000. For charities with less gross income, a review by a certified public accountant is sufficient, although where annual income is less than $100,000, an internally produced financial statement is adequate. Financial statements should include a breakdown of expenses (such as salaries, travel, and postage) that also shows the portion of the expenses allocated to program, fundraising, and administration.

A charitable organization is to "avoid accumulating funds

that could be used for current program activities." Net assets available for program use should not be more than the greater of three times the size of the prior year's expenses or three times the size of the current year's budget. "Material conflicting interests" involving the board and staff are prohibited. At least 65 percent of total expenses must be for program; no more than 35 percent of contributions may be expended for fundraising. An organization that cannot comply with these percentages is permitted to demonstrate that its use of funds is nonetheless reasonable.

The organization's board of directors must be composed of at least five voting members. There must be at least three board meeting each year, "evenly spaced," with a majority in attendance. Only one of these meetings can be by conference call.

No more than one individual on the board, or 10 percent of the board, whichever is greater, can be compensated by the organization. The chair and treasurer of the entity cannot be compensated. One of the transgressions embedded in these standards is failure to respond promptly to matters brought to the attention of the Alliance or local Better Business Bureaus.

The media, funders of charitable organizations, and governmental agencies tend to embrace and rely on standards such as these. As federal and state governments evolve best practices guidelines, it may be anticipated that some of these rules will take on the force of law. As an illustration of this probability, the staff of the Senate Finance Committee in mid-2004 prepared a discussion draft of proposals for reforms in the law of tax-exempt organizations, including best practices. These proposals included rules (or guidelines) that boards of these organizations be composed of between 3 and 15 individuals, that no more than one board member could be compensated by the organization, that the board's chair or treasurer could not be compensated, and (in the case of public charities), that at least one board member or one-fifth of the board would have to be independent. In addition, an individual that is not permitted to serve on the board of a publicly traded company due to a law violation could not be a member of the board of a tax-exempt organization. An individual convicted of a federal or state charge of criminal fraud or comparable offense could not serve on the board or be an officer of an exempt organization for five years following the conviction. An exempt organization and its officers that knowingly permitted such an individual to be a board member would be subject to a penalty.

SUMMARY

This chapter focused on existing and emerging concepts of what has become known as corporate governance. These principles primarily concern the matter of the boards of directors of charitable organizations: their functions, duties, and responsibilities. Abuses in the for-profit sector and resultant statutory law have created governing principles that are quickly being imported into the realm of nonprofit organizations. The chapter also addressed the subject of legal liability for nonprofit organizations and board members personally; as to the latter, the chapter sketched steps that board members can take to minimize (or maybe eliminate) personal liability. The chapter also revisited the law as to nonprofit organizations' use of management companies. The chapter concluded with a look at the import in this context of watchdog agencies' guidelines. This chapter describes a body of law that is poised to be most informed and expanded by law as yet unwritten but imminent—law that is about to be manifested in emerging statutes, regulations, rules, and forms, all of which could significantly transform the law of nonprofit organizations.

Index

CPSIA information can be obtained
at www.ICGtesting.com
Printed in the USA
BVOW06*1518280917

495978BV00007B/31/P